The heart has its reasons which reason does not know.

Blaise Pascal

Reasons of The Heart

Joy and The Rationality of Faith

Rick Howe

Books by Rick Howe

Path of Life: Finding the Joy You've Always Longed For, 2012, University Ministries Press Revised Edition, 2017. 279 pages.

River of Delights: Quenching Your Thirst For Joy, Volume 1, 2015, University Ministries Press Revised Edition, 2017. 230 pages.

River of Delights: Quenching Your Thirst For Joy, Volume 2, 2015, University Ministries Press Revised Edition, 2017. 250 pages.

Living Waters: Daily Refreshment for Joyful Living, 2017, University Ministries Press. 393 pages.

Reasons of the Heart: Joy and the Rationality of Faith, 2017, University Ministries Press. 250 pages.

For Small Group Studies

Enjoying God: Discovering the Greatest of All Pleasures, University Ministries Press, 2017. 122 pages.

Love's Delights: The Joys of Marriage and Family, University Ministries Press, 2017. 104 pages.

Sacred Patterns: Work, Rest, and Play in a Joyful Vision of Life, University Ministries Press, 2017. 122 pages.

Kingdom Manifesto: A Call to Joyful Activism, University Ministries Press, 2017. 104 pages.

Joy and the Problem of Evil, University Ministries Press, Boulder, 2017. 122 pages.

For more information, visit www.rickhowe.org.

UNIVERSITY MINISTRIES PRESS

BOULDER, COLORADO
University Ministries Press, 2017

ISBN: 978-0-9987859-7-4

DEDICATIONS

To Gene Dunmire, who believed in me before there was sufficient evidence.

To Paul and Shirley Piper and the Piper family, whose generosity has made much of my ministry to the university community possible.

To Dave Horner and Garry DeWeese, friends and former colleagues. If I were a philosopher, I would want to be like them.

ABBREVIATIONS

ESV   English Standard Version

KJV   King James Version

JB   Jerusalem Bible

NASB   New American Standard Bible

NIV   New International Version

NRSV   New Revised Standard Version

RSV   Revised Standard Version

CONTENTS

AUTHOR'S NOTE

Most of this book is new to my publishing efforts. Because they are foundational to this project, I have also drawn from these earlier works on joy:

> Rick Howe, *Path of Life: Finding the Joy You've Always Longed for* (Bloomington, IN: WestBow Press, 2015)

> Rick Howe, *River of Delights: Quenching Your Thirst For Joy, Volumes 1 and 2* (Bloomington, IN: WestBow Press, 2015)

There are many endnotes in *Reasons of the Heart*. They include references to Scripture, scholarly works, as well as my own comments. My suggestion is that you read *Reasons of the Heart* first without interacting with the endnotes in order to trace the flow of thought without interruption, and then read it again with those references.

The "Questions for Thought and Discussion" at the end of each chapter reflect my hope that you will study this book with others, my belief that learning in community is the best way to learn, and my prayer that God will use this book to create communities of joy.

Some have said that my books on joy are virtually C.S. Lewis readers. I freely admit his influence. I gladly stand in his shadow. Though I interact with many others, Lewis' words often come to mind. If my books encourage others to read him, it will be a small payment on a very large debt.

Finally, I make no pretense of offering a disinterested study of joy and its implications for the rationality of faith. I write as one who has sought joy and truth and found them in the same place. I write as one who has been persuaded and who hopes to persuade others. My joy will be greater if that includes you!

PREFACE

I f there is no truth to it, it is extremely odd that millions of people over the centuries and around the world have claimed to know God in a way that empowers them to live with joy, even in the face of adversity. An account must be given. Reason demands it. But what if there is something to these claims? What if joy is what it seems to be to those who know it well? What if it is an encounter with a joyful God? What if it is the fragrance of his presence? A glimpse of his beauty? An echo of his voice? What if joy turns out to be a clue to the meaning of life? What if a full, robust joy in God is the ultimate goal of our existence? If this is even possibly true, it is worthy of serious inquiry. Reason demands it.

PART ONE

PRELIMINARY MATTERS

CHAPTER 1

GETTING OUR BEARINGS

A DRUNKARD ON A HORSE

O f all the changes we are living through in our day, one of the most significant is the way we approach claims to truth. For more than three centuries the Western world has been dominated by the Enlightenment and its assertion that reason – and reason alone – gives us objective, universally true beliefs about the world. That paradigm is being challenged and eclipsed by new ways of thinking known collectively as *Postmodernism*.[1] In stark contrast to its predecessor, Postmodernism maintains that reason has no access to a world that exists apart from our engagement with it. We are embedded in subjective, linguistic, social, and economic situations that result in an all-encompassing relativism.

If either of these models (which I will call *Rationalism* and *Relativism*) provides a true account of our knowledge, you should stop reading now and find something better to do with your time.[2] On both accounts joy is merely subjective. It tells us nothing about the world. Talking about joy and the rationality of faith would be folly, and this book, the errand of a fool.

I, for one, however, would not accept a theory of knowledge that is self-defeating from the start. If we say with Rationalists, "The foundation of knowledge must be self-evident truth," that assertion is not self-evident and must be dismissed. Or if we say, "Only beliefs that are evident to our senses can be the foundation of knowledge," that belief must be excluded on its own terms. In either case, we can't even begin.[3] Relativism fares no better. Take its central assertion: "All truth-claims are relative." If this claim is true, then it is relative on its own terms and cannot be taken as a universally true statement. If it is true, then it cannot be true, which is simply incoherent. This isn't all that is wrong with these views, but it should be enough to encourage us to continue.

C.S. Lewis wrote, "For my own part I hate and distrust reactions not only in religion but in everything. Luther surely spoke very good sense when he compared humanity to a drunkard who, after falling off his horse on the right, falls off it next time on the left."[4] Here, the Western world is the drunkard who falls off his horse on one side (Rationalism) only to remount and fall off on the other (Relativism).

I advise staying sober and in your saddle. Rationalists are right in affirming that the world exists in an objective relation to us,[5] and that reason plays an important role in our understanding of it, but wrong in denying that there are other significant factors at play in our beliefs. Relativists are right in acknowledging that our beliefs are shaped by more than reason and that we cannot fully escape this, but wrong in denying that a knowable world exists independently of our interaction with it.[6]

We will stay clearheaded and on our horse if we grant that knowledge of the world is both possible and provisional. We will prepare for a great adventure if we affirm that the prospects of knowledge are increased as we engage in critical interaction with the world and in reflective conversation with other truth-seekers.[7] We will be fruitful in our quest if we make the best use of reason we can and at the same time come to grips with all of the factors that shape our beliefs. There will be uncertainties ahead, but there will also be surprising discoveries. We will face our limitations, but we will also learn things that astonish us.[8] If we let these bearings guide us in our quest, we will not only avoid the misdirection of the Enlightenment and the confusion of our contemporary culture, we may well meet joy along the way.[9]

NARNIAN DWARFS IN OUR WORLD

Bertrand Russell, a famous atheist of the last century, was asked upon the celebration of his 90th birthday what he would do if, when he died, he found himself face-to-face with the Creator. Russell responded, "Why, I should say, 'God, you gave us insufficient evidence.'"[10] Daring presumption, if I were to speak for God I would respond with these questions: "What counts as evidence for God and who decides that?" and "What is sufficient evidence, and who decides when evidence has that property?"

Consider this: Russell was an activist for justice and peace. He wrote, "For love of domination we must substitute equality; for love of victory we must substitute justice; for brutality we must substitute intelligence; for competition we must substitute cooperation. We must learn to think of the human race as one family."[11] Clearly, Russell did not regard these moral judgments as evidence for a Deity. I would argue that they are theistic contraband in his philosophy-without-God. Equality, justice, and concern for others fit well in a Christian vision of life, but not in a godless world governed inexorably by the survival of the fittest. That he could passionately advocate such views, I suggest, is evidence for the God whose existence he denied.[12]

One has to wonder if an actual postmortem encounter with the Creator would count as sufficient evidence for Russell, or if he would continue his unbelief in whatever afterlife he found himself, evidence to the contrary. I am reminded of the Dwarfs in *The Last Battle*, by C.S. Lewis. As the story draws to a close, the Dwarfs – who refuse to be taken in by claims about Aslan, the true Ruler of Narnia – are in a wide-open, sunlit field, but believe themselves to be in a cramped, dark stable. The great Lion comes to them and sets the air shaking with a long, low growl, but the Dwarfs hear only a loud, unpleasant noise. We pick up the story here:

> Aslan raised his head and shook his mane. Instantly a glorious feast appeared on the Dwarfs' knees: pies and tongues and pigeons and trifles and ices, and each Dwarf had a goblet of good wine in his right hand. But it wasn't much use. They began eating and drinking greedily enough, but it was clear that they couldn't taste it properly. They thought they were eating and drinking only the sort of things you might find in a Stable. One said he was trying to eat hay and another said he had got a bit of an old turnip and a third said he'd found a raw cabbage leaf. And they raised golden goblets of rich red wine to their lips and said, "Ugh! Fancy drinking dirty water out of a trough that a donkey's been at! Never thought we'd come to this."[13]

Aslan responds to this sorry state of affairs: "They will not let us help them…. Their prison is only in their own minds; yet they are so afraid of being taken in that they can not be taken out."[14]

There are Narnian Dwarfs in our world. Many of them are very bright. Many have impressive credentials. Many are professors and experts in their field. You will know them not by their stature, but by their strident protests that God has not met them on their terms. You will know them not by their honest search for evidence, but by their rejection of any possible evidence for God.[15] You will know them not by their open minds, but by their motto, "Dwarfs will not be taken in!" You can join their club and sing their song, or explore the possibilities of joy (which, I will argue, turns out to be significant evidence for God). You must choose one or the other.

POSTPONING GOD

More than three hundred years of Western intellectual tradition have made it easy and even respectable for people to postpone making decisions about God. Although René Descartes (famous for the assertion, "I think, therefore I am.") was seeking to refute skepticism in his day, his methodological doubt created a strategy for skeptics to avoid making commitments until no doubt remains.[16] W.K. Clifford, the 19th century British philosopher argued that it is "wrong always, everywhere, and for any one to believe anything upon insufficient evidence."[17] Unless and until sufficient evidence can be marshaled for a claim, the intellectually responsible thing to do is to reject it.

If you wait until all possibility of doubt is removed, or you are sure that there is sufficient evidence to believe in God, you will wait until you draw your last breath. Then, if Christians are right, you will meet your Maker and you will no longer ask questions about sufficient evidence. Your doubts will not avail you. (If Christians are wrong, there will be no meeting. Your insistence on certainty will die with you, mocked by a coffin, a grave, and a tombstone with an epitaph beneath your name: "Died waiting.")[18]

BETWEEN THE PROBABLE AND THE PROVED

You would be unwise to subject many of your beliefs to Descartes' methodological doubt or to Clifford' standards of sufficient evidence: your belief that existence is a good thing, that life is worthwhile, that you should be faithful to your marital vows, that your children have a right to your loving involvement in their lives, that you should invest time and money helping poor communities in Africa or trafficked children in Mexico City, that you should sell your house and move to another state to pursue a dream job, or that you should jump into a river to rescue a drowning child.[19]

Momentous beliefs, beliefs that define who we are and shape our lives most profoundly, include uncertainty and risk. This is nowhere truer than our beliefs about God, whatever they may be.

Let me illustrate with the story of American author, Sheldon Vanauken, as it is recounted in his autobiographical work *A Severe Mercy*.[20] Vanauken and his wife, Davy, were happy pagans. If there was any god in their lives, it was their love for each other, enshrined in a vow they called the "Shining Barrier" – a commitment in which they promised to share everything and to bind themselves to each other so tightly that nothing could come between them.

Their world without God changed when they moved to England, where Vanauken studied at Oxford University, and they became friends of C.S. Lewis. Through this friendship Davy converted to Christianity. Vanauken, reluctant, but willing in the spirit of the Shining Barrier, asked questions, and Lewis, in his inimitable way, gave answers. Their interaction chipped away at Vanauken's confident paganism and led him to consider the possibility that Christianity might be true. The evidence and arguments became persuasive, but brought him to a chasm he knew he would have to leap to cross. Then, standing at the brink, he saw his situation differently. He could no longer simply return to the halcyon days of his unbelief. There was not only a gap before him, but behind, and the ground beneath him was giving way! One way or another, he would have to leap. Later he wrote:

> Between the probable and proved there yawns
> A gap. Afraid to jump, we stand absurd,
> Then see behind us sink the ground and, worse,
> Our very standpoint crumbling. Desperate dawns
> Our only hope: to leap into the Word
> That opens up the shuttered universe.[21]

Whatever your belief about the existence of God, whatever philosophy of life you embrace, whatever ultimate concern you may have,[22] you have no choice but to deal with the gap between the probable and the proved, between evidence and commitment. It is the human situation. You must leap.[23] The only question is what awaits you at the end of your jump.

REASONS OF THE HEART

As we move toward the topic of joy and the rationality of faith, let me recommend the wisdom of Pascal. There are two equally dangerous extremes, he wrote: "to exclude reason," and "to admit reason only."[24] In the chapters that follow, we will bring reason to the evidence, but not reason alone. We will let our hearts have a say. Like it or not, our most important beliefs are shaped by our longings and desires, our interests and concerns, our hopes and fears, and our dreams and aspirations. What we believe is influenced by experiences we have had and the way we respond in deep and hidden places. Pretending otherwise is just that.

Pascal also wrote, "The heart has its reasons which reason does not know."[25] Our exploration will include matters of the heart. Our inner world is at least as important as our interaction with the world around us, and the evidence we find there is at least important as evidence that we find in the world. When I look within, I find a yearning for purpose, a longing for significance. I find strong beliefs about what is right and wrong, just and unjust, good and evil. I find delight and disdain, love and hate, sorrow and joy. I discover exhilaration in my success and disappointment in my failure. I see regret and remorse over things that I have said and done, or have left unsaid and undone. I discover pleasure in small victories and steps forward in my pursuit of the good life. I find a deep and indelible awareness of my Maker and Redeemer.

You will have to look within for your own accounting. Whatever you find, it is important. As best you can, you should lay those cards on the table and acknowledge that they influence what you believe.

THE SIGNIFICANCE OF SEEKING

When we talk about sufficient evidence it is fair to ask, "Sufficient for what?" Evidence that is sufficient to warrant a nod to the Deity, but that allows one to continue living as if there were no God? I don't know that God is interested in providing that kind of evidence. If we are talking about the God of the Jewish and Christian Scriptures, I am quite sure that he is not.

If that God exists, what is he looking for? Mere intellectual assent? The Epistle of James includes this startling claim: "You believe that God is one; you do well. Even the demons believe and shudder!"[26] In this regard, better to be a demon than someone with an uncommitted, incidental faith. What if God is there and he is looking for more than that? What if he is looking for people who seek him with a whole heart and will revel in their discovery if and when it comes? Ancient Scriptures say that this is so:

> You will seek the LORD your God and you will find him, if you search after him with all your heart and with all your soul. (Deuteronomy 4:29)

> You have said, "Seek my face." My heart says to you, "Your face, LORD, do I seek." (Psalm 27:8)

> May all who seek you rejoice and be glad in you! (Psalm 70:4)

> But seek first the kingdom of God and his righteousness, and all these things will be added to you. (Matthew 6:33)

> Ask, and it will be given to you; seek, and you will find; knock, and

it will be opened to you. For everyone who asks receives, and the one who seeks finds, and to the one who knocks it will be opened. (Matthew 7:7-8)

And without faith it is impossible to please him, for whoever would draw near to God must believe that he exists and that he rewards those who seek him. (Hebrews 11:6)

Seeking puts us in a position to discover what others may never learn from theirs.[27] Pascal put it this way:

[Thus] willing to appear openly to those who seek Him with all their heart, and to be hidden from those who flee from Him with all their heart, He so regulates the knowledge of Himself that He has given signs of Himself, visible to those who seek Him, and not to those who seek Him not. There is enough light for those who only desire to see, and enough obscurity for those who have a contrary disposition.[28]

Maybe you wouldn't describe yourself as a seeker. I appreciate your honesty. I hope that you will not be offended by mine: Unless you are open to the possibility that God exists and, if so, that you might have life-changing encounters with him, you would be better served to sell this book and use the money for something you do believe in. Better yet, you could keep reading with an open mind.

Questions for Thought and Discussion

1. What are the strengths and weaknesses of the author's alternative to Rationalism and Relativism?

2. Discuss the characteristics of Narnian dwarfs. Where do you see them in your world?

3. What is the significance of the gap between the probable and the proved, between evidence and commitment?

4. How does seeking God differ from an intellectual assent to his existence, and why is this important?

5. How do reasons of the heart play out in your beliefs about the world?

CHAPTER 2

ON SECOND THOUGHT

RETHINKING EMOTIONS

I f you are like many, you separate the rational and emotional dimensions of human nature. Philosophers and theologians sometimes distinguish between "faculties" or "capacities" of the soul, such as intellect, emotion, and will. Maybe you aren't that theoretical. Still, you may think that reason and emotions belong in different categories. They aren't the same kind of thing. Emotions are subjective; reason, objective. Emotions are partial; reason, impartial. Emotions happen to us; reason is deliberate and intentional. Emotions are a spontaneous, and reason, a studied, way of interacting with the world. So most of us have been taught.

For some, emotions belong in the same class as hunger, thirst, and full bladders. They are something we share with the animal world. According to this view, emotions are distinct from our cognitive faculties.[1] They are impulsive, capricious, and unreliable. They are not only irrelevant to the rational dimensions of life, they must be governed like unruly children, kept silent and subservient while reason goes about its more important tasks.

Is this an accurate appraisal of our emotions? I don't think so. Emotions are more than feelings tethered to physical states.[2] They are an intricate fabric woven from threads of belief, feeling, and desire.[3] If I love my wife, I *believe* that her existence is a good thing,[4] I experience pleasurable *feelings* in her company, and I *desire* to be with her and to contribute to her well-being. If I am jealous, I *believe* that my entitlement to the affection of another has been violated, I experience *feelings* of resentment, and I *desire* to prevent him from continuing to undermine my rights. If I am anxious, I *believe* that my future may be imperiled by something over which I have little or no control, I experience *feelings* of apprehension, and I *desire* to avoid or to overcome the uncertainties I envision.

Some emotions arise so swiftly that we are not aware of the factors that bring them about. Nevertheless, they follow the same pattern. If I am angry, I *believe* that I have been wronged, I experience *feelings of agitation*, and I *desire* to even the score. The progression can be lightning-fast. If I am frightened, I *believe* that my well-being is threatened, I *feel* a rush of adrenaline, and I have a strong *desire* to fight or to flee. All of this can happen in a split second. Even if we are unaware of the process that gives rise to these emotions, they are configured in the same way.[5]

Emotions are rooted in our thought life. This is so because they are interpretive in nature. We don't delight in things unless we *perceive* them as something to be desired. We don't fear things unless we *regard* them as a threat. We don't become angry with someone unless we *construe* their actions to be contrary to our expectations or desires. We don't lament the loss of someone or something unless we *see* ourselves bereft of something we value.[6] Without this interpretation, this process of thought, we wouldn't have emotions as we know them.

The interpretations that shape our emotions don't exist in isolation. They are part of a larger body of beliefs about the world and our place in it.[7] Even if we give little thought to the nature of reality, the meaning of life, and what is valuable and right or wrong, we all have beliefs about these things, and these beliefs shape the interpretations that shape our emotions.

Although we can (and should) think *about* these essential beliefs, more often than not we simply think *from* them. In the experience of an emotion we are probably not aware of them at all. Nevertheless, they are integral to our emotions. As Robert Roberts puts it: "Human life, even when it is far from intellectual, is fundamentally a life of the mind."[8]

RETHINKING REASON

Contrary to Descartes, at our core we are more than thinking beings.[9] Contrary to Kant, there is no such thing as reason alone.[10] We are rational and affective creatures. Both dimensions come into play in our beliefs about the world.

Emotions are shaped by beliefs. The opposite is also true. If we step back from our beliefs for a moment, we will see that they include a spectrum of emotions: indifference, boredom, ambivalence, reluctance, doubt, aversion, contempt, scorn, curiosity, interest, excitement, fascination, or wonder.[11] If you engage the text as you read and ask yourself if my claims are believable, your response will likely include at least one of these emotions. We are so accustomed to this arrangement that we may take little notice of it, and attach little significance to it. We seriously misunderstand ourselves as a result. This is the truth of the matter: *Beliefs are lifeless until they engage our emotions. They are mere abstractions until they interact with our affections.*

Let's explore this. When we think of reason, we usually think of the *content* of beliefs and logical or empirical relationships between them.[12] It is also important to understand the *status* and *role* of beliefs in our interior life.

If we do, we will see the importance of our emotions in what we may have regarded as reason's domain.

Emotions and the status of beliefs. Not all beliefs are equal. Some are trivial and others are crucial. I believe that I had a bagel and cream cheese for breakfast this morning, that my car is slate gray, that Wyoming is north of Colorado, et cetera. I also hold these beliefs: God created the universe. Humans have been created in the image of God. Marriage is an institution designed and ordained by God. Children are a blessing from God. I ought to steward the resources of the earth for the glory of God and the good of all. I ought to seek the welfare of the poor and the oppressed.

There are two important differences between these sets of beliefs: their status in my values and the emotions that accompany them. Suppose I remember that it was yesterday, and not this morning, that I had a bagel for breakfast. I would not regard this change of beliefs as important. The only emotion I might have is amusement, or mild irritation, at my forgetfulness. Suppose, however, that I no longer believed that the universe was created by God, or that I came to believe that I was nothing more than the product of eons of time, blind chance, and the interplay of the survival of the fittest and mutations in the gene pool from which I emerged. This would be very important to me. I would have very different emotions about the world and about myself. I can imagine hopelessness, desolation, and despair.[13]

Consider again my beliefs about marriage, children, stewardship of the earth, and compassion toward the poor, and now these related emotions: Delight in a wedding celebration. Grief over the divorce of close friends. Thankfulness for my children when I tuck them in bed at night. Frustration at seeing children disadvantaged by the neglect of their parents. Admiration of people who conserve and protect natural resources and habitats. Anger over the despoiling of the earth. Sorrow over the plight of homeless people in my community.

If I were you I would underline or highlight the next sentence. *The more significant the belief, the stronger the accompanying emotions will be; the more momentous the belief, the more powerfully our emotions will be engaged in affirming it.*

Emotions and the role of beliefs. Some beliefs are part of our noetic structure – the sum total of all that we believe – but have little bearing on the way we see and respond to things.[14] I believe that George Washington was the first president of the United States, but it has little practical significance for me. Other beliefs are more powerful. They are "control beliefs."[15] They govern our readiness to accept other claims to truth, direct our values, priorities, and actions, and shape the way we interpret and respond to situations in life. Let's say that I have a control belief that my wife is faithful to me. If that is so (and it is), it will influence the way I see her talking to a tall, tanned, handsome man in the produce section of the grocery store. I will probably think that he is seeking her advice on kumquats. Even if I think that he might be dallying, I will not suspect that she is flirting with him. I will not imagine them hiding behind the fruit stand, planning a later rendezvous. Control beliefs work that way.

We use the language of *conviction* to talk about control beliefs. Convictions are *firmly* held beliefs. We are *fully* persuaded of their truth. We *truly* believe them. If you give this a moment's thought, you will see that the words *firmly, fully,* and *truly* aren't about what we believe, but the way we believe. They refer to emotions that shape and animate our beliefs. If I say that I *truly* believe that God is good, I am describing not only the content of my belief, but its status and role in my interior life, and emotions that are interwoven with my belief, such as gratitude and humble trust.

Convictions are beliefs that are shaped and energized by strong emotions. Let me return to my conviction that children are good gifts from a good God. I delight in them. I love interacting with them. I take great pleasure in watching them grow and develop new skills in life. I am disturbed when I see them ignored. I am angered when I see them mistreated. I am enraged at the very thought of partial-birth abortion, child pornography, and child trafficking. Unless you have let your heart grow cold, or you have trained yourself in disciplines of apathy, you will find examples in your own life.

Emotions and sufficient evidence. Our modern Western distortions have led us to be unwitting and sometimes dishonest about the role of emotions in our beliefs about the world. Do you remember the issue of "sufficient evidence" in the last chapter? If beliefs seem inconsequential to us, such as our belief that all bachelors are unmarried men, or that water boils at 212 degrees Fahrenheit if we are standing on an ocean beach, our emotions may not factor significantly in our judgment of their truthfulness. Not so when we move beyond those limited parameters. A scientist may claim that there is insufficient evidence to disprove a theory that he has published, and the most powerful factors in play (and suspected by his peers) are pride and a fear of losing face. A historian may argue that there is insufficient evidence to believe that Jesus was the figure described in the Gospels, and behind that judgment we discover the painful death of a loved one, or a traumatic adolescent experience at a church camp, and residual bitterness and resentment.[16] A scholar may reject an argument or a factual claim, and may even give you reasons for her rejection, but if the truth were fully known, the proposal conflicts with control beliefs she already has that are buttressed by strong, enduring emotions.[17]

Evidence belongs to the realm of rational inquiry; as soon as we attach the words *sufficient* or *insufficient* to it, emotions are likely involved. If we point these things out, we will be scolded for engaging in *ad hominem* criticism.[18] We should never dismiss evidence and arguments because we suspect that subjective factors may also be in play. Nevertheless, it is wise to acknowledge that significant beliefs are *de homine*.[19] They are not shaped by evidence and arguments alone. They engage an inner world of emotions.[20]

A SENSE OF THE HEART

In the eighteenth century, Jonathan Edwards wrote, "There is a distinction to be made between a mere *notional understanding*, wherein the mind only beholds things in the exercise of a speculative faculty; and *the sense of the heart*, wherein the mind not only speculates and beholds, but *relishes* and *feels*."[21] Some of our beliefs involve only a notional understanding: that the earth travels around the sun, that the area of a triangle is its base multiplied by its height divided by 2, or that Socrates is mortal if he is a man and all men are mortal. But that is not true of other beliefs: my belief that a sunset over the Rockies is beautiful, that events in my life have a purpose, that terrorism and cancer are great evils in our world, or that racism and sexism crush the human spirit. *The more life-shaping the belief, the more it involves a sense of the heart.*

If you feel uncomfortable talking about your heart in the context of reason and rationality, it is probably because you see the word "heart" and think only of emotions, and you have a deficient view of emotions. I've done my best to address this. The ancient Hebrews had a richer, more robust view of our interior life. For them, your heart (Hebrew, *lev*) is the innermost dimension of who you are.[22] It is the center of your being. It is the place where you think and feel and choose before anyone else (but God) knows. It is the secret place within, where your values are forged, your priorities are formed, your beliefs are shaped, and your decisions are made. Your heart is cognitive, affective, and volitional. The strands are interlaced and cannot be undone.[23] The beliefs you embrace, the desires you pursue, the decisions you make, and the quests you undertake, course from your heart – which is why the Proverb rings true: "Keep your heart with all vigilance, for from it flow the springs of life."[24]

QUESTIONS FOR THOUGHT AND DISCUSSION

1. How has this chapter challenged and possibly changed your understanding of emotions?

2. How do you see emotions at play in important beliefs in your life?

3. What difference does it make to think about reason and emotions disjunctively (either/or) or conjunctively (both/and)?

4. How does the Hebrew conception of our heart differ from the way you have thought about your interior life?

5. Discuss the contrast between a notional understanding and a sense of the heart in important beliefs that you hold. How do you see this playing out in your beliefs?

CHAPTER 3

A THEOLOGICAL PRIMER ON JOY
PART 1

In this chapter and the next I will introduce you to joy in the Jewish and Christian Scriptures and the Christian theological tradition. I write this as one who has embraced Christian faith and often feasted at joy's table, but I offer it to anyone who wishes to learn more about the experience that I will argue plays a significant role in the rationality of faith.[1]

THE HIGHEST AND BEST OF ALL PLEASURES

Joy and the pleasures of life. If you were to ask, "What is joy?" of the ancient Jewish Scriptures, the answer you would get is that joy is a kind of pleasure. You would learn, perhaps to your surprise, that sacred prophets, poets, and historians esteemed it as the highest and best of life's pleasures, and the one Pleasure that embraces and enhances all other pleasures given by God.

This is illustrated by the following Psalm. To appreciate its significance you should know that Hebrew poets did not rhyme words, but ideas: in this case with a second line echoing the thought of the first. Addressing God, David wrote:

> You have shown me the path of life.
>   In your presence there is *fullness of joy;*
>   in your right hand are *pleasures for evermore*.[2] (Psalm 16:11)

"Fullness of joy" and "pleasures for evermore" are two ways of describing the same thing. When David thought of joy, images of exquisite and enduring pleasures came to mind. When he thought of such pleasures, the word "joy" best summed them up.

Writers of the Old Testament not only thought of joy as a kind of pleasure, they were not at all uncomfortable likening joy to earthy delights. The Psalmist, for instance, could say that God had put "more joy" in his heart than the unrighteous have "when their grain and wine abound."[3] Joy is like the pleasures of food and potent drink, but is distinguished by the fact that it is much greater.[4] Joy is likened elsewhere to the pleasure of a feast,[5] the pleasure of wealth,[6] and the delight of a bridegroom in his bride.[7] Joy surpasses these pleasures but is significantly like them.

Like the Scriptures he revered, Jesus drew analogies between joy and other pleasures. He likened the joy of salvation to the excitement of discovering a priceless treasure,[8] and the future joy of the Kingdom to the gaiety of a wedding celebration.[9] He found common ground between the joy of God over a sinner's repentance and a shepherd's pleasure in finding a lost sheep, a woman's delight in finding a lost coin, and the elation of a father in the return of his lost son.[10] He invited people to a greater understanding of joy by likening it to other pleasures and delights in life.

The apostolic company responsible for the New Testament drew from the same well. You can see it in the words they chose to describe their joy. They borrowed a number of terms from the Greek vocabulary of pleasure, from sensual pleasure in general to the delights of food and drink, to a raucous, merrymaking celebration of life.[11] True, these words were transformed when they were put to use in describing Christian experience; nevertheless, they were considered the right place to begin thinking and talking about joy. As they were brought into the service of a fledgling Christian movement they came laden with nuances of pleasure that the pagan world sought and that found their true fulfillment in the overflowing, life-encompassing experience of joy.[12]

Not only did ancient people of faith view joy as a kind of pleasure, they saw clearly how it related to the yearning that lay beneath their world's quest for the good life. Pleasure is the best way to begin thinking about joy, and common pleasures begin to give us an idea of what we are talking about. Joy is like, and yet far surpasses, the many pleasures that enrich our lives and bring us delight.

The scope of joy. Some Christians put a halo over joy. They limit joy to contexts they consider *sacred*, which they define very narrowly. Not so the Scriptures! There we discover that joy encompasses all of life's wholesome pleasures. It is not only the highest and best pleasure, it is the one Pleasure that embraces and ennobles other pleasures given by God. Take the Hebrew word, *sameach*, for instance. It is used to depict joy in God.[13] It is also used to describe romantic delight in one's betrothed,[14] the sexual pleasures of marriage,[15] pleasure in one's youth,[16] one's work,[17] one's wealth,[18] in all that one does under the blessing of God,[19] and in all the gifts God bestows in life.[20] Joy and these pleasures belong together.

Popular distinctions between what is spiritual and what is not break down before the biblical understanding of joy. Joy welcomes other pleasures.

It receives them gladly, exalting them as the good gifts of a good God. Joy orders and unites all the healthy pleasures of life. By its very nature joy affirms every wholesome delight. It hallows our gladness in the good things of life by directing our hearts to God in thanksgiving and praise.[21]

Joy and sensory pleasures. Some Christians envision a great chasm between joy, which, they think, is spiritual, and the pleasures of our senses, which, they are sure, are not. To change the metaphor, as they see it the oil of joy cannot be mixed with the water of sensory delight. This is not what we find in the Scriptures:

> And there you shall *eat* before the LORD your God, and you shall *rejoice*, you and your households. (Deuteronomy 12:7)

> And if the way is too long for you, so that you are not able to carry the tithe, when the LORD your God blesses you, because the place is too far from you, which the LORD your God chooses, to set his name there, then you shall turn it into money and bind up the money in your hand and go to the place that the LORD your God chooses and spend the money for whatever you desire—oxen or sheep or wine or strong drink, *whatever your appetite craves*. And *you shall eat* there before the LORD your God and *rejoice*, you and your household. (Deuteronomy 14:24-26)

> Then you shall keep the *feast* of weeks to the LORD your God . . . and you shall *rejoice* before the LORD your God. (Deuteronomy 16:10-11)[22]

The link between joy and pleasures of the palate in these texts provides us with a paradigm for joy's relationship to other pleasures, as well.[23] If they are framed by the goodness and wisdom of God, and they are received as his blessing, they are not only compatible with joy they are enriched by the touch of that higher pleasure. Joy is honored by the retinue of other pleasures. They become nobler in its royal presence.

Joy and the transposition of pleasure. In *The Imitation of Christ*, Thomas á Kempis gave us the principle that in spiritual things the highest does not stand without the lowest.[24] C.S. Lewis used this with great insight in his study of love.[25] The highest love, *agape*, he said, ascends to its height upon the steps of the lower loves: *storge, philia,* and *eros.* It also transforms and perfects the lower loves so that they more fully realize the unique role that God has ordained for them. They are transposed, given a new and higher place, by the touch of *agape*.

The same principle illumines the relationship between joy and other pleasures. What *agape* is to other loves, joy is to other pleasures in life. It is the highest of all pleasures,[26] reaching its throne upon the stairway of life's many delights, transforming them into something greater than they could ever have been without its touch, enabling them to be more fully what the Creator meant them to be. Joy does not negate lower pleasures; it fulfills them. It does not drive a wedge between the good gifts of God; it unites and orders them, and lifts them to the highest plane possible in God's good and wise design.

Degrees of joy. Luther wrote: "Not even the more perfect saints have a full and constant joy in God."[27] Joy can fall anywhere along a great continuum. The Bible speaks of joy, rejoicing greatly,[28] an exceeding joy,[29] an exceeding great joy,[30] the fullness of joy,[31] overflowing with joy,[32] one's highest joy,[33] and an "unutterable and exalted joy."[34] What is enjoyed in part can be experienced more fully. If Christians are right, even our greatest pleasures and most robust joys in this life are but a glimpse and a taste of pleasures without end that await us in the hand of a loving God.[35]

The Fulfillment of Happiness

Is joy like or unlike happiness? We should first be clear about what we mean by happiness. Unfortunately, there are as many opinions about what happiness is as there are people in pursuit of it. Aristotle observed this long ago:

> When it comes to saying in what happiness consists, opinions differ, and the account given by the generality of mankind is not at all like that of the wise. The former take it to be something obvious and familiar, like pleasure or money or eminence, and there are various other views; and often the same person actually changes his opinion: when he falls ill he says that it is health, and when he is hard up that it is money.[36]

Centuries later, Augustine saw the same diversity of opinion in his day: "The desire for happiness is certainly universal, though the great variety of beliefs as to what constitutes happiness proves that the knowledge of it is by no means equally so."[37]

Because philosophers in antiquity gave serious thought to the nature of happiness, this would be a good place for us to start. Two views presented themselves to the ancient Greek mind. One envisioned happiness as an *activity* of the soul; the other saw it as a desirable *state* of being. Aristotle taught the first[38] and the Stoics the second.[39]

Aristotle on happiness. Let's begin with Aristotle's version of happiness-as-an-activity and see how joy compares with it. To understand Aristotle, we must begin with his notion of the "function of man."[40] We know the functions of musicians and artists. They are to perform music and to create art. But is there a function that belongs to humans-as-such? There is, according to Aristotle. It is to live a life of reason and virtue. Happiness is *doing* this. It is a flourishing in life that coincides entirely with this enterprise. Happiness is living well, and living well is pursuing reason and virtue.

Is this what Christians mean by joy? Joy has much to do with functioning well and flourishing in life. It is a sign that our hearts are working the way God intends them to. Joy results from a harmony between our desires, decisions, and deeds, and the congeniality of our hearts with God's. When it is ours, we live robustly in God's world. We flourish in life beneath his good hand.

There is a rational dimension to joy.[41] As a Pleasure of Appreciation joy involves our minds. It engages our thoughts in reflective delight. When Aristotle thought of the rational life, he had in mind the cultivation of intellectual virtues,[42] and a life informed by the disciplines of physics, metaphysics, ethics, and the like. We can experience joy in these rational endeavors. (Augustine reminds us: "All good and true Christians should understand that truth, wherever they may find it, belongs to their Lord."[43]) We are closer to the target, however, if we see joy emerging in the more focused project of loving God with our minds, seeking to honor him in all of our thinking (which will involve intellectual virtues and may include academic disciplines).

For Aristotle, happiness coincides with the pursuit of virtue. Joy has ethical dimensions, too. Again, however, there are significant differences between Aristotelian and Christian views. Aristotle's understanding of virtue – a human enterprise from first to last – includes such dispositions as courage, temperance, liberality, and so forth, defined by the rational calculation of a mean between two extremes.[44] For followers of Jesus, joy's focus is the imitation of God's character and obedience to his commands. It is a harmony of wills. A heartsong whose meter is the beat of God's own heart. It is the beatitude of love for God. Pleasure in his purposes. Delight in his designs.[45]   These facets of joy make a world of difference, because,

Christians believe, joy hails from another world – one whose terrain Aristotle seems not to have known.[46]

Let's get to the more fundamental point: Is joy an activity? Yes and no. Joy is a dance of the heart: a dynamic movement of thought, will, and affection in harmony with the music of Heaven. In this sense joy is active rather than static. It is more like play than sleep. More like a flowing fountain than a motionless pond. It is an effervescence of spirit that spills out in songs of thanksgiving and praise.[47]

Joy is active, but it isn't an activity as Aristotle thought of it. It isn't something we do, like swinging a baseball bat, riding a bike, or singing a song. These things are largely up to us: our decisions, our actions. Aristotle thought of happiness this way.[48] Here we come to a fork in the road: Aristotle's version of happiness takes us in one direction, and the joy God offers us will take us down a very different path. Joy is a "fruit of the Spirit."[49] It occurs only as God gives himself to us. If we were to choose between *active* and *static*, we would say that joy is active. If we distinguish between *active* and *passive*, we would have to say that joy is passive. It is the gift of God. We are its recipients.[50] Aristotle would have said that we are not talking about the same thing.

The Stoics on happiness. If Aristotle emphasized the active dimension of happiness, the Stoics stressed its character as a desirable inner state. Stoicism viewed the ideal inner life as a state of tranquility undisturbed by, and utterly indifferent to, the events and circumstance of life.[51] Many Christians have been influenced by this view in their understanding of joy. Commenting on the Beatitudes in the Sermon on the Mount, one scholar describes this ideal state as "serene and untouchable, and self-contained" and "completely independent of all chances and changes of life."[52]

My reading of that Sermon sees Jesus' understanding of joy moving in a very different direction. He says, "Blessed are those who mourn, for they shall be comforted."[53] Joy (or *beatitude* to use the more technical term in this context) belongs to those who mourn. It is difficult for me see how one who mourns and is in need of comfort is someone whose experience is "serene and untouchable, and self-contained." No, joy is much more than inner tranquility. It is an experience granted in and through life's realities, harsh as they sometimes are. It transforms our experience of them, but is not untouched by them.

Happiness and the fulfillment of desire. Joy is not the same as Stoic imperturbability. The Stoics weren't the only ones to think of happiness as a desirable inner state, however. In contemporary culture, many think of happiness as a pleasurable state that results from a *gratification of desires.* Is this the same as joy? Let's start with some qualifications. You may think that I am quibbling over words, but the *fulfillment* of desire seems to me to be a better candidate for talking about joy than *gratification* or *satisfaction.* You can be satisfied but not fulfilled. It depends on how easily you allow yourself to be satisfied! It is possible to be satisfied with mediocrity, but mediocrity is not fulfilling. Pornography might gratify your sexual desire, but it cannot fulfill your sexuality. If happiness is linked to mere satisfaction or gratification of desire, we are very far from joy.

We are also far from joy if we are only talking about superficial interests in life. If the desires we have in mind are for a style of clothing, the make of a car, the size of a house, or a vacation destination, we are not within shouting distance of joy. If joy is an alpine summit, these desires are marshes in the vale. Happiness must be more than this if we are to compare it with joy. In the best sense of the word, if someone asks, "Are you happy?" she wants to know whether the more significant desires in your life are being fulfilled, and if that in turn has made you glad to be alive, to be who you are, doing what you are doing. Is this the same thing as joy? Yes and no. Let's take the latter first.

Some would say that this is not joy because it involves the contingencies of life. Whether your desires are fulfilled depends upon the shifting sands of circumstance. For them, this is what distinguishes happiness from joy. I disagree. The real problem with equating joy with this version of happiness is not that the fulfillment of desire is contingent upon circumstances and joy never is, but that our desires are often skewed. Even if they are good, often the way in which we seek their fulfillment is not.

If happiness is based upon unhealthy desires, or healthy things pursued wrongly, it cannot be what Christians mean by joy. Augustine put it this way: "In so far as all men seek the happy life they do not err. But in so far as anyone does not keep to the way that leads to the happy life, even though he professes to desire only to reach happiness, he is in error."[54] This is an important observation. Once we make it, however, what should we say about a scenario in which our desires align with God's good and wise design, and we see their fulfillment as his gift to us? Is it fitting to speak of this as joy? *Yes!*

Joy can be ours in the worst of circumstances. The prophet Habakkuk gave words to this experience:

> Though the fig tree do not blossom,
>   nor fruit be on the vines,
> the produce of the olive fail
>   and the field yield no food,
> the flock be cut off from the fold
>   and there be no herd in the stalls,
> yet I will rejoice in the LORD,
>   I will joy in the God of my salvation.
>   (Habakkuk 3:17-18, RSV)

But what should we say if the fig tree blossoms in our lives, there is fruit on the vines, the produce of the olive flourishes, and so forth, and we enjoy this as a gift from God? Some may insist that this is happiness, and not joy, but it is no longer meaningful to differentiate between the two. If, as Augustine saw it, happiness is "the satisfaction of all wants when nothing is wanted wrongly,"[55] and it is received thankfully, distinguishing between happiness and joy is a distinction without a difference.[56]

This puts us in a position to answer the question that began this section. Is joy like or unlike happiness? How are the two related? When happiness is the fulfillment of significant and wholesome desires, and that fulfillment is received as a gift from God, happiness enters joy's domain.[57] Happiness and joy become nuances of the same experience: "Delight yourself in the LORD (the centerpiece of joy) and He will give you the desires of your heart" (the essence of happiness).[58] When it is experienced in relation to God, happiness becomes joy in one mode, just as pleasure becomes joy in another. Joy is more than happiness, but often includes it, just as joy is more than other pleasures in life, but can include them. *Joy is the consummation of both.*[59]

Happiness and pleasure point to joy (for it is greater than they), and find their true fulfillment in joy (for it gladly includes them in its court when they acknowledge its royal status). Joy transposes happiness-as-a-gift-from-God in the same way that it transposes pleasures-enjoyed-in-relation-to-God. The lower is caught up in the higher and becomes part of it. Happiness and joy are not meant to be competitors for our hearts, but partners in the dance of life.

POSTSCRIPT: ENJOYING GOD

Joy is the greatest of all pleasures, and the enjoyment of God is the greatest of all joys.[60] Joy is the best gift we can possibly receive, because the Giver offers himself in his gift, and he is supreme.

The enjoyment of God is not only the greatest of all joys, it is the Joy in every joy. Wherever there is true joy, God is in it, whether he is beheld in the enraptured gaze of our hearts, or is the Light by which other pleasures are illumined and experienced as his good gifts.[61] Joy always has to do with God. Always. *Whether we know it or not, our experience of joy in every instance is a connection with God.*[62] If we are held in hushed wonder before a forest ablaze with autumn color, we have encountered the Creator in his artistry. If we revel in a sumptuous meal and find ourselves savoring the experience with a thankful heart, we have tasted his goodness. If we find pleasure in people, it is an enjoyment of God mirrored in them.[63]

There is no joy apart from God. It is not even possible. To speak of joy without speaking of God is a desecration of language. If we knew the true nature and dimensions of joy, we would see that it is always, and never less than, our heart's encounter with the Joyful One. Joy is the touch of God. The fragrance of his presence. A glimpse of his beauty. An echo of his voice.

To say that we were created for God, and that we were made for joy, is to say the same thing in different ways. In words now famous, Augustine wrote, "You have formed us for yourself, and our hearts are restless until they find rest in You." [64] We are vagabonds, wandering restively in pursuit of something that beckons and yet eludes us until we find our hearts' true home in God. Pascal saw our quest for joy ending here:

> There once was in man a true happiness of which there now remain to him only the mark and empty trace, which he in vain tries to fill from all his surroundings, seeking from things absent the help he does not obtain in things present. . . . But these are all inadequate, because the infinite abyss can only be filled by an infinite and immutable object, that is to say, only by God himself.[65]

The greatest joy in this world (and the next) is our hearts' delight in God.[66] For those who know it, nothing enriches life more. Nothing pleases more fully. Nothing satisfies the longings of our hearts more profoundly than a joy that is at the same time adoration and awe, reverence and rapture, breathtaking wonder and soul-satisfying pleasure. It is a delight in the beauty, majesty, and splendor of God, and then a joy that so great and glorious a God is ours.[67] The enjoyment of God leaves us incredulous, marveling, *"Surely this is too good to be true!"* But it is supremely good and it is true. It is a pleasure-filled wonder (or wonderful pleasure) that there should be such a God, and even greater pleasure and greater wonder that he offers himself to us for our joy.

QUESTIONS FOR THOUGHT AND DISCUSSION

1. How do you see the relationship between joy and pleasure after reading this chapter?

2. If you have never put joy into the context of pleasure in your thinking, can you identify beliefs that have kept you from that?

3. How do you see the relationship between joy and happiness after reading this chapter?

4. If you have tended to separate happiness and joy in your thinking, can you identify the sources of influence that have shaped your understanding?

5. What do you think of this quote: "Joy always has to do with God. Always. *Whether we know it or not, our experience of joy in every instance is a connection with God.*" How does it challenge or change your understanding of joy?

CHAPTER 4

A THEOLOGICAL PRIMER ON JOY
PART 2

JOY AND OUR EMOTIONS

Joy is a Godward pleasure. It includes the vast array of wholesome pleasures in life when they are shaped by thanksgiving and praise. Another dimension of joy is the experience that follows when God grants the significant desires of our hearts, which is what we call happiness. Joy is the consummation and crown of happiness and pleasure. Now we can add that joy engages and enriches our emotional life. Joy is to our emotions what truth is to our minds. Our emotions were made for joy as our minds were made for truth. As truth is the fulfillment of our minds, joy is the fulfillment of our emotions. As truth enlightens our minds, joy illumines and enhances our emotional life.

The transforming touch of joy. Joy spans a range of emotions, from cheerfulness to hilarity, from gladness to jubilation, from delight to ecstasy, from exuberance to rapture.[1] However it is experienced, joy leads us to say with Augustine, "You introduce me to a most rare affection, inwardly, to an inexplicable sweetness, which, if it should be perfected in me, I know not to what point . . . life might not arrive."[2]

Although we can think of joy in its own right, it is usually found in the company of other emotions.[3] Joy caresses our emotions. They are enriched by its touch. When it takes them up in its dance it changes them. Joy transforms love from duty to delight. Courage becomes a cheerful confidence. Humility becomes the pleasure of honoring others. Joy makes peace a celebrative serenity. It transforms gratitude into a song of thanksgiving.

Varieties of joy. Joy is not a single flower, but a garden with winding paths and many species bursting with fragrance and color. Some pleasures command our attention, and though we gladly give it to them for a time, we could not endure their intensity for long. Others are amiable company with whom we would enjoy spending an entire day. Some joys are like that. There are times when joy calms the turbulent waters of life, and brings with it a refreshing serenity. It is experienced as a peaceful joy. There are contemplative joys: the delight that arises in our hearts when we direct our thoughts to God. There are grateful joys, when thanksgiving and joy give rise to each other.

Some joys inspire action. There is a courageous joy, found in the exhortations, "Be of good cheer!"[4] "Cheer up!"[5] "Take heart!"[6] "Take courage!"[7] And "Have courage!"[8]

There is musical joy:

> Make a joyful noise to the LORD, all the earth;
> break forth into joyous song and sing praises!
> Sing praises to the LORD with the lyre,
> with the lyre and the sound of melody!
> With trumpets and the sound of the horn
> make a joyful noise before the King, the LORD! (Psalm 98:4-6)

There is a joy that inspires a movement-in-harmony of body and soul in the celebration of life before God. In the sacred dance of joy, one's body becomes one's instrument, and one's movements become the lyrics of worship offered in joyful adoration of God.[9] There are times when joy is expressed outwardly in playfulness and laughter.

There is a joy so pure and so powerful that it is beyond words. It is a "joy unspeakable and full of glory,"[10] as Peter described it. We have no lexicon with which to approach it. It would be like trying to describe a field of wild flowers or a rainbow with the words "black" and "white." To approach this joy with words is to profane it. To describe it would only demean it. It is too heavy for words; they cannot bear its weight. It is too lofty; they cannot reach its heights. It is too profound; they cannot plumb its depths. At best they convey the merest glimpse of a breathtaking beauty. They impart only the barest taste of a rapturous feast. The only response worthy of this joy is hushed wonder.

When joy crowds and spills over the limits of our human frame, it becomes an experience of ecstasy. It is no longer merely pleasant; it is virtually unbearable. It is possible to be enthralled by joy, intoxicated with its elixir. The experience is disorienting, unsettling, and overwhelming. To be in this state is to be "overjoyed." Filled beyond the capacity of our human vessel. It is the joy experienced by Pascal on November 23, 1654, recorded, sewn into his coat, and not discovered until after his death:

From about half past ten in the evening until about half past twelve,

FIRE

God of Abraham, God of Isaac, God of Jacob, not of the philosophers
and scholars.
Certitude. Certitude. Feeling. Joy. Peace.
God of Jesus Christ.
Deum meum et Deum vestrum.
"Your God shall be my God."
Forgetfulness of the world and of everything else, except GOD.
He is to be found only by the ways taught in the Gospel.
Greatness of the human soul.
"Righteous Father, the world has not known You, but I have known
You."
Joy, joy, joy, tears of joy.[11]

If ecstatic joy crowds the limits of our human frame, there is also a joy that
dances just outside, elusive, beckoning, luring, and even haunting. It reveals
something of itself in the pleasures of life, but only enough to let us know
that it includes but transcends them. It is something more. Something better.
We taste it in happiness, but the experience leaves even the happiest person
feeling bereft, hungry for the greater reality to which happiness points, and in
which happiness finds its true fulfillment. This joy is a hand that beckons,
and a finger that points beyond this world to the next. It is a voice "from far
more distant regions," in the words of C.S. Lewis, inviting and even
summoning.[12] It is a taste of the "powers of the age to come,"[13] a sample
which, savored, creates a longing that nothing in this world can satisfy. It is
both a filling and a void. Having and wanting. Joy and joy desired. Gift and
promise. Already and not yet.[14]

Lesslie Newbigen wrote, "Joy is a visitor who comes when she will, and
who sometimes calls when we least expect her and sometimes fails to turn up
when we were sure she was coming."[15] That is true of some joys. They may
come once in a lifetime, and maybe not at all. Others are like old college

friends, surprising us occasionally with a visit, and then moving on. But that isn't true of all joys. Some make the heart a home.

Joy can become a disposition, orienting and inclining our hearts toward God. It can be a foundational emotion. A shaping and empowering affection. It can be a slow, steady current that flows beneath the surface of all that we experience. The more it is ours the more we experience life as it was envisioned in the apostle's exhortation: "Rejoice in the Lord always!"[16]

POSTSCRIPT: AN EPISTEMOLOGY OF JOY

This will be a brief, in-house exploration of how we come to know joy. If you find yourself on the outside looking in, I hope that you will not be offended by language that addresses readers in the Christian community. Consider it an invitation to a better understanding (a *notional understanding* in Edwards' terms) of a Christian perspective on joy.[17]

Joy is more than an ordinary emotion, but not less. It is an emotion that bears the presence of a joyful God to us; nevertheless, we experience joy as an emotion, and that is an important observation. Like other emotions, joy is perspectival.[18] It is interpretive in nature.

Joy flourishes and is most robust in a God-centered vision of life.[19] Josef Pieper wrote, "Man can (and wants to) rejoice only when there is a reason for joy. And this reason, therefore, is primary, the joy itself secondary."[20] We enjoy God *because* we believe that he is our Creator and Redeemer. We enjoy the world *because* we believe it to be the amazing work of an amazing God. We rejoice in our circumstances *because* we see them as the work of a sovereign God for our good. We rejoice in redemption *because* we regard it as the highest and best gift that could ever be given to us in our plight. These are the reasons for joy. Embrace them (because they are true), and joy will follow. Reject them (or prove them false), and joy will vanish like mist on a hot summer day.

This is the pattern of joy as early Christians saw it:

> Not only that, but we *rejoice* in our sufferings, *knowing that* suffering produces endurance. (Romans 5:3, RSV)

> You *joyfully* accepted the plundering of your property, *since you knew* that you yourselves had a better possession and an abiding one. (Hebrews 10:34, RSV)

> *Count it all joy*, my brothers, when you meet trials of various kinds, *for you know* that the testing of your faith produces steadfastness. (James 1:2-3, RSV)

Do you see the condition for joy in these texts? It is described as a kind of knowing.[21] This is another way of talking about faith. It is an orientation of our hearts that results from habituating our thoughts and affections – here, in the truth that God is at work in every situation, seeking to shape our character. Joy is secondary in the sense that it follows this. It cannot take the lead.[22] Joy flourishes in a vision of life in which our hearts are formed and informed by the knowledge of God and his ways.[23]

The explicit condition for joy is that you know that God intends to shape your heart in positive ways through difficult circumstances in life. The implicit condition is that this is important to you. You must understand the significance of trials, but this, in turn, must be significant to you. If you don't value the development of your character in a Godward life, you will never experience joy in trying times. If you don't aspire to a life of moral excellence, you will remain a stranger to joy in challenging circumstances that come your way.

Joy is not only contingent upon the status of certain beliefs (such as believing that God is present in our circumstances and sovereign over them) but upon the role they play in our interior life. An existential context for joy is created when these beliefs engage us deeply, illumine our thoughts, kindle our affections, and govern the decisions we make.[24] It is not sufficient to possess information. It is not enough to have a *notional understanding.* Joy comes as we embrace truth and let it shape the way we interpret and respond to life as it unfolds.[25] It comes when our beliefs about God and his ways become a *sense of the heart.* [26]

Positioning ourselves for joy includes having right beliefs and believing rightly. It also involves (and cannot be divorced from) the shaping of our hearts and the development of our character.[27] Joy is bound together with a pursuit of virtue: moral excellence that becomes characteristic of us and is expressed outwardly in a way of living in the world. Virtue involves our emotions, motives, intentions, values, and desires, and the consistent, habitual manner in which we live with them.[28] Virtue is in view in the commandments to love God and to obey him with *all of our heart* and *all of our soul.*[29] It is the whole of our inner life brought into harmony with God and his design for life. When this happens, even in small and imperfect ways, joy follows.[30] It is a sign that our hearts are working the way that God intends them to. The result is that we flourish in life, whatever our circumstances may be.

Aristotle taught that virtue is not just doing the right thing; it includes having the right emotions about doing the right thing.[31] A virtue is present only to the extent that we take pleasure in it.[32] To the degree that we are at odds with a trait of moral excellence, and move toward it grudgingly, reluctantly, or from a sense of duty, it is not yet a virtue in us. Virtue involves the integrity of our hearts, when our desires, decisions, and deeds sing in harmony and dance in step. Joy is the pleasure we experience when this is so.

There is greater virtue in loving virtue and enjoying its pleasures. In fact Augustine went so far as to say that there is no devotion, no good life "unless it be also delighted in and loved."[33] If we don't find pleasure in it, it is not the good life we think it is. *This is an important dimension of joy.* Jonathan Edwards wrote, "And in every degree of an act of the will, wherein the soul approves of something present, there is a degree of pleasedness; and that pleasedness, if it be in considerable degree, is the very same with the affection of joy or delight."[34]

QUESTIONS FOR THOUGHT AND DISCUSSION

1. Describe misunderstandings of joy you my have had that saw it disconnected from your emotional life.

2. Describe your understanding the relationship between joy and emotions after reading this chapter?

3. How does joy relate to other emotions in your own experience?

4. How does the author's understanding of the epistemology of joy in this chapter relate to discussions in the first chapter? The second chapter?

5. Discuss this claim: "The common factor in all joy is the interplay of important beliefs and fruitful character formation in a Godward life." How does this differ from joy as you have understood it in the past?

CHAPTER 5

IMPORTANT DISTINCTIONS

A s we prepare to explore joy and the rationality of faith, let me introduce you to distinctions that will keep our thinking clear.

KNOWING AND SHOWING

Suppose that you saw me in a restaurant after I had finished the last bite of my meal. Following an exchange of obligatory small talk you asked what entrée I would recommend, and I said, "I just finished the Beef Wellington. You can't go wrong with it." You probably wouldn't do this, but imagine asking, "How do you know that you had Beef Wellington and not Wiener schnitzel?" I would surely respond, "I know because I ate it, morsel by delicious morsel! I remember what it looked and smelled and tasted like!" If you were to ask me such a question, my experience would count heavily in my claim that it was Beef Wellington, and not Wiener schnitzel, that I enjoyed for dinner.

Now suppose that you changed the question slightly and asked it again: "How do *I* know that it was Beef Wellington that you ate and not Wiener schnitzel?" This is where the distinction between *knowing* and *showing* comes into play.[1] To satisfy you I might ask my fellow dinner guests to confirm my claim. I might call the waiter, ask for my check, and show you that Beef Wellington was recorded thereon. I might tell you from memory everything that came with that entrée and invite you to look at the menu to see for yourself. I might point out that Beef Wellington is served with herbed rice, and Wiener schnitzel with baby potatoes, and that if you looked closely you would see a kernel of rice hiding beneath the parsley on my plate.

That is the difference between knowing something to be true (from experience) and showing it to be true (by examining evidence and arguments). Many claim to know God in experiences of joy. We will explore the significance of this. I will also endeavor to show you that these claims, all told, are strong evidence for the existence of God.

RATIONALITY AND TRUTH

Rationality and truth belong together, but are not bound together.[2] It is possible to be rational in believing something that is false, and possible to come to a true belief irrationally. Let me illustrate. Suppose, after listening to days of evidence and arguments, that a jury reached the verdict that Mr. Smith killed his wife. Given the case that was presented to them, and their open and honest evaluation, let's grant that it was the rational thing to do. That belief could be false. We have all heard of guilty verdicts that were later overturned when new evidence surfaced that vindicated the defendant. Suppose that Mr. Smith had an identical twin brother who actually committed the heinous crime and fled the country, leaving his look-alike brother to take the rap. You would have people who are rational in a belief (given the evidence presented in court and their open-minded and careful evaluation) that is false (because Mr. Smith didn't do it).

Suppose, however, that one member of the jury secretly believed that Mr. Smith was innocent. If, in fact, Mr. Smith's twin brother set him up to take the blame for the murder, that juror would have a true belief. But let's say that he did not reach his conclusion by considering the evidence and arguments presented in court. Imagine instead that he violated the court's order not to discuss the trial with anyone, and that he told his wife, who in turn consulted a medium, who, in a séance, purportedly asked the dead woman if she had been killed by her husband, and was purportedly told that someone else had done the dastardly deed. Most of us would agree that this juror's belief in Mr. Smith's innocence is true (because Mr. Smith didn't commit the crime) but irrational (because it was not formed in a rational way).

To be rational and hold true beliefs is the ideal to which intellectually virtuous people aspire. I will seek to show you that joy not only makes believing in God a rational thing to do, it provides significant evidence for the truthfulness of that belief.

PLEASURE-STATES AND TAKING-PLEASURE-IN

Aristotle made a distinction between these two kinds of pleasure. [3] Sometimes pleasure is a conscious state with a beginning and an end. A dip in a pool on a hot summer day (sensory pleasure), appreciating a Renaissance masterpiece (aesthetic pleasure), and solving a mystery before the author gives it away (intellectual pleasure), fall into this category. Pleasure-states enrich our lives for a time, and then pass.

Taking pleasure in someone or something is different from this. It is a way of viewing and valuing, of seeing and savoring. If I take pleasure in a friendship, I see my friend in a positive light. I enjoy his sense of humor, his unique way of doing things, and his interest in things that also interest me. It may include a memory or an anticipation of shared pleasures, like a meal at a favorite restaurant or summiting a mountain peak together; in itself however, it is not so much a conscious state with a beginning and end as it is enduring sense of appreciation and esteem.

These two kinds of pleasure often occur together. I might take pleasure in the arts and enjoy aesthetic pleasure-states as I stroll through an art gallery or listen to a concert. I might take pleasure in a friendship and enjoy emotional pleasure-states in our fellowship of shared interests and experiences. This is no coincidence. I am most likely to enjoy pleasure-states in a friendship if I take pleasure in people, if sharing life with others is important to me. I am most likely to enjoy pleasure-states in viewing works of art if I take pleasure in the arts, if they are an important part of my interests and values. Put the other way around, an uncouth person is unlikely to experience pleasure-states in the arts. A recluse is not likely to experience pleasure in personal relationships.

Joy is like other pleasures in these ways. It can be a delighted awareness of God in the events of life (a pleasure-state), or savoring a relationship with God in all of life (a taking-pleasure-in).[4] These joys are found in each other's company. In fact, taking-pleasure-in-God seems to be an existential prerequisite for most pleasure-states of joy. If you do not take pleasure in "the things of God," as Jesus put it, you are not likely to experience God in pleasure-states of joy.[5]

I will seek to persuade you that the existence of God is the best explanation for the pleasure-states of joy. I will also argue that the relationship between these two kinds of pleasure explains why experiences of joy are not universal. It defeats the so-called argument from negative experience, that is, a case for the non-existence of God because some have not experienced him.[6]

NEED-PLEASURES AND PLEASURES OF APPRECIATION

In his classic work, *The Four Loves*, C.S. Lewis made a distinction between these two kinds of pleasure.[7] `Need-pleasures are preceded by a sense of lack or deficiency. There is a compulsion in the pleasure, a drive toward the fulfillment of a need. Many of our bodily pleasures fall into this category. Pleasures of Appreciation, on the other hand, have no antecedent need. They are simply pleasurable. The aesthetic pleasures of beauty and sound, and the intellectual pleasures in learning and discovery, fit this description. We do not need these things as we need food and water. They are examples of what I will call "surfeit pleasure." They do not replenish deficits. They serve no other purpose than to adorn and enrich life.

I will argue that a worldview without God can make sense of Need-pleasures, but fails in its account of Pleasures of Appreciation, and of joy as it is experienced as both.[8] A Christian vision of the world is superior on this score.

THE SOURCE OF JOY AND THE OBJECT OF JOY

From a softly hummed tune to a symphony that fills the room with sound, joy brings with it a sense that it has come from God. It seems that God himself is behind the pleasure, that he is joy's Source, that he is the Giver and joy is the gift. It is also often the case that joy not only seems to come from God, but to be about him. He is not only the Source of joy; he is its chief Object. Joy conveys a sense that God has drawn near. It delights in the presence of God and exults in who he is.[9] As I enjoy a friend who comes for a visit and delight in his adventurous spirit and gift for telling stories as we sit together in my living room, so I enjoy the presence of God and revel in his wisdom, goodness, and providential care as I encounter them in meditation and worship.

I am not asking you to believe these claims, but to acknowledge that there are many who make them, and that they should be taken seriously. To preview arguments to come, an account must be given of these two facets of joy. An explanation must be given, and we should accept the best proposal set before us.[10]

NATURAL AND NUMINOUS DIMENSIONS OF JOY

This distinction will play a very important role in all that follows. For our purposes an experience is natural if it involves the tangible world and the ordinary use of our faculties. C.S. Lewis described numinous experience this way:

> Those who have not met this term may be introduced to it by the following device. Suppose you were told there was a tiger in the next room: you would know that you were in danger and would probably feel fear. But if you were told "There is a ghost in the next room," and believed it, you would feel, indeed, what is often called fear, but of a different kind. It would not be based on the knowledge of danger, for no one is primarily afraid of what a ghost may do to him, but of the mere fact that it is a ghost. It is "uncanny" rather than dangerous, and the special kind of fear it excites may be called Dread. With the Uncanny one has reached the fringes of the Numinous. Now suppose that you were told simply "There is a mighty spirit in the room," and believed it. Your feelings would then be even less like the mere fear of danger: but the disturbance would be profound. You would feel wonder and a certain shrinking – a sense of inadequacy to cope with such a visitant and of prostration before it – an emotion which might be expressed in Shakespeare's words "Under it my genius is rebuked." This feeling may be described as awe, and the object which excites it as the *Numinous*."[11]

Numinous experience does not always come as a profound disturbance. Rudolf Otto, the first major thinker to make use of the idea of the numinous in an analysis of religious experience wrote:

> [It] may at times come sweeping like a gentle tide, pervading the mind with a tranquil mood of deepest worship. It may pass over into a more set and lasting attitude of the soul, continuing, as it were, thrillingly vibrant and resonant, until at last it dies away and the soul resumes its 'profane,' or non-religious mood of everyday experience.[12]

For our purposes, an experience is numinous if it involves an awareness of something real but utterly intangible. There are no physical properties involved. Ordinary modes of perception do not come into play. Numinous experience is presented to its subject as a direct awareness of the Spiritual, the Transcendent, the Supernatural, or, in our context, God himself.[13] (Again, I am not asking you to acknowledge that such experience is possible. At this point it is enough for you to understand what I have in mind.).

This puts us in a position to understand the natural and numinous dimensions of joy. Joy often has natural dimensions. It interfaces with the tangible world as it is experienced in relation to God. It embraces and transposes sensory and aesthetic pleasures. Lower pleasures are caught up in a higher pleasure as the heart rejoices in the world as a tangible token of the goodness of God. It seems at once to be a pleasure in the world and in the world's Maker. It is not that joy follows other pleasures in a sequence of experiences. They are part of the same experience in a twofold perception of senses and spirit, a double pleasure in creation and the Creator.[14]

Joy may or may not have natural dimensions; all joy includes the numinous. It may be a steady incandescence or may flicker briefly and disappear. It may come as a boisterous waterfall or a tiny ripple on a quiet country lake. It may be a ravishing beauty, a heavenly radiance, or a clarion sound. It may be a faint whisper, a lingering fragrance, or the glimmering of a gossamer thread on the boundary of our awareness.[15] However it is experienced, a numinous awareness of God is the defining characteristic, or distinguishing mark, of joy.[16] Without it we are talking about something else.[17]

In his important work, *The Existence of God*, Richard Swinburne explores five types of religious experience:[18]

1. Perceiving a common or public phenomenon in a "religious" way.
2. Perceiving an uncommon phenomenon in a "religious" way.
3. Having private sensations that can be described in normal vocabulary.
4. Having private sensations that cannot be described in normal vocabulary, i.e., are ineffable.
5. Having a direct awareness of God that is not the result of any sensations or phenomena.

Joy, with its numinous properties, has examples in all five categories. The fifth might be described as numinous experience proper, but the same dimension, with nuances, is present in the other four. In every case it is the awareness of God (with its numinous qualities) that distinguishes joy from other pleasurable experiences.

Imagine an atheist and a believer parked at a roadside vista appreciating the same beautiful scenery (Swinburne's first category of religious experience). It is the pleasurable awareness of God in relation to the beauty that makes the believer's experience joyful as well as aesthetic, while the experience of the atheist is merely aesthetic. The numinous feature of the experience makes the difference.

Consider the Gospel story of an encounter between Jesus and his disciples in a closed room following his death and their discovery of the empty tomb (Swinburne's second category). Seeing a man they loved and knew to be dead now demonstrably alive and standing before them overwhelmed the ordinary use of their faculties. The text says that they "disbelieved for joy."[19] Their minds reeled from the numinous dimensions of joy. The experience was uncanny, unnerving, and freighted with joy.

Joy is often a private experience that can be described in normal vocabulary (Swinburne's third category). Biblical writers used ordinary language to describe joy when they compared it to common pleasures of food, drink, and other delights.[20] You may be a stranger to joy, but if you know the pleasures of wine, wealth, or romantic love, you know something akin to it by virtue of the analogy. What you miss, by the nature of the case, is joy's numinous character.

When joy has no analogue in ordinary experience it becomes ineffable (Swinburne's fourth category). At best words point to the experience, like Pascal penning the exclamation "Fire!" after an unusual experience of joy.[21] This joy pulsates with numinous qualities. It is experienced as a crowding and spilling over the limits of normal human capacity. Because it conveys a sense of being outside the bounds of ordinary experience, it is ecstatic (the literal meaning of the word). Because there is no vocabulary for this experience, it is unspeakable.

This brings us to Swinburne's fifth category of religious experience, seeming to have a direct awareness of God that is not the result of any sensation. This is numinous experience in its purest form. It is joy when one is aware that God is not only behind the pleasure, but present in it, and the encounter elicits delight. One may have doubts when the numinous properties of the experience fade and ordinary modes of consciousness and perception return, but it does not seem possible to doubt the reality of God in the experience itself.

In the chapters that follow, my argument will be that the numinous dimensions of joy, presented as an encounter with God, make belief in God rational for those who have the experience. The fact that many claim to have this experience is significant evidence that this belief is true.

QUESTIONS FOR THOUGHT AND DISCUSSION

1. How would you explain the difference between knowing something to be true and showing it to be true? Why is this distinction important?

2. What is the difference between being rational in your beliefs and demonstrating that they are true? Why is this important?

3. How would you explain the difference between joy as a pleasure-state and joy as taking-pleasure-in?

4. Discuss the difference between God as the Source and the Object of joy. Why is this important?

5. If this chapter introduced you to the Numinous, how would you describe it to someone else?

PART TWO

ARGUMENTS

CHAPTER 6

JOY AND THE RATIONALITY OF FAITH

I might reason to the existence of a beautiful woman who shares my life in a state of matrimony from feminine clothing that takes more than its fair share of the closet in my bedroom, make-up and bottled fragrances in the bathroom drawers, his and her towels on the towel rack, certain purchases recorded in my checkbook, the ring on the fourth finger of my left hand, a picture that hangs on the wall, and a certificate that is filed away in a cabinet in my house. I do not, however, base my belief in her existence on any of these things, but on the fact that I have held her in my arms and at this very moment enjoy memories of shared experiences with her.

I might also give you a reasoned case for the existence of God.[1] Rational arguments, however, are not the basis of my faith. I believe that God exists because I have encountered him in an array of experiences, including joy.[2]

I maintain, further, that experiences of joy, with their numinous properties, make it rational for those who have them to believe in God. You will recall from earlier discussion that it is possible to be rational in a belief that is actually false. I am not yet seeking to show you that my belief in God is true.[3] I am not arguing that others have an epistemic duty to believe in God because of my experience. My claim is modest but significant: Unless there are persuasive reasons to believe otherwise, it is rational for a person who seems to encounter God in experiences of joy to believe that God exists.

The issue of rationality has to do with the relationship between a truth-claim and conditions that must be met for one to believe reasonably that the claim is true. John Hick puts this into the context of our discussion:

> Thus the question of the rationality of belief in the reality of God is the question of the rationality of a particular person's believing, given the data he is using; or that of the believing class of people who share the same body of data. Or putting the same point the other way round, any assessing of the belief-worthiness of the proposition that God exists must be an assessing of it in relation to particular ranges of data.[4]

As a Christian, the "data" I use in assessing the "belief-worthiness of the proposition that God exists" include what I take to be an encounter with God (among other things) in experiences of joy. The "believing class of people who share the same data" is the Church, or Christian community. I find that others have experiences like my own, with the result that my joy, their joy, and our shared joys produce a "body of data" that makes belief in God rational *for us*.

After discussing the compelling characteristic of some religious experiences, like those of the Old Testament prophets and the apostle Paul, Hick continues:

> Our question concerns, then, one whose "experience of God" has this compelling quality, so that he is no more inclined to doubt its

veridical character than to doubt the evidence of his senses. Is it rational for him to take the former, as it is certainly rational for him to take the latter . . .? Are the two features noted above in our sense experience – its givenness, or involuntary character, and the fact that we can successfully act in terms of it – also found here? It seems that they are. The sense of the presence of God reported by the great religious figures has a similar involuntary and compelling quality; and as they proceed to live on the basis of it they are sustained and confirmed by their further experiences in the conviction that they are living in relation, not to illusion, but to reality. It therefore seems *prima facie*, that the religious man *is* entitled to trust his religious experience and to proceed to conduct his life in terms of it.[5]

With this in mind, let me refine my claim: It is rational – *prima facie* – to believe in the existence of God if one has experiences of joy in which God seems present.[6] This follows from the nature of joy and what Richard Swinburne calls the "principle of credulity."

JOY AND THE PRINCIPLE OF CREDULITY

If you are not familiar with it, let me introduce you to the principle of credulity. Richard Swinburne puts it this way: "I suggest that it is a principle of rationality that (in the absence of special considerations) if it seems (epistemically) to a subject that X is present, then probably X is present; what one seems to perceive is probably so."[7] As I type these words it seems to me that I perceive them on the screen of my laptop computer. Unless there are special considerations that defeat my belief, it is rational for me to believe that they are probably there. If you knew me well and knew that when I am very hungry I claim to see things that aren't there, and you pointed out that I hadn't eaten all day when I made the assertion about seeing words on my computer screen, that would count against the rationality of my belief. In the absence of such factors, it is rational for me to believe that my perception connects truthfully with the world.

What significance does this have for joy? Though it may vary in nuance, to the attentive heart joy brings with it a sense that God is not only the Source but the Object of the experience. It is presented numinously as an encounter with God. A delighted awareness of God. An enjoyment of God. He draws near, summons our attention, and joy results from the encounter.[8] I have in mind the joy described classically by Thomas à Kempis:

> Blessed may You be, heavenly Father, the Father of my Lord Jesus Christ, for You have vouchsafed to remember me, Your poorest servant, and sometimes You comfort me with Your gracious presence. . . . O my Lord God, most faithful Lover, when You come into my heart, all within me rejoices. You are my glory and the joy of my heart . . . .[9]

The principle of credulity establishes the *prima facie* rationality of believing in God for those whose awareness of God in experiences of joy seems compelling to them. In the absence of special considerations, if it seems that God is present, then it is rational to believe that he probably is. If you disagree, you might argue that there are special considerations that undermine my claims. For instance, if you could prove that God does not exist, that would defeat all claims to have experienced him! Your proof, however, would have to be more than an assertion that there is insufficient evidence, since the experiences of joy are a claim to just such evidence.[10] You might seek to prove that I am emotionally disturbed, or am subject to delusions or hallucinations. Even if you could demonstrate that your diagnosis is true in my case, you would have to establish the same for all who make similar claims. If your evidence of instability were an alleged experience of God, you would only have assumed what you must prove.[11]

Your other option would be to challenge the principle of credulity. You might dismiss it outright, but that would be a Pyrhhic victory. You would lose too much in winning. You would land in complete skepticism about everything beyond your own conscious states. As Swinburne rightly points out, it is a fundamental principle of rationality. If you are going to play the game of reason – or at least the acquisition of knowledge through experience – you must play by this rule.

Perhaps the principle can be construed in a way that excludes numinous experience. You might challenge the claim that such experience is similar to sensory perception. You must, of course, move beyond the obvious fact that the numinous does not have a sensory "filling"[12] or "presentation."[13] An accounting of its characteristic traits does not include properties that are familiar to our senses: colors, textures, sounds, smells, tastes, motion, dimensions, weight, et cetera. Nevertheless, there is a structural similarity between sense perception and numinous experience.[14]

In its simplest terms, there are three components to sensory perception: the perceiving subject, the perceived object, and the phenomenon or appearance of the object as it is presented in perception.[15] Importantly, we can add that it is possible to act in fitting ways to what is given in perception.

Suppose that I watch a college football game on a Saturday afternoon in September. I am the subject of the perception, the football field is the object of my perception, and the phenomena in the perception are what seem to be little people (because my seat is high in the stadium) in helmets and lumpy uniforms running across the field. I can respond to this visual perception in suitable ways, cheering if I see my team score, or booing what I regard as a bad call by a referee.

Now suppose that on the next Saturday afternoon in September I hike through an aspen forest in the Rocky Mountains. As I enjoy the solitude, golden leaves quaking in an early autumn breeze, and the sun-dappled path before me, my awareness shifts from the beauty of this alpine setting to a sense of its Creator, present with me, and presented to me in goodness and creative wisdom and power – as it were, the phenomena of my experience.[16] I respond to this spiritual perception suitably in worship, thanksgiving, and reflective delight.

The parallels are clear.

If you grant that there is a perceptual structure to numinous experience, you might seek to discount such experiences on other grounds. Arguments of this sort usually focus on special characteristics of numinous experience, such as our inability to test it as we can other claims:

> If someone says, "There is a fire burning in the fireplace," it would not normally occur to me to doubt that he really does *perceive* a fire in the fireplace. On the other hand, I might at that very moment observe that there is, in fact, no fire in the fireplace. But there is a big difference between saying, "There is a fire in the fireplace," and saying, "I have had an experience with the divine." The difference is, of course, that I can go and see for myself whether there is a fire in the fireplace, whereas there is no possible way to verify or confirm, say, mystical experience; such a claim is by its nature subjective and private.[17]

Let's think about this. First, the comparison isn't quite accurate. Both claims should be made in the first person: 1) "I perceive a fire burning in the fireplace." and 2) "I perceive the presence of God." I maintain that just as it is rational for me to believe that there is a fire in the fireplace if it seems to me that I see it and am warmed by it, so it is rational for me to believe that

God exists if I have experiences in which it seems that he is present and I experience joy in the encounter.

You might object that there is no way to "get outside" of numinous experience to test its truthfulness. But this is also true of sense experience. Suppose that you decided to test the claim that there is a fire in the fireplace. Any test you devise would involve checking one experience by another, such as approaching the fireplace and checking for warmth, going outside to see if smoke is rising from the chimney, or waiting until the next morning to see if ashes have replaced the logs. At what point do you get outside sensory experience in the checking process? You never do. You simply move from one private sensory experience to another. How do you know that the experience you use to check another experience is itself trustworthy?

Nor would it help to appeal to the sensory experience of others. How do you know that two or more people share the same properties of experience? Checking someone else's claim to sensory perception involves the same endless (and fruitless) process that we have already described. George Mavrodes states the case this way:

> In some particular circumstance I may have doubt about some putative experience, perhaps my apparent seeing of a piece of blue paper. In that case I might resort to photography or to the testimony of friends to resolve my uncertainty. This procedure does not enable me, however, to substitute a "checked" experience for the unchecked variety. It enables me, rather, to substitute one unchecked experience for another. If I do not rely upon my vision of the paper, I do rely upon my vision of the photo, or upon my sense of touch, or upon the accuracy of my hearing when I listen to my friends' report. I can, perhaps, seek a check for any of these that I wish but to look for a check for all of them is self-stultifying. If I cannot rely upon some unchecked experience of my own, I just

cannot get anything out of experience and I must give up the empirical route to knowledge.[18]

At some point, to avoid an "infinite regress," you must affirm that sensory experience is trustworthy unless there are special considerations that warrant a contrary belief. *Claims to an encounter with God in experiences of joy deserve the same consideration.* The exclusion of numinous experience from the principle of credulity, if not arbitrary, would destroy all rational enterprise if applied for the same reasons to the experience of our senses.

In the absence of persuasive evidence to the contrary, it is rational, *prima facie,* for one to believe in the existence of God if one has experiences of joy in which he seems to be present. In the chapters that follow we will explore arguments that this belief is also true.

QUESTIONS FOR THOUGHT AND DISCUSSION

1. If you are a believer, what role does religious experience play in your faith? Your experience of joy? If you aren't, find someone who is a believer and ask these questions of him or her.

2. If you don't agree with the principle of credulity, what are the implications of rejecting it?

3. If you accept the principle of credulity, how would you critique a claim that it cannot be used in evaluating religious experience?

4. What do you think of the author's comparison of ordinary perception and numinous experience?

5. What do you think of the author's comparison of these statements? 1) "I perceive a fire burning in the fireplace." and 2) "I perceive the presence of God."

CHAPTER 7

ON THE THRESHOLD OF JOY

W e turn now from the rationality of believing in God to evidence for the truth of that belief. This is where the distinction between *knowing* something to be true and *showing* it to be true becomes important. My belief in God is not based upon these arguments, but they confirm it and offer reasons for faith to others who have not enjoyed the same experiences. My claim is not that the evidence compels belief in God, but that it points to him. The evidence is explained best by the existence of God. Joy leaves serious problems if there is no God.

THE PROBLEM OF BEAUTY

"Flowers are not fragrant and colorful for our aesthetic pleasure. These features serve only to attract insects which, in the process of seeking their own survival, unwittingly contribute to the survival of these plants." The lecture was closer to a sermon. The instructor, an aspiring Ph.D. student, was intent on making converts, on dissuading a classroom of university freshmen from what he saw as the mythical, theistic notion that we live in a world made for us, urging us instead to look at the world through the pristine lens of Darwinism.[1]

Beauty reduced to utility. It was my first encounter with the ugliness of a world without God. I thought, "Why are color and fragrance the mechanisms that serve the interests of survival? Why not something with no aesthetic dimension? It seems more than would be necessary for the perpetuation of a species. It seems extravagant." When I asked this question, I was told (in a demeaning tone) that our subject was biology, not philosophy. The instructor saw an opportunity to enlighten me. His response was something like this: "What you think of as beauty and fragrance are aesthetic construals that have no meaning for the insects that carry out their survival tasks, and merely respond to visual and olfactory stimuli. You are imposing an anthropomorphism on a purely physical process in the life of a bug."

That only led to a deeper question: "Even if what you say about insects and flowers is true, it is still the case that beauty has meaning for me. (An appeal to anthropomorphism only shifts the question to *anthropoi*.) If floral species can exist without us, and our species can exist without them (that is, neither species is essential to the survival of the other in a natural environment), how is it that we enjoy their beauty and fragrance for no other reason than the appreciative pleasure we experience?" I was probably the only one who left thinking that our pleasure in nature's beauty is sheer surfeit in a world with no God, where everything can be reduced to the bottom line of survival. Whatever else it may explain, Darwin's theory fails to elucidate our experience.[2]

Could it be that flowers are exquisite because they are the handiwork of an Artist and Perfumer who creates things for their survival value and for the joy of his creatures? That the Maker designed things to be beautiful as well as useful? This is exactly what we find when we turn to the book of Genesis:

"The LORD God made to spring up every tree that is pleasant to the sight and good for food."[3] Beautiful (*pleasant to the sight*) and useful for survival (*good for food*). In fact, if there is significance to the order, beauty is first in the Creator's interests and concerns for his world.[4]

The tangerine beauty of a sunset. The shimmering beauty of moonbeams on a lake. The distant beauty of a star-spangled sky. The brilliant beauty of sun-glistened snow. The lush beauty of a forest canopy. The arid beauty of a desert. The majestic beauty of mountains. The winged beauty of geese in flight. The underwater beauty of coral gardens. The thundering beauty of cascading waterfalls. The lustrous beauty of earthen gems. Beauty in the world is the glory of God. If it is not, it is a cruel hoax. Beauty is incomprehensible or an expression of the extravagant benevolence of our Creator. Joy in nature's beauty fits in a world created by God, and is a serious misfit without him.[5]

THE PROBLEMS OF PLEASURE

The problem of surfeit pleasure. If needs and pleasures were a matched set (with no needs that do not have corresponding pleasures and no pleasures without corresponding needs), it could all be accounted for under the rubric of survival. At least on this point we could be comfortable atheists. Be prepared to be uncomfortable: There is more pleasure in the world than can be explained by the survival of the fittest. To make use of an earlier distinction, Need-pleasures fit well with the needs and demands of survival. Pleasures of Appreciation do not. In a world driven by needs, they are extras.

Aristotle pointed out that not even all bodily pleasures derive from deficiency or need.[6] There are pleasures of sight, smell, and sound that go beyond the needs of survival. Enjoying a birdsong, delighting in the fragrance of a flower, and admiring the beauty of a sunset will not add a day to our lives, or make it any more likely that our genes will pass to the next generation. Even if all pleasures were physical, the residual pleasure after physical needs and drives are accounted for makes pleasure a serious problem.

Whether it is enjoying the harmonies of an a cappella choir, delighting in the subtle shapes and textures of a sculpture, savoring the colors and hues of a painting, appreciating the intricate plot of a murder mystery, or smiling with satisfaction at the solution to a riddle, aesthetic and intellectual pleasures compound the problem for the atheist. Unlike Need Pleasures (pleasures that match biological needs and drives), Pleasures of Appreciation do not serve our continued existence in the world. They enrich. They enhance. They create a robustness that cannot be measured or weighed. If we were bereft of them we would see ourselves diminished and poorer, but we can live, pass on our genes, and die of old age without them.[7] They have no bearing on the challenges of survival.[8]

The surfeit of pleasure in the world is either a quirk or a clue. It is either inexplicably odd or a key to the nature of reality. It is, as Clark Pinnock put it, "as if the Maker wanted to see us glad."[9]

The paradox of hedonism. There is another problem with pleasure. We have such a strong attraction to it that it is fair to say, as Aristotle did, that pleasure is essential to our humanity.[10] But here we encounter something strange: The more we give ourselves to the pursuit of pleasure, the more the endeavor goes bad on us. Philosophers call this the "paradox of hedonism." Aristotle asked, "How is it . . . that nobody feels pleasure continuously?" His answer was that the "cause is probably fatigue. No human faculty can be continuously active, so pleasure is not continuous . . . ."[11] In other words, the problem is that we are under-equipped for a life of perpetual pleasure. We aren't up to it.

The real answer to the paradox of hedonism is the opposite of this. We are not under-equipped. We are over-endowed.[12]

The pursuit of pleasure often leads to frustration and guilt: to the first when one's designs are thwarted, and to the second when moral boundaries are crossed in the quest. If it manages to escape these fates, the pursuit of pleasure ends, nevertheless, and inevitably, in boredom. A malaise of discontent. Boredom emerges from the incongruity between human potential and the pleasures of the world, from the disparity between the transcendent longings of the heart and the mere appeasement of immediacy, from the false equation of sensual gratification and existential fulfillment.

The problem is not that there are not enough pleasures in the world. Nor is it that we lack strength and endurance to take full advantage of them. If experience teaches anything, a life of perpetual pleasure would be like a steady diet of candy bars and soda. It doesn't matter how much we consume. We cannot live on sugar, or pleasure, alone.

What does pleasure tell us about human nature? Why are we attracted to it, but in the end discontent with a life devoted to it? Why is it that we can be enriched, but not sustained, by it? There are two answers, and you must choose one: Either we are tragically under-equipped for a life of pleasure, if atheism is true, or we are wonderfully over-endowed, if God exists and is the One to whom all pleasure points and the One in whom all pleasure finds its fulfillment. Pleasure terminates in boredom or fatigue, or points to something beyond itself that will fulfill our human potential and satisfy our deepest longings and aspirations.

I invite you to consider the possibility that pleasure is meant to point our hearts to joy. Pleasure is good, which explains why we are attracted to it, but it is not our Greatest Good, which explains why we are not fulfilled by it. Our *summum bonum* is the One in whose presence there is fullness of joy and in whose right hand are pleasures for evermore.[13]

SEHNSUCHT

The Germans have a word for deep yearnings of the heart: *Sehnsucht.* C.S. Lewis used this term to describe a recurring experience in his life. In the preface to *The Pilgrim's Regress,* he wrote:

> What I meant was a particular recurrent experience which dominated my childhood and adolescence and which I hastily called "Romantic" because inanimate nature and marvellous literature were among the things that evoked it. I still believe that the experience is common, commonly misunderstood, and of immense importance: but I know now that in other minds it arises under other stimuli and is entangled with other irrelevancies and that to bring it into the forefront of consciousness is not so easy as I once supposed.[14]

Lewis described *Sehnsucht* as an inexorable longing, an aching of the heart, a captivating desire. Even if there were no hope of satisfaction, those who know it would prize it above all else. The inexperienced and inattentive might identify it with mundane desires and their matching pleasures, but that is a mistake, Lewis contended. The experience can be evoked by a number of things, but they are not the true source or object of this desire. They leave one longing for something not yet given. Lewis himself sought to fulfill this yearning in everything from books to eroticism, from knowledge to a craving for real magic and occultism. None of these things, he concluded, is adequate for this desire, because it seeks something that is not of this world.[15]

"Maybe Lewis ended his quest prematurely," you say. "Perhaps the object of his longing is supplied by the world, but he missed it in his search." He would have given two responses to this, I think. First, when it is examined carefully, this desire is always for something *other*, something *beyond.* By its very nature it is a longing for something that is not of this world. It is a yearning for the Transcendent. Second, and more importantly, Lewis' quest did end – not in the world, but in the world's Maker. In his own words, he discovered God to be the "source from which those arrows of Joy" had been shot at him from the days of his childhood.[16]

Accounting for our desires. You may or may not want to follow Lewis as an existential guide. For the moment that is beside the point. My intent is to investigate the significance of this experience even for those who have not had it. We are not yet to the problem of joy. We are only at its threshold: the longing that many have discovered to be fulfilled in the experiences of joy. How do we account for this existential desire?

Consider the following argument:

(1) If p, then q;
(2) p;
(3) Therefore, q.

This is a mixed hypothetical syllogism known as *modus ponens.* Its two premises consist of a hypothetical statement followed by a categorical statement. If the premises are true, the conclusion necessarily follows. Let's add content to it:

(1) If I have a desire for X, then X exists to fulfill my desire;
(2) I have a desire for X;
(3) Therefore, X exists to fulfill my desire.

If we stipulate that X is something not of this world, then my desire for X establishes that something not of this world exists to fulfill my desire.

To deny the conclusion, you must deny one or both of the premises. You could reject the categorical statement: "I have a desire for X, that is, for something that is not of this world." You might deny that you have this desire and therefore deny that I do, but one does not follow from the other. You would have a better hope of success if you focused on the hypothetical statement: "If I have a desire for X, then X exists to fulfill my desire." Is it true that desires always have objects that fulfill them? No. If I awoke in the night with a compelling desire to ride a unicorn through my neighborhood, it would not imply that a unicorn exists to fulfill my longing.

To succeed, the argument must be qualified. Peter Kreeft has done that by distinguishing between two kinds of desires: natural or artificial, innate or conditioned:

> We naturally desire things like food, drink, sex, knowledge, friendship, and beauty, and we naturally turn away from things like starvation, ignorance, loneliness, and ugliness. We also desire things like Rolls Royces, political offices, flying through the air like Superman, a Red Sox world championship, and lands like Oz. But there are two differences between the two lists. First, we do not always recognize corresponding states of deprivation of the second, as we do with the first. And, most important, the first list of desires all come from within, from our nature, while the second come from without, from society, or advertising, or fiction. . . .
>
> The existence of desires of the second class does not necessarily mean that the objects desired exist. Rolls Royces do, Oz does not. But the existence of desires of the first class, in every discoverable case, does mean that the objects desired exist. No case has ever been found of an innate desire for a nonexistent object.[17]

If you grant this distinction, it must still be demonstrated that *Sehnsucht* falls into the first class and not the second. In some cases it might seem that a yearning for the Transcendent comes from one's social setting, or religious propaganda, or religious fiction. To use postmodern language, one might argue that *Sehnsucht* is a social construct. On the other hand, it may be that social factors merely awaken a desire that is already present, but latent, and that is, in fact, innate. Consider the fact that many who were raised in atheistic, agnostic, secular, or nominally religious families and social contexts have reported a yearning for the Transcendent. Lewis himself was an atheist from his early teens. This desire is as wide as the world and as old as humanity itself.[18] It crosses time, places, and cultures. Like a fingerprint at a crime scene, it is significant evidence. Lewis would say that it is a token of another world that transcends and yet interfaces with our own.

What should we make of the argument in light of this? If the premises are true, the conclusion follows: There must be an object – not of this world – that fulfills yearnings of the heart for something that is not of this world. Lewis was right in sizing up the argument this way:

> The Christian says, "Creatures are not born with desires unless satisfaction for those desires exists. A baby feels hunger: well, there is such a thing as food. A duckling wants to swim: well, there is such a thing as water. Men feel sexual desire: well, there is such a thing as sex. If I find in myself a desire which no experience in this world can satisfy, *the most probable explanation* is that I was made for another world.[19]

Calculating the consequences. Before you make up your mind about this, let me give you another argument.

(1) If p, then q;

(2) not q;

(3) Therefore, not p.

This is another mixed hypothetical syllogism, known as *modus tollens*. If the premises are true, the conclusion necessarily follows. Let's give it content:

(1) If nature makes nothing in vain, then every natural or innate desire has a matching object that will satisfy it;

(2) The natural or innate desire for the Transcendent has no matching object that will satisfy it;

(3) Therefore, it is not the case that nature makes nothing in vain (or stated positively, it is the case that nature makes things in vain).

My reason for presenting this argument is to persuade you that the stakes in this matter are very high. First, if the argument is successful, it refutes a claim as old as Aristotle. Under these premises, nature makes things in vain. Second, and more significantly, there are dreadful implications if the argument succeeds. In the words of Peter Kreeft, the cost of conceding that nature makes things in vain is a "meaningful universe, a universe in which desires and satisfactions match." "In other words," he writes, "God can be avoided. All we need is to embrace 'vanity of vanities' instead. It is a fool's bargain, of course: Everything is exchanged for Nothing – a trade even the Boston Red Sox are not fool enough to make."[20]

Richard Purtill calculates the cost of a godless universe:

> If reason left us no alternative to such a view, intellectual honesty might force us to accept it. But if this view is true, reason has no force. If morality impelled us to take such a view, integrity might make us choose it. But if the view is true, morality has no force. If the deepest needs of our nature were satisfied by this view, then our nature might

compel us to accept it. But if this view is true the deepest needs of our nature are illusory. In sum, there can be no reason for accepting . . . (that) view of the universe, for that view destroys all reasons.[21]

The other option, of course, is to reject this view of the world and embrace our deepest desires as evidence that points us to the One who alone can fulfill them.

QUESTIONS FOR THOUGHT AND DISCUSSION

1. What do you think of beauty as a problem? Compare and contrast evolutionary naturalism (survival of the fittest) and a Creator as rival explanations.

2. What is the problem of surfeit pleasure? What are the strengths and weaknesses of the author's view on this?

3. What is the significance of the paradox of hedonism? How is this relevant to our culture?

4. What do you think of C.S. Lewis' argument for God from *Sehnsucht*?

5. What do you think of the author's analysis of the implications of denying the argument from *Sehnsucht*?

CHAPTER 8

JOY AND THE EXISTENCE OF GOD

PART 1

Any view of the world that fails to account for the significant experiences of its inhabitants is inferior to one that does. If a yearning for the Transcendent were all we had to go on, it would give us reason to believe that we were created for something more than this world offers. But that is only part of the story. Millions of people, young and old, male and female, rich and poor, from every imaginable background and place on the earth, have found their longings for the Transcendent fulfilled in experiences of joy. It seems compelling to them that their joy is a gift from God and a connection with him. What are we to make of these claims?

Experiences of joy may differ from each other (like snowflakes, no two joys are the same), but they have the common feature, for those who are attentive, that they seem to come from God.[1] Either this is true, or it is not. We can diagram our analysis this way:

Joy

Not Caused   Caused

Not God   God

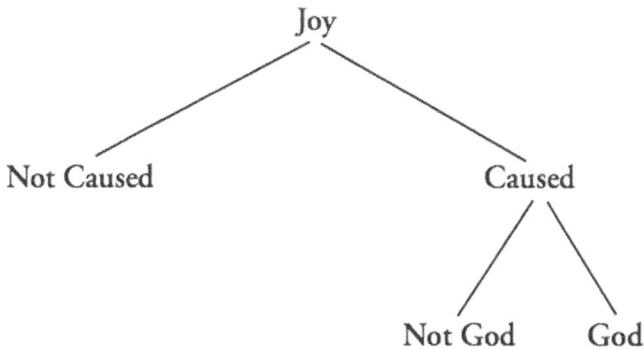

In an earlier chapter I introduced you to Aristotle's distinction between two kinds of pleasure: a pleasure-state, and taking pleasure in someone or something.[2] Joy is like other pleasures in this regard. It can be a delighted awareness of God in the events of life (a pleasure-state), or savoring a relationship with God in all of life (a taking-pleasure-in). In the following we will view joy as a pleasure-state, a distinct experience of delight with a beginning and an end.

Let's start with the possibility that joy has no cause. You could hold this position in theory, but not credibly. You would have to make a persuasive case that joy is the kind of thing that appears out of thin air. It is a brute fact. But that runs counter to our experience. Pleasure-states don't just happen. If you saw a small child at a table, smiling, with chocolate frosting on her face and hands, and a chocolate cake on a table within her reach, you would make a causal inference from the chocolate-laden smile to the cake. If you came upon people in a park looking raptly into the sky, you would follow their gaze and expect to see a rainbow, a sunset, geese in flight, or something that would explain their apparent pleasure.[3]

Pleasure-states point beyond themselves. Maintaining that joy is anomalous to this makes your position look more like gamesmanship than a serious attempt at rational explanation. Contending that joy has no causal factors (and is therefore incapable of rational explanation) gives it an *ad hoc* status, a weakness for any theory. At least on this point, any view that makes sense of this experience would be superior. The more serious objection to this position, however, is that here, as everywhere, nothing comes from nothing. Claiming otherwise cuts against the grain of uniform experience.

Let's move to the second set of options. If joy has causal factors, either God is one of them or he is not.[4] If you accept the view that God is the ultimate Source of joy (that is, that God and joy are related as Cause and effect), you have an explanation that fits all instances of the experience. If you reject that explanation, you must give another account. You might claim that the pleasure-states of joy are entirely like mundane pleasures, and therefore do not require another explanation. The Jewish and Christian Scriptures invite this challenge when they compare joy to other pleasures. It is like the pleasure of wine, wealth, food, and romantic love, they say, but better.[5] Not just better, however. Joy is different in ways that require another explanation.

Let me illustrate. On the day of Pentecost, according to a story passed down from the early church, the disciples of Jesus were accused of being drunk in public because of the unusual, ecstatic nature of their joy (praising God in languages not previously known to them).[6] They believed that their experience was the result of an unprecedented presence and work of the Holy Spirit (one causal explanation); their critics believed it to be the result of too much wine (another causal explanation). The stubborn fact was that they were not inebriated. ("These men are not drunk, as you suppose, since it is only the third hour of the day.") Their experience may have borne similarities to the intoxicating pleasures of wine; among other things, however, it lacked the same causal factors.[7] Another explanation was demanded.

If you reject the believer's explanation of joy, you must find a causal factor or package of factors that are 1) common to all experiences of joy and 2) found consistently in other pleasures that do not involve God. The diversity of experience, and the diverse background of millions of people who have claimed the experience, make your task herculean. If you do nothing more than assert that such an explanation is possible, you mask the weakness of your position. Believers have an explanation that fits, and you don't.

We could stop at this point and wait for critics to produce a convincing counter-explanation of joy, but we would never get around to anything else. For the sake of argument, let's suppose, contrary to fact, that they are successful in their endeavor. Let's say that X is the set of causal factors found in all pleasure-states of joy, and that X is also found in other pleasure-states, all of which are mundane (that is, entirely of this world). If this common causality were established, it would strengthen the explanatory power of a non-theistic point of view. It would not, however, address the claim that joy also has a transcendent causal factor, which we might designate as T. Believers are willing to acknowledge X in many experiences of joy, but insist that a full explanation will always be $X+T$.

This is not a "God of the gaps" argument, invoking God to explain something that is otherwise explicable in natural terms. Joy seems to come from God. Even if other factors are involved, the property of seeming-to-come-from-God must be included in a complete account. To exclude the most significant feature of joy for those who know it well would be a serious flaw in any explanation. It would be like describing a skyscraper but omitting any reference to its height. The report might be true as far as it goes, but it would be seriously incomplete. The pleasure-states of joy seem to come from God. It seems that he is the Giver and joy is his gift. If you reject the believer's explanation of joy, you must offer another account of the pleasure (for which we are still waiting) that includes the captivating sense for those who experience joy that its Source is God.[8]

PART 2

If you spent a lifetime tallying claims to a joyful encounter with God, you would run out of breath before you ran out of claims. I argued earlier that it is rational for those who have such an experience to believe that God exists. My argument now is that this claim – because it is made by so many and by such a great variety of people – is evidence for the existence of God that rational people must account for whether they have had the same experiences or not.

Even if you do not believe the claims to be true, it is astonishing that millions of people from so many nations, ethnicities, backgrounds, and social stations, with such a remarkable diversity in personality, temperament, and disposition, claim to have encountered God in experiences of joy. What are we to make of this?

Our situation is illustrated in *The Lion, the Witch and the Wardrobe*, by C.S. Lewis. In this story Peter and Susan are seeking counsel about their younger sister, Lucy, from a professor in whose countryside mansion they are staying during the World War II bombing of London. Lucy claims to have gone through a wardrobe into the land of Narnia, where she entered an enchanted wood and met a Faun. Their younger brother, Edmund, also ventured into Narnia through the wardrobe, but now claims that it was all make-believe. In their conversation with the professor, Peter and Susan explore the possibility that Lucy is lying about Narnia, or that she might have gone mad. The conversation ends here:

> "Logic!" said the Professor half to himself. "Why don't they teach logic at these schools? There are only three possibilities. Either

your sister is telling lies, or she is mad, or she is telling the truth. You know she doesn't tell lies and it is obvious that she is not mad. For the moment then and unless any further evidence turns up, we must assume that she is telling the truth."[9]

Like Peter and Susan, we are faced with a set of choices:

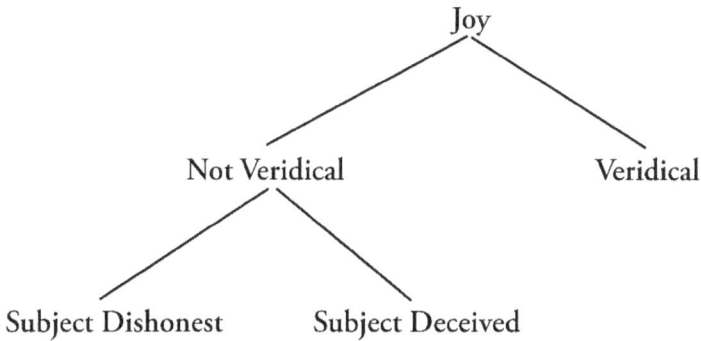

Joy

Not Veridical   Veridical

Subject Dishonest   Subject Deceived

Although it may vary in clarity, prominence, and degree, all joy seems to be a connection with God. There is a sense that he is not only the Source of joy but its chief Object. Either this experience is what it seems to be or it is not.

The dishonesty hypothesis. If you are not yet convinced that joy is veridical, that is, that at least some who have claimed an encounter with God in experiences of joy have had such a meeting, you must provide a persuasive, alternative explanation. One possibility is that those who make such claims are dishonest about their experience. They know it to be one thing, but pass it off as another. I can think of a few reasons why one might do this, but none that would apply to everyone who has made the claim. People who profit from religious claims (including writing books about joy) might do it. In Christian communities in which one's status is judged by claims to religious experience, I can imagine some people making claims that don't square what they know to be the case.

You might be able to think of other reasons why someone would be dishonest about experiences of joy. First, however, finding a motive for dishonesty does not prove the lie. Second, even if it were the case that some people are dishonest about their claims, it does not follow that all claims are therefore spurious. Third, in fact, counterfeits usually imply a genuine article. Forgeries imply an authentic work. False claims imply true. Fourth, people who are dishonest about religious claims usually have other noteworthy flaws, such as the marital infidelity of televangelists in the 1980's, and adulterous pastors in our own day. *Causes célèbres* like these are a far cry from the piety of most believers. Finally, in the words of the proverb, "You can fool all the people some of the time, and some of the people all the time, but you cannot fool all the people all the time."[10] If everyone who has ever made a claim to encounter God in an experience of joy were dishonest about it, it is unlikely that Christianity could have outlived the lie, and survived and flourished for twenty centuries.

The deception hypothesis. It appears that you will have to supplement the dishonesty hypothesis with your other option, that those who claim an experience of God in their joy are deceived. They believe that they are connecting with God, but it is not so. You might accept the principle of credulity, that in the absence of special considerations our perceptions should be regarded as trustworthy, but argue that there are, in fact, special considerations that make it more probable that claims to encounters of God in experience are mistaken than that they are true.

This could take a number of forms. One is the old wish-fulfillment argument. Perhaps the longing for a joyful encounter with God is so great that an imaginary god is reified, or given real status, and this fictional god becomes the fulfillment of a desire. In other words, joy is pleasure in a psychological projection. However, if wishing something does not make it true, neither does it make it false. If I have a profound wish to meet the President of the United States, or to attend a Wimbledon tennis championship, the wish does not entail the non-existence of the President or of that prestigious tennis tournament. Wishing proves nothing about truth one way or the other. Moreover, if you take this path, it leads you back to the problem of *Sehnsucht*. If you explain joy in terms of a deep desire for it, you must then give a fitting explanation of the desire.

Another argument seems at first glance to be more generous than saying that joyful people are deceived. Perhaps what Christians call *joy* eastern traditions call *nirvana* and pagans are content to call *personal peace* or *happiness*. The disagreement is not about facts, but what to call them. The differences are not about *what* is experienced, but *how* it is interpreted, and in the name that is given to it.

John Hick's parable of the Celestial City illustrates this approach to religious experience.[11] In his story two men are walking together on a road. One believes that the road leads to a Celestial City; the other that it leads nowhere. As they travel down the road, both men experience moments of refreshment and delight, and both interpret them in light of their convictions about the end of the road. The first man sees them as encouragements along the way, and the other man sees them simply as good things to be enjoyed on an aimless ramble. The difference between them is not one of experience, but interpretation. They do not differ about the facts, only about their meaning.[12]

This approach is beguilingly *tolerant,* to use a term in vogue today. In fact, it is patronizing and dogmatic, and in the end a repetition of the claim that people who seem to have encountered God in experiences of joy are deceived. It involves two debatable assumptions. The first is that there is no difference in what is experienced.   The second is that the experiences,

REASONS OF THE HEART

interpretations aside, are mundane; that is, they can be explained entirely by natural factors. It is not the non-religious person who makes experiences out to be less than they really are, but the religious person who makes them out to be more.

Let's address the first assumption, that there is no difference in what is experienced. If you recall Swinburne's five-fold classification of religious experience in an earlier chapter, to an observer this claim might be plausible in the first two cases, and perhaps the third. Imagine one person viewing a sunset and seeing a world "charged with the grandeur of God,"[13] while another sees only the refraction of light through clouds or dust in the air (Swinburne's first category). Or imagine two people responding to a sudden and surprising restoration of the health of a dying friend. One responds joyfully, seeing it as an answer to her prayers. The other responds with cheer, but with skepticism about the existence of a prayer-answering God (the second category). Or imagine one person describing her joy in terms that another person might use to describe an experience of romantic love (the third category).

Even if it is plausible to someone on the outside of these experiences looking in that the only difference is one of interpretation, the more numinous an experience purports to be, the less that explanation fits. To rewrite Hick's parable, if one traveler has an experience of ecstasy that he is unable to communicate and that causes him to fall to his knees and begin praising the King of the Celestial City, and the other stands alongside, bewildered (Swinburne's fourth category), the difference between them is not merely one of interpretation. They have not had the same experience. If one traveler sees nothing unusual on the road, but the other stops, transfixed and trembling, and exclaims that he has just had a vision of the King (the fifth category), you might doubt his claim, but you surely would not say that his experience is the same as his fellow traveler's.

Another refutation of the claim that joy is a common experience interpreted differently is the report of adult converts to Christianity. More than anyone, they are in a position to judge whether their post-conversion experiences and pre-conversion experiences are the same. The autobiography of C.S. Lewis, *Surprised by Joy*, illustrates this point. Lewis claimed that he discovered in God the joy he sought and had not found. If you ask them, you will learn that the experience of believers is not a religious rehash of what they knew before they came to faith.

The most powerful evidence that joy is not the same experience others have with a different name is the fact that it often occurs and even flourishes in situations of suffering and pain. Where else do you find that? I'm waiting for an answer, but not holding my breath for one. In fact this is one of the chief characteristics of joy. [14] Courageous resolve, a habit of Zen-like detachment, and Stoic indifference may be commendable in their own ways, but they are not the same as joy in suffering. Joy in the midst of pain and distress is unnatural. Unnatural, I suggest, because it is supernatural. It draws from a well that is not of this world.

The second assumption, that what all people experience – interpretations aside – is entirely mundane, is an assertion without an argument. It could just as well be the case that atheists make less of an experience than the facts warrant as it is that believers are exaggerating. A colorblind person who rejects the claim that a flower has color and hue makes less of the facts than they warrant. So it is – believers contend – with those who live in the world without a sense of God. Their experience is deficient. They see less than is really there. [15]

Back to the argument. If you are unable to prove that God does not exist, which would defeat all claims that joy is veridical, and you are unable to demonstrate that all who claim an encounter with God in experiences of joy are dishonest, your only other option is to say that they are deceived in their belief. Of course you must do more than assert this if you care about the rationality of your claim, or you hope to persuade others that your explanation is true. You must demonstrate that the most likely explanation of these religious claims is that those who make them have experienced some form of fantasy, illusion, or hallucination.

Your demonstration will require two test groups. The first will feature subjects who have experienced life-altering illusions of a non-theological nature. As scientifically as possible, you must identify the psychological factors common to them. The second group will be people who claim to have a life-altering awareness of God in experiences of joy. It will have to be a large group, since it must represent the diversity of joyful believers around the world, including their gender, ethnicity, culture, education, economic and social status, and personality type. Now, with equal rigor, you must demonstrate that the factors found in the first group are present in every case in the second. In other words, you must demonstrate, without exception, that joyful believers fit the psychological profile of someone who is prone to abnormal, life-changing states of consciousness.

I wish you good luck in the task, should you undertake it, and urge you not to do anything rash like pledging yourself to a fast until you succeed.[16]

Unless there is compelling evidence that those who claim to have encountered God in experiences of joy are dishonest or deceived, their claims should be given the benefit of the doubt. It is what rational people do. Richard Swinburne refers to this as the "principle of testimony."

> It is another basic principle of rationality, which I call the principle of testimony, that those who do not have an experience of a certain type ought to believe any others when they say that they do – again, in the absence of evidence of deceit or delusion. If we could not in general trust what other people say about their experiences without checking them out in some way, our knowledge of history or geography or science would be almost non-existent. In virtue of

the principle of testimony, there become available to those of us who do not ourselves have religious experiences the reports of others who do, and to which, therefore, we can apply the principle of credulity. In the absence of counter-evidence, we ought to believe that things are as they seem to be to other people; and we do, of course, normally so assume. We trust the reports of others on what they see unless we have reason to suppose that they are lying, or deceiving themselves, or simply misobserving. We ought to do the same with their reports of religious experience.[17]

You can get some mileage out of the argument that those who claim an experience of God in their joy are dishonest, and some out of the argument that they are deceived. The critical question is whether the combined mileage of the two is enough to get you to the conclusion that an awareness of God in experiences of joy is never veridical. I don't think so. Short of proving that God does not exist, I don't see how the arguments can be stretched to reach that conclusion. An exception would not prove the rule; it would destroy it. If one person is not dishonest or deceived about encountering God in experiences of joy, then God exists.[18]

We can put the argument into a syllogism:

(1)   If there are credible claims to an encounter with God in experiences of joy, then God exists.
(2)   There are credible claims to an encounter with God in experiences of joy.
(3)   Therefore, God exists.

If the premises are true, the conclusion follows. You will have to make a judgment call on the credibility of claims to a joyful encounter with God. Perhaps you still have questions that must be answered, or objections that demand a response. I have tried to anticipate four of them that I will address in the next two chapters.

QUESTIONS FOR THOUGHT AND DISCUSSION

1. What are the problems with saying that joy has no cause?

2. If you reject the explanation that God is causally behind the experiences of joy (even hypothetically), how would you go about crafting an alternative explanation?

3. How would you evaluate the argument that all those who say that they have encountered God in experiences of joy are being deceptive?

4. How would you evaluate the argument that all those who say that they have encountered God in experiences of joy are mistaken in their belief?

5. What do you think of Swinburne's "principle of testimony?" How do you see this playing out in conversations with your family, friends, peers, and colleagues at work?

CHAPTER 9

ANSWERING OBJECTIONS, PART 1

THE PROOF-VALUE OF JOY

A common objection to arguments from religious experience is that it is impossible to prove the existence of God from them. One philosopher asks, "But what good is religious experience as a proof or demonstration of God's existence?" and then responds, "The answer is, None."[1] He is right. Only propositions *entail* other propositions. Experiences may be factually significant, but they are logically barren. It isn't until we make statements about them that the laws of valid reasoning can be introduced and proofs developed. While this is an important observation, its significance can be overstated. The objection is true of all experience. Experience alone proves nothing.

It is also true that when statements about experiences of joy become premises in an argument, they are open to dispute. We saw this argument at the end of the last chapter:

(1) If there are credible claims to an encounter with God in experiences of joy, then God exists.

(2) There are credible claims to an encounter with God in experiences of joy.

(3) Therefore, God exists.

The argument is formally valid, but the conclusion isn't certain because the premises are open to debate. Granted, but this isn't nearly as significant as it is made out to be. A proof can fail in the strict sense of the word, and still be strong, as I contend this argument is. Proofs are not an all-or-nothing affair. To ask that of them is to ask too much. Rem Edwards has written:

> It is sometimes maintained that unless a very strict proof or set of related proofs is offered, nothing is proved at all. For example, it is sometimes held that unless all the premises of an argument are absolutely certain and the pattern of reasoning indubitably valid, the proof is utterly worthless. If one adheres strictly to this rigid deductive ideal, however, one is forced to conclude that there are *no* worthwhile proofs anywhere . . . . Certainly there are no such proofs to be found in natural science or in philosophy.[2]

My claim is not that the existence of God is logically entailed in a set of assertions about joy, but that the existence of God, compared to rival explanations, best illumines and explains the phenomena of joy. This is the case behind the second premise of the syllogism that there are credible claims to an encounter with God in experiences of joy. It is known as an argument to the best explanation.[3] It is the kind of reasoning we routinely (and rationally) use when factual claims are involved. A jury concludes that Mr. Jones committed an armed robbery from the evidence of motive, weapon, opportunity, and an eyewitness. You conclude that it has rained from the evidence of clouds in the sky, lightening and thunder in the area, wet surfaces wherever you look, and water racing downhill on the streets of your neighborhood. Other explanations may be possible, but one is more likely than the others.

My argument is not an inference from premises that are beyond dispute, but a conclusion reached by comparing rival explanations and a range of data. In this case the data involves experiences of joy. Joy, in turn, is part of the larger field of evidence known as "religious experience," and religious experience is just one line of evidence among many. When the field of data is expanded to the full range of human experience and interaction with the world, and rival explanations are compared, a strong, cumulative case for the existence of God emerges.[4] It does not prove that God exists; it strengthens the belief-worthiness of the assertion that he does. There is much that is subjective on our part, and even more that is mysterious on God's; nevertheless, the path of evidence takes us as far as reason can go, and then points beyond to forest-clad mountains and snow-capped peaks where we will find the treasure for which our hearts long.

THE INTERPRETIVE NATURE OF JOY

This is a "Give-me-the-facts-and-nothing-but-the-facts" objection. Joy may be more than other emotions – and I maintain that it is – but it is an emotion nevertheless. Like all emotions, it is interpretive in nature. It is a perspectival experience. It occurs most robustly when it is framed by beliefs that include a God with a particular character, and theological concepts, such as creation, providence, and redemption. This is what skeptics find objectionable. Their argument is that there is no way to get to the facts of the experience that believers call joy, precisely because it is *believers* who have it. There is no way to untangle the facts from their theological interpretation.

This is not the same as the argument in the last chapter that religious experiences are nothing more than common, mundane experiences dressed in theological clothing. These critics grant that there may be such a thing as religious experience. Their objection is that the theological orientation of the people who have such experiences makes it likely that they will have them, and that there is no way to remove the religious beliefs that frame the experience and evaluate the experience itself.[5] If this is true, they say, then we can't make anything more of religious experiences than that some people seem to have them.[6]

There are two ways in which joy can be interpretive. To explain this, let me introduce a distinction between *retrospective* and *incorporated* interpretation. Retrospective interpretation is what takes place, according to Caroline Franks Davis, "when an experience is understood in the light of subsequent reflection or new information."[7] My first response to a painful situation might be frustration or sorrow. Later I remember apostolic exhortations to rejoice in the trials of life because God is seeking to bring good from them. In a posture of prayerful thanksgiving I experience peace and joy that eclipse the original frustration or sorrow.[8]

The skeptic probably has another kind of interpretation in mind. It is incorporated in the experience from the very beginning. All joy, ostensibly, has a numinous dimension. There is a sense of God in the experience. The critic claims that the facts of this experience are not available to us apart from their theological construal.[9] I acknowledge the interpretive dimension of joy, but I insist that in this matter joy is like any other experience. Either the presence of interpretation counts against all experience, or it cannot count against joy.[10]

All experience is interpreted from the start.[11] The interpretive act organizes and shapes the data of experience. Knowledge would be impossible without it. This is not just true of numinous experience; it is true of all experience. For instance, I do not see black shapes appearing on a screen as I type, I see words. The seeing is both a visual experience *and* a way of construing it. I do not see a body-like shape with long blond hair and blue eyes on the other side of a brown, rectangular object, I see my wife at the dinner table. Visual sensation and interpretation are inseparable in the experience. This follows naturally, unobtrusively, and inevitably from the fact that we are cognitive and sentient creatures. There is an interpretive dimension to everything we experience. Either this counts against all experience, or it cannot count against joy.

Ordinarily, people do not distinguish between the discrete properties of visual experience and their interpretation of what they see; nevertheless, the interpretive dimension is always present. Franks Davis claims, "Interpretation, far from being an extraneous element imposed from without, is absolutely essential to there occurring a perceptual experience at all."[12] To return to the common act of reading, except for the fact that I have called your attention to it, it probably would not occur to you as you read this that you are not seeing words. You are interpreting small black squiggles on white paper or a digital screen. The squiggles are all that appear to you in your sense experience. The rest is interpretation. If the interpretation is a good fit, the visual properties and the interpretive dimensions of your experience come to you in a single package. You may only be aware of the distinction between them if you engage in the kind of thinking that we are doing right now.

In the same way, believers don't usually distinguish between the numinous properties of their experience and their construal of them in theological terms. The two fit so well that they are experienced as one.[13] Consider the following examples.

As Ted Brown drives home from work, thinking about his family and the many good things he enjoys in life, he has a numinous experience that matches the psalmist's exclamation, "O taste and see that the LORD is good!" [14] He has a compelling awareness of a Personal Presence, a Superabundant Goodness, before whom he is a delighted beneficiary. The experience elicits a prayer of thanksgiving. His theological construal of the experience is distinct from its numinous properties, but fits them in a way that seems entirely natural.

Alone on a cabin porch high in the Rocky Mountains, gazing into a cloudless night sky with stars beyond count, Bob Bennett has a numinous experience in which it seems to him that he is enveloped in the presence of a Being of grandeur and might. He experiences a profound sense of contingency, dependence, reverence, and awe in the presence of such creative wisdom, artistry, and power. He whispers the ancient words of the Apostle's Creed, "I believe in God the Father Almighty, Maker of heaven and earth." The numinous "filling"[15] of his experience and its construal are analytically distinct, but experienced as one.

In a Sunday morning worship service Susan Smith has a numinous experience in which she is aware of a Being of utter holiness, and she responds, involuntarily, as the prophet Isaiah did, with a sense of loathing over her moral failures. [16] She feels unraveled. Undone. Profoundly humbled. Heart-pierced with remorse. These are the numinous dimensions of the experience and her response to them. She identifies the object of her experience as the Triune God of Christian faith. This interpretation does not seem artificial, and it occurs without any difficulty or conscious deliberation. The experience and its construal can be separated when we think about them, but they take place together without a gap or a seam.

As she ponders her future, recently divorced, unemployed, and the mother of three young children, Anita Johnson prays for strength, and in the course of her prayer has the numinous experience of being upheld, sustained, and protected by a transcendent Source of power and loving care. It has not come from her; it has come to her. A wave of peace washes over her, even though she has no answers to the practical questions before her. She says to herself, "Ah! This is the 'peace of God that passes all understanding.'"[17] The connection seems compelling. It does not enter her mind to think that it could be otherwise.

As he lies in bed at night, long after everyone else in the house has fallen asleep, Stan Brown finds himself wide-awake. His mind is alert and his senses are keen. Sounds that would normally fall below his threshold of hearing seem magnified. Nothing escapes his attention. A light moves across the ceiling and down the opposite wall as a car rolls down the street in front of his house. In those dimly lit moments he sees the menagerie of porcelain cats his wife has collected and placed on a cedar chest. He muses on the fact that he has never really paid much attention to them, but now finds his focus riveted on them in the middle of the night. He is thoroughly awake, but does not mind being so. In this highly sensitive state he becomes aware of a Presence in the room. It is not his wife, a child, a pet, or an intruder. He does not see it, smell it, or hear it, yet it seems almost tangible. He cannot say why, but he knows it to be the presence of God. In the stillness and darkness of the room, his sense of the divine Nearness lingers, joy fills his heart, and he thanks God for the Visitation.

Jennifer Roberts gets away for a weekend of solitude and meditation at a mountain retreat. After spending time in prayer and reading the Bible, she gives herself fully to reflection on the attributes of God. In her contemplative pleasure she loses sense of time and place. At some point, her meditation upon God becomes a numinous awareness of God. In the words of William James, she possesses the object of her faith not in the form of a mere conception that her intellect accepts as true, but "rather in the form of quasi-sensible realities directly apprehended."[18] She experiences a tremulous joy, which she regards as an encounter with God.

I offer these examples of numinous experience because I believe that they are common. In each case the numinous constituents of the experience and their construal are analytically distinct, but experienced as one. The structural analogies between numinous and visual experience are clear. In fact the similarities are so striking that I must repeat: Either interpretation counts against all experience, or it cannot count against experience that is numinous in nature.[19]

"But surely," you say, "we must be able to draw a line at some point. Hallucination, mirage, and illusion are possible explanations of an unusual perception." True. This is where the principle of credulity cuts the other way. To review, Swinburne says: "I suggest that it is a principle of rationality that (in the absence of special considerations) if it seems (epistemically) to a subject that X is present, then probably X is present; what one seems to perceive is probably so."[20] In the case of hallucinations, mirages, and illusions, in which the interpretive dimension has gone askew, one can usually identify the "special considerations" that count against the veridical character of the experience. To rule out an entire category of experience (numinous experience) in advance, however, without clearly and persuasively identifying the special considerations that count against it, is like calling a third strike before a player steps into the batter's box. It is a hollow victory at best.

All experience is interpreted. All experience is construed in the larger framework of a worldview or belief-system. We should not jump to false conclusions, however. One is that we are so trapped in our worldviews that we cannot appraise them. We can and do. Another false conclusion is that an analysis of worldviews can never be more than an evaluation of one view by another.[21] There are evaluative criteria embedded in worldviews *as such*.[22] The common criteria arise from the nature of these epistemic projects.

It is possible to assess worldviews in terms of their internal fitness (consistency and coherence of core beliefs), external fitness (explanatory power and pragmatic fruitfulness), and existential fitness (enabling those who hold them to flourish in life). The outcome of such a comparative analysis will not be an objective declaration of a "winning worldview," but a greater sense of belief-worthiness for those who seek to be rational in their beliefs in an honest and serious pursuit of truth. The result will be a closer approximation to the truth that emerges from the best thinking we can bring to these important issues.

QUESTIONS FOR THOUGHT AND DISCUSSION

1. What do you think of the author's statement that proofs "are not an all-or-nothing" affair? What difference does this make in the way you advance or critique arguments for the existence of God?

2. Do you see the distinction between "retrospective" and "incorporated" interpretation in some of your own beliefs? If so, describe examples of each.

3. Discuss the author's claim: "Either the presence of interpretation counts against all experience, or it cannot count against joy."

4. Discuss the author's claim: "Believers don't ordinarily distinguish between the numinous properties of their experience and their construal of those properties in theological terms. The two fit so well that they are experienced as one."

5. Discuss the author's statement: "It is possible to assess worldviews in terms of their internal fitness (consistency and coherence of core beliefs), external fitness (explanatory power and pragmatic fruitfulness), and existential fitness (enabling those who hold them to flourish in life)." How would you assess your own worldview by these criteria?

CHAPTER 10

ANSWERING OBJECTIONS, PART 2

THE PROBLEM OF COMPETING CLAIMS

The principle of credulity does not discriminate on the basis of creed. It is not exclusive to the beliefs of any religious community. What implications does this have for a world in which there are many competing religious claims?

To use nomenclature from the first chapter, Rationalists and Relativists say that if the principle of credulity applies to one religious experience, it applies to all. Rationalists contend that this puts advocates of such arguments in a "no-win" situation, because contradictory truth-claims cannot all be true. Relativists see it as an "everyone-wins" scenario by shifting the notion of truth to whatever an individual or religious community believes to be true.[1] Both sides are mistaken.

First, the principle of credulity does not referee claims to truth. It is about the rationality of forming and holding beliefs that are regarded as true. As we saw in an earlier chapter, one can be rational in coming to a belief that turns out to be false. They are distinct issues. Rationalists and Relativists wrongly conflate them.

Second, both sides are mistaken in thinking that the principle of credulity applies to all religious experience. Let me explain and address the issue of competing claims by showing how the principle plays out in this assortment of religious experience:

1. A man senses himself absorbed into the One, wherein the subject-object distinction ceases to hold.

2. A woman senses the unity of all things and that she is nothing at all.

3. The Buddhist monk who is an atheist senses the presence of the living Buddha.

4. A person senses the presence of God, the Father of our Lord Jesus Christ.

5. The Virgin Mary appears to S (in a dream).

6. The Lord Jesus appears to Paul on the road one afternoon, though no one else realizes it.

7. A man senses the presence of Satan, which convinces him that Satan is the highest reality.

8. The goddess Athena appears to Achilles. He believes her to have sprung from Zeus's head. She promises that he will win the battle on the morrow.

9. Allah appears to S and tells him to purify the land by executing

all infidels (e.g., Jews and Christians) whose false worship corrupts the land.

10. A guilt-ridden woman senses the presence of her long-deceased father, assuring her that he has forgiven her for her neglect of him while he was aging and dying.

11. A mother senses the presence of the spirit of the river. It tells her that her deformed infant belongs to the river and that she should throw it back.

12. A man senses the presence of the Trinity and understands how it could be that three persons are one God, but he cannot tell others.

13. A person senses the presence of the demiurge who has created the universe but makes no pretense of being omnipotent or omnibenevolent.

14. An atheist senses a deep, infinite gratitude for the life of his son without believing in the least that a god exists.

15. An atheist has a deep sense of nothingness in which she is absolutely convinced that the universe has manifested itself to her as a deep void.[2]

Does the principle of credulity apply to all of these experiences? No. It is relevant only to experiences that are analogous to ordinary sense perception. Being "absorbed into the One" must be excluded because it negates the subject-object distinction essential to perception and the principle of credulity. Nor can the principle be used to support profound feelings of oneness, gratitude, or nothingness *per se*, since they do not parallel ordinary perception. It may be possible to establish the rationality of believing that

Reality is an undifferentiated One, despite appearances to the contrary, or that there is no God, despite evidence to the contrary, but you will have to take another path than an appeal to religious experience and the principle of credulity.

That leaves us with alleged experiences of the divine, the demonic, and the dead. Let's take the last first: reported experiences of the Buddha, the Virgin Mary and a departed father. Although Gautama Buddha and Mary are religious figures, they lived and died, and in that regard they belong in the same category as the father who died neglected and alone.[3] The first thing to say about any postmortem encounter is that even if the principle of credulity establishes the rationality of believing that it occurred, it does not establish the truth of any message delivered by the departed. Unless it can be demonstrated independently that dead people never lie and are never mistaken, we would have to evaluate the truthfulness of their statements apart from the extraordinary fact that they seem to have made them from the other side of the grave.

A postmortem encounter is not a competitive claim for people of Christian faith. The Bible reports such events.[4] J.B. Phillips, New Testament scholar, translator, and contemporary of C.S. Lewis, told the story of how Lewis, shortly after his death, appeared to him twice in his home. He described Lewis as "ruddier in complexion than ever, grinning all over his face and, as the old-fashioned saying has it, positively glowing with health."[5] As a supernaturalist, I acknowledge that such a thing is possible. As one who accepts the principle of credulity, unless special considerations proved otherwise, I grant that Phillips was rational in believing that Lewis was present in the situations he reported.

What about visions of Mary, the mother of Jesus? If they involve a configuration of clouds, rocks in a streambed, or burn marks on a fried tortilla, the principle of credulity has no relevance. Some, however, claim to have seen the Virgin herself, and have found encouragement, comfort, strength, and peace from the experience. Whether or not such visions connect with an objective reality, I cannot say. There may be special considerations that must be taken into account. If not, I grant that those who make such claims are rational in their belief that they have seen her.

What should we make of the experience of the Buddhist monk? To repeat an important point, even if we grant that he is rational in believing that he has had an encounter with the Buddha, it would imply nothing about the truth of Buddhism or of anything the Teacher might say postmortem.[6] The principle of credulity does not even establish the truth of the claim that an encounter took place. It says only that the monk is rational in believing in a living Buddha in the absence of special considerations that would defeat it or make it less likely.[7]

What about an alleged encounter with Satan? In itself it is not a competing claim for people of Christian faith. Only the belief that Satan is the highest reality is. But how could we possibly know that from such an experience? It is conceivable that a malevolent being might make such a claim, but why should we believe him? At any rate, the claim would have to be assessed independently. If one wished only to establish the rationality of believing in Satan from alleged encounters with him, that case can be made, and it would not be a competing claim for Christians.

Apart from encounters with the risen Christ and the triune God of Christian faith, this leaves us with a Greek goddess, a finite creator, a river spirit, and an infinitely powerful God who commands his worshipers to kill in his name. At the risk of being redundant, even if the principle of credulity establishes the rationality of believing that one has had an encounter with a deity, it does not imply anything about the truth of a message delivered in such a meeting. (Despite the violence of Jidhadists in the name of Allah, peace-loving Muslims reject the claim that their God would give such commands.) That is another matter. The issue before us is the rationality of believing in a deity based upon alleged encounters with him or her.

If one has a religious experience that is analogous to ordinary perception, barring special considerations, it is rational to believe that it is trustworthy. This implies a duty to respect people of other faiths – a very important point to be made in our pluralistic world. It does not, however, entail a duty to affirm the truthfulness of their beliefs. I trust that you see this by now.[8] Some religious experiences provide a *prima facie* basis for a rational belief. To say more than this, we would have to look at all the relevant evidence for a truth-claim, and ways in which the claim might be defeated.[9]

It is possible to grant the authenticity of a religious experience and to reject the theological system that frames it. Ronald Nash puts it this way:

> It is possible to maintain that religious experiences in competing religions point to the existence of the object (God) without requiring us to believe that the competing conceptual systems within which the experiences occur are equally true or false. The similar religious experiences of people in conflicting religious traditions may be a sign that humans can tap into a reality beyond the human or that this reality can break into human consciousness.[10]

Or there is Peter Kreeft's understanding of the situation:

> Hinduism's name for God is "Brahma." Like a rose, A God by any other name will smell as sweet, though not, perhaps, sound as clear. In other words, although the Christian has important theological disagreements with Hinduism, the Hindu experience of Brahma is apparently a real experience of God.[11]

Not all Christians would be willing to go as far as Nash does; perhaps even fewer would agree with Kreeft. There is no need to agree with either. The apostle Paul, for instance, acknowledged that people in antiquity who claimed to converse with "gods" and "lords" were in touch with the supernatural realm. He believed that these were not petty deities, like Greek gods and goddesses, which their human devotees believed them to be, but demonic beings masquerading as the divine.[12]

George Mavrodes has written:

> The Christian tradition, both in the New Testament documents and in later theological developments, seems to me to take seriously the idea that human beings are not the only rational creatures in the realm of existence. And in particular it seems to countenance the existence of powerful and nonembodied intelligences. At least, that is how I understand the references to angels and devils within the Christian tradition. . . .
>
> Are any of these beings – could any of them be – the gods of some actual religion? Now that I come to think of it (and my thinking of it is very recent), I don't think of any strong reason for returning a negative answer. Playing such a role might, of course, be a usurpation of divine prerogatives. But I think that the possibility of such a usurpation is not entirely foreign to Christian thought.[13]

I leave you to your own conclusions.

The principle of credulity plays an important role in establishing the rational status of some religious beliefs. It creates confusion only when it is misused, as it often is in contemporary discussion. It has no bearing on the truth-status of beliefs. It is irrelevant to religious experience that is not similar to ordinary perception. It has nothing to say about an alleged message given in a religious experience. Claims to the contrary may seem impressive, but so does running very fast into the wrong end zone. It draws cheers only from those who don't understand the game.

THE PROBLEM OF NEGATIVE EXPERIENCE

If an experience in which God seems to be present is evidence for the existence of God, is the absence of such an experience, or an experience in which God seems notably absent, evidence that he does not exist? [14] Not by itself. If there were no claims to an encounter with God, that would give strength to the argument. In the face of such claims, however, the absence of experience has no evidential value. This is so because there are other possible explanations for an experiential deficit. [15]

Suppose that on a Saturday morning in June men and women on my block are working on their front lawns, and I on mine. I look up from my work, clippers in hand, and between the houses across the street I spot a brightly colored hot air balloon rising from a field nearby. I call to my neighbors, "Look!" and point in the direction of the balloon, thinking that they will welcome a respite from their work. To my dismay, none of them can see it from their yard. I am alone in my experience. That I see the balloon is evidence that there is such a thing; that they do not is not evidence to the contrary.

All experiential knowledge is conditional. To have the experience of seeing the hot air balloon, my neighbors might have to come to my house and stand where I stand to see what I see. That would be a geographical condition. I can't force them to come. Perhaps they are enjoying their yard work and don't want to be bothered, or maybe they are rushing through their tasks because they have another commitment and don't want to be distracted by anything that keeps them from their objective. That would be an interest condition. Suppose that one neighbor comes to my house to see the balloon, but is so nearsighted that he can't make anything of the phenomenon to which I direct his attention. That would be a physical condition.

I intend no offense, but if you have never encountered God in experiences of joy it may be that you have not met conditions for doing so.[16] We saw in an earlier chapter that taking pleasure in something is often a condition for experiencing complementary pleasure-states. If you have not experienced God in pleasure-states of joy, it may be because you do not take pleasure in such things. If you are honest, the possibility of encountering God is more likely to bring a yawn than to inspire a great quest.

If you have never had a joyful encounter with God, there may be other factors in play, as well. C. Stephen Evans has written:

> It is . . . difficult to say when the objective conditions for experiencing God have been satisfied. The difficulty is that God is not a passive object to be observed. He is like Aslan in C.S. Lewis's Narnia books; Aslan is "not a tame lion." Things like trees and books just sit there to be seen. People and animals have some initiative. If they do not want to be seen, they can hide and make things difficult for a would-be observer. God, however, being omnipotent and perfectly free, has the greatest possible degree of initiative. It seems impossible that anyone should experience God unless God wills it to occur. And it seems difficult or impossible for us to say when God will do this.[17]

Joy fits the pattern of all theistic experience: The knowledge *of* God can only be knowledge *from* God. Unless he reveals himself, our claims to knowledge are guesses. God can only be known as he gives himself in sovereign self-disclosure. As William Alston put it: "God does not passively sit for His portrait; we cannot just stare at Him, not in this life at any rate. If we come to know God through experience at all, it is through His works, including, pre-eminently, His works in human lives."[18] C.S. Lewis said much the same thing: "When you come to knowing God, the initiative lies on His side. If He does not show Himself, nothing you can do will enable you to find him."[19]

"If the initiative lies with God," you may ask, "why does he not reveal himself to all people?" The apostle Paul would have said that he does. He put it this way to a pagan audience: "In past generations . . . (God) allowed all the nations to walk in their own ways; yet he did not leave himself without witness, for he did good and gave you from heaven rains and fruitful seasons, satisfying your hearts with food and gladness."[20] All good things that sustain us, enrich us, and enable us to flourish in life are revelatory signs. Even if their meaning is missed, they are gifts from God, point to God, and find their fulfillment in the enjoyment of God.[21]

"Why doesn't God make the signs clearer?" If I were to venture an answer, it would be that God is not content merely to have people believe in him, or give a passing nod or an intellectual assent to his existence. He seeks seekers.[22] In seeking God, we find him, and in finding him, we discover joy. If we saw things clearly, we would see that there is no other way that it can be.[23]

QUESTIONS FOR THOUGHT AND DISCUSSION

1. How do your peers talk about the competing and contradictory claims made by different religions? How do they solve this problem? Would they say, "All religious claims are true for the people who make them" or "It's all rubbish"?

2. What significance does the distinction between rationality and truth make for the above questions?

3. What do you think of alleged encounters with people who have left this world? How does the principle of credulity speak to this?

4. Would you agree with Kreeft, Nash, or Mavrodes on alleged claims of people to an encounter with God in other religious traditions? None of them? Do you have a nuanced view?

5. How do you show respect for people of other faiths without necessarily agreeing with their theological claims? What are the cultural challenges to this?

PART THREE

JOY & THE PROBLEM OF EVIL

CHAPTER 11

A TALE WORTH TELLING,
A STORY WORTH DEFENDING

J oy fits in a world created and governed by a benevolent, wise, all-powerful God. If the arguments that I have advanced are successful, it is rational to believe that such a God exists. But our world also features pain, suffering, and a troubling array of moral evil. No discussion of joy is complete without coming to grips with these stubborn facts. There can be no happily-ever-after ending to the story unless joy meets these foes on a field of battle and survives the ordeal.

There are more books and articles on the problem of evil than you could read even if you wanted to. Apart from the fact that you paid for it, why should you venture into this last section with me? This is why: My exploration will keep joy paramount in our thinking, and you won't find that in many treatments of the subject. I am not interested in defending mere theism, or any version of Christian faith that does not see joy at the center of God's purposes for us. Nor do I have any interest in defending a vision of life that does not take seriously our cultural mandate and stewardship of the earth, which, I believe, factor significantly in the Creator's design for our joy. The final chapter of the section is not a defense, but a rallying call to followers of Christ to take action against evil as agents of God's Kingdom. It is a summons to live out Kingdom commitments to righteousness, peace, and joy in the Holy Spirit. If addressing the problem of evil does not end here, I have no desire to begin.

Let me begin by telling you the Story of joy as I understand it. The narrative opens with a preface about its Author.

THEOLOGY 101: A JOYFUL GOD

God loves being God. He enjoys being God. He takes immeasurable pleasure in simply being God. Can you really imagine a God who didn't like himself? Who was frustrated or bored with having to be the Supreme Being? Can you really envision the Creator of the universe wishing that he could be someone else, somewhere else, doing something else? I can't.

The joy of God begins with his overflowing delight in himself. Augustine declared, "Thou art an everlasting joy to Thyself!"[1] Aquinas wrote: God "possesses joy in Himself and all things else for His delight."[2] It is the essence of God to be joyful.[3] He exults in his excellence. He rejoices in his regal splendor. He takes boundless pleasure in his infinite perfection. It's a good thing for us that he does! There would be no joy anywhere in the universe if he did not. Before the first word of creation, God existed eternally in a state of unimaginable, immeasurable delight.

The joy of God is Trinitarian in nature. To say that God is a Trinity is to affirm that the one God is a community of Persons – Father, Son, and Holy Spirit – who delight in each other and revel in the beatitude of their shared love.[4] There never was a time when this was not so. There never will be. If we could glimpse what angels behold, we would see that this

Fellowship of Joy is a "great fountain of energy and beauty spurting up at the very centre of reality."[5] All joy flows from these Headwaters.[6]

CREATION, FALL, AND REDEMPTION

Original Joy. Once upon a time, or before there was time, there was God, and only God. Then he created. He sang a pure and powerful song, and suddenly angels surrounded his throne. Myriads of heavenly creatures. Countless ranks. As they joined his song, lending harmony to the Maker's creative melody, galaxies and stars and planets, billions upon billions, came into existence.[7] And then his musical mandate brought forth a particular world, our own, filled with plants, insects, and animals – sea-swimmers, land-walkers, and sky-flyers – as many and varied as the luminaries in the night sky. Nearly finished, he sang once more and fashioned the crown of his handiwork, humans – a man and a woman – to mirror him in his world, and to steward and rule it in his stead.

Why did God create? The answer can't be that he was lonely or bored, that it was a whim or an inadvertence, that he was somehow compelled to do it, or that there was a deficit in his existence that could only be remedied by creating a universe. None of this can be true of the Supreme Being.[8] God's life was full and complete before he spoke the first word of creation. This is the right answer to our question: God created from the plenitude of his pleasure. He created from the overflow of his joy. The universe is a surplus to him. It is "gloriously superfluous."[9] As Louis Smedes put it: God was "free to create or not to create. He did it out of his own good pleasure, for the divine fun of it."[10] This is the deep truth of the universe: God created because it was sheer delight to do so.[11]

Sometimes my heart aches for Eden. For that ancient *garden of delights.*[12] I long for the world God first created. A world unspoiled and unsullied by sin. A world filled with tokens of the divine Presence, from the shimmering light of stars overhead to the cool, crystalline dew beneath one's feet at the dawning of the day, each and every one pointing vividly and irresistibly to its Source. I yearn for the world in which the knowledge of God was untrammeled, and every blink of the eye brought one into touch with some new dimension of his glory. I long for the day long past when no distinction was even possible between sensual and spiritual, when all pleasures were joyful, directed to God in thanksgiving and praise, and joy pulsed with pleasure in the Creator and the good world that he created.[13]

Joy Lost. Alas, that world did not survive. Its brevity is linked to the mystery of human freedom. The unthinkable happened. Our forebears chose the Creator's good gifts over the Creator himself. They chose to forge their own future rather than embrace the adventures God had in store for them. They chose to write their own story rather than play a part in God's. Though it was sheer folly to do so, they turned their will away from the will of God. The harmony between Being and being was destroyed. Real pleasures were lost, and sensual idols took their place. The joy that bound creatures together and all created things to the Creator became a wistful memory. A whisper that few still hear, beckoning the heart to a better time and a better world.

Our freedom made joy possible. Our misuse of that gift shattered the fragile and precious jewel. Only shards remain, bits and pieces strewn over the sands of human experience like the remains of a long-lost and once-glorious civilization.

What great loss the Fall brought to our race!

We are used to living with our sin, like skunks at home with their own stench. We take as normal fare what the Bible treats as a great horror and scandal.[14] Nothing could be more abnormal than humanity in its fallen condition. Nothing more unnatural. In our sinful state we have exchanged the glory of God for smudgy little gods of our own making, and the wine of joy for the waste of our own perversions: an obscene draught, which, though it offends the sensibilities of heaven, we have come absurdly to prefer.

The Psalmist declares: "Those who choose another god multiply their sorrows."[15] To limit this to images of wood and stone is to miss the point. To make a god of anything other than the living and true God is to forsake the Fountain of Joy.[16] It is to drink instead from the fetid marshes of our own folly. Idols of the heart are not only tokens of defiance, but monuments to our insanity. The self-inflicted wounds of idolatry, in fact, are its greatest irony. Make a god of money and you will pierce your heart with many pangs.[17] Make a god of pleasure and you may as well try to grasp the wind in your hands.[18] Whatever our god, at whatever self-made shrine we bow, we forgo by that choice the joy for which we were created, and embrace a course that will lead only to sorrow beyond anything we can imagine. As Peter Kreeft put it, "Since an idol *is* not God, no matter how sincerely or passionately it is treated as God, it is bound to break the heart of the worshipper. . . . You can't get blood from a stone or divine joy from nondivine things."[19]

The temptation of our first parents was to become like God.[20] They were enticed to leave their station under his wise and generous rule, and to chase something they foolishly thought would be better. They thought they were pursuing a greater good; what they found was a Curse: alienation from the Creator, from themselves, from each other, and from all other creature-life. They made themselves petty deities, and, in that choice, multiplied their sorrow. Day after day brought forth new grief, from the painful memory of Eden-lost to the horrors of their own growing evil. It is an ancient story. Every chapter tells the same tale. Only the times, places, and characters change. We are all sons of Adam and daughters of Eve. We have all shared in their sin and know their consequent sorrow.

This is the condition of fallen humanity. This is what it means to be "by nature children of wrath."[21] The wrath of God is not a bolt of lighting, thrown Zeus-like from the heavens to punish wrongdoers. *Wrath is joy rejected.*[22] Peter Kreeft is right: "But the opposite of true joy is far worse than anguish . . . . In fact, its opposite is hell."[23] Jesus' description of perdition is no pre-scientific fiction. It is as realistic as anything can be. Hell is a place of weeping and gnashing of teeth.[24] Ultimate sorrow and grief. If joy is found only in the undimmed presence of God,[25] and hell is the darkness of eternal separation from him,[26] there is no other way that it could be. Hell is the place of divine wrath: joy refused and forfeited with finality. It is the unending, unmitigated sorrow of choosing another god.[27] It became one of two destinies the day our first parents took their first steps from the Garden.[28]

Joy Regained. Fallen earth is neither Eden nor hell. Sin accounts for the first, and grace for the second. Short of hell, joy lost can be regained. In fact, this is the heart of redemption. It is God's loving action to restore sinners to the joy for which they were created.

The joy of salvation begins with the joy of the Savior. Here, as everywhere, our joy is sourced in the overflowing joy of God. His mercy is not meager, his goodness never grudging. It is lavish. Profuse. A cascading waterfall. A coursing river. A fathomless, brimming well. A life-saving, thirst-quenching drink poured into dry and desolate hearts in desperate need of refreshment.[29]

Christians believe that in Jesus God has drawn near to us, so near that he became one of us. Why? The Nicene Creed answers with the words, "For us human beings and for our salvation."[30] Our sin and misery created the need for God's action in Christ. But there is another question we should ask: Why would God do this?[31] Our need did not create an obligation for him. He could have left us in our sin and been fully just in doing so. Why did he script the drama of salvation, and in Jesus Christ step onto the stage of human history as its central character? Because it was his joy to do so!

With a sense of wonder the prophet Micah asked, "Who is a God like you, pardoning iniquity and passing over transgression?" No one! This is astonishing! Not at all what sinners should expect from a holy God! But there is an even greater wonder when we ask why God would deal with us so. Micah's answer takes us to the heart of God: "because he delights in steadfast love."[32] There is unimaginable pleasure here that only God can know. This insight into the heart of God leapt to life in the assuring words of Jesus: "Fear not, little flock, for it is the Father's good pleasure to give you the kingdom."[33] And, "Just so, I tell you there is . . . joy in heaven over one sinner who repents" (a joy pictured with music, dancing, and a feast).[34]

So great was Christ's joy in bringing salvation to the world that even the agony of the cross was compelled to yield to it. The author of Hebrews wrote of him: "For the joy that was set before him [he] endured the cross, despising the shame, and is seated at the right hand of the throne of God."[35] It was the vision of his redemptive work completed that brought him such joy, even in the hour of his greatest suffering and pain. If we cannot fathom his passion (and we cannot), we will never plumb his greater pleasure in its outcome. Nevertheless, the joy of salvation begins here. Our boon in redemption lies in the bountiful joy of the Redeemer.

God enjoys bringing salvation to sinners, and sinners to salvation. It is a joy for him to renovate human hearts, opening them to all he has done, all that he is now doing, and all that he has pledged to do. Our joy starts here. When grace triumphs in us, we come to revel in our need for God. Our plight brings us pleasure.[36] We experience grace as a feast offered to poor, famished, thirsty wayfarers a step away from perishing in their desperate want:

Ho everyone who thirsts,
    come to the waters;
and you that have no money,
    come, buy and eat!
Come, buy wine and milk
    without money and without price.
Why do you spend your money for that which is not bread,
    and your labor for that which does not satisfy?
Listen carefully to me, and eat what is good,
    and delight yourselves in rich food.
Incline your ear, and come to me;
    listen so that you may live. (Isaiah 55:1-3, NRSV)

In our sin we are utterly lost and ruined, without hope because we fully deserve the trouble we are in and can do nothing to change it. Nothing to escape it. We cannot see a light, and could not move toward it even if we did. Sin brings only unrelenting darkness and despair. And then. And then God. And then God transforms our troubled lot. He pardons us! Rescues us! Delivers us! He reaches down to us when we could not reach up to him. He meets us in our misery. He sings to us, sings over us, and puts his song within us. We are enchanted by the music. He washes away the filth that caked us. Mends our brokenness. Dresses and heals our wounds. Clothes our nakedness in robes that befit royalty. Fills our aching and empty souls. Quenches our terrible thirst. Then, to our utter amazement, he invites us into an "ecstasy of love and delight," C.S. Lewis wrote, "compared with which the most rapturous love between a man and a woman on this earth is mere milk and water."[37] Hands that covered our face in shame now lift in grateful praise, and we join Mary's song: "My soul magnifies the Lord, and my spirit rejoices in God my Savior!"[38]

The joy of salvation is a restoration of joy in the Triune God. It is not the kind of joy we experience in viewing a sunset or a meadow of alpine flowers. It is more like the gaiety of a wedding dance: delighting in one's beloved and the celebration of love and life together. The joy of salvation is a participation in God's joy: the Father's joy in the Son and the Spirit, the Son's joy in the Father and the Spirit, the Spirit's joy in the Father and the Son, and the shared joy of the Three-in-One. Sin destroyed the communion of joy our kind once shared with this Three-Personal God.[39] Redemption restores it. We are brought back to, and drawn into, this Fellowship, or Dance, of joy. Joy is then experienced in its highest and purest form as love's delight: joy in God's Triune love for us, our small, growing love offered back to the Father, Son, and Holy Spirit, and the love and joy we share with all who have entered into the life of God.[40]

JOY AND OUR CULTURAL MANDATE

Joy's Story is not complete unless we include God's vision for the world and the role he has called us to play. The Creator has plans for us. Some have your name on them. Some have mine. But he also has purposes for image-bearers-as-a-whole, also known as the human race. His design embraces all people, and the earth as our shared habitat. This finds expression in a mandate that was given at the beginning of our story.

> Then God said, "Let us make man in our image, after our likeness. And let them have dominion over the fish of the sea and over the birds of the heavens and over the livestock and over all the earth and over every creeping thing that creeps on the earth." (Genesis 1:26)

> So God created man in his own image,
>   in the image of God he created him;
>   male and female he created them. (Genesis 1:27)

> And God blessed them. And God said to them, "Be fruitful and multiply and fill the earth and subdue it, and have dominion over the fish of the sea and over the birds of the heavens and over every living thing that moves on the earth." (Genesis 1:28)

The world is not ours; it is God's.[41] We are managers, not owners. An important part of what it means to be made in God's image lies in the charge to rule the earth in God's stead, fulfilling his vision for our planet and the human project. We obey this mandate from the Creator when we discover resources and develop the potential he put into his world, when we harness all things for his glory and the good of all, and we do it in a way that honors, protects, and preserves the world he made and has entrusted to us.

Goodness, beauty, and truth. The ancient Greeks saw goodness, beauty, and truth as pure, transcendent realities that shape our experience in the world.[42] Whatever we find to be good in our world is an instance of the Good, which is timeless and supreme. The beautiful in our experience participates in Beauty, above and beyond our sentience. Whatever is true is grounded in absolute, eternal, and unchanging Truth. Augustine and other theologians embraced this, but taught that the one God, the Creator of the world, is the transcendent Source of all goodness, beauty, and truth in it.[43]

The people of faith whose stories and songs are written in the Bible didn't think about these things abstractly (or if they did, they didn't leave us a record of their thoughts). But if you had asked them if God is good, they would have said, "Taste and see!"[44] If you asked if God is beautiful, they would have said, "Breathtakingly!" And if you had asked them if God is truthful, they would have exclaimed, "Absolutely!" If you asked them how they knew these things, they wouldn't have constructed a chain of reasoning to get them to those conclusions, they would have talked about God's gracious self-disclosure and their matching experience in worship and life.

Goodness, beauty, and truth are united in our Creator. They are treasures from him and portals to him. They are structural to the world that he intends for us. They are essential to the mandate he has given us and are central to our joy. They are meant to shape and inform all that we do as his image-bearers. In every endeavor we should ask, "Does this reflect the goodness of

God, and his commitment to the well-being of all people? Does it reflect God's commitment to beauty in the world? Does it align with what God has revealed to be true about himself, our world, and the nature and purpose of human life?"

If our cultural mandate were put into a global mission statement, it would look something like this:

- Vision: to become a fully developed world in harmony with God and his purposes.

- Mission: to steward the resources of the world for the glory of God and the good of all.

- Core Values: goodness, beauty, and truth.

- Intended Outcome: Global joy.

Can you imagine a world in which all endeavors seek to bring this vision about? A world in which all projects are harnessed to this mission? A world in which all enterprises are shaped by these foundational values? A world that flourishes in joy as a result? This is what God has purposed for us from the beginning.

STEWARDS OF THE EARTH

If we look at the world through the lens of joy we will see God in all that we behold. In its vastness we will see his immensity. In its great antiquity we will see his eternal power. In its grandeur we will see his glory. In its wonders we will see his wisdom. In its intricacies we will see his genius. In its wildness we will see his sovereign freedom and surprising ways. In its pleasures we will see his goodness to us. If we see the world as it truly is, we will see it enchanted with the presence of God.[45]

If our first response to the world is anything but reverence, wonder, and awe, we haven't seen it truly. We are out of touch with reality. There is much that we will miss and much that we will misuse because we misunderstand the true nature and significance of the world. We will live in it like witless thugs throwing fine crystal into the air for target practice.

God invites us to savor his world and calls us to steward it. Our first calling as bearers of God's image is to govern the world as a theater for his glory.[46] We should do nothing to diminish it. Nothing to disgrace it. Nothing to sully it. Nothing to spoil it. We should do everything we can to protect it. Everything we can to preserve it. We should use but not abuse. We should enjoy but not exploit. Because it bears the presence of God, the earth is sacred. Because it is a habitation of God, it is holy. Our stewardship begins here.

Our responsibility to steward the earth includes managing its resources for the good of all. God does not intend that some (who happen to have and control wealth) should enjoy the benefits of his world and others (who do not) should not. Nor does he intend that one generation should tap the resources of his world in a way that deprives future generations of them.[47] It isn't our planet. We don't have that right:

> The earth is the LORD's and the fullness thereof,
>   the world and those who dwell therein. (Psalm 24:1)

> One generation shall laud your works to another,
>   and shall declare your mighty acts. (Psalm 145:4)

It should come as no surprise that our stewardship of the earth is meant to reflect the two great commandments we have been given: to love God fully and supremely, and to love our neighbors as ourselves.[48] We are called to manage the resources of the world as an expression of love for its Maker and ours. We are summoned to steward its provisions as an expression of love for our neighbor – near and far, present and future. This is integral to our joy and God's glory in the world.

Joy and The Good Life

Why should we embrace this Story? First, because it is true, and then because we will flourish in life if we do. First, because it truly illumines the landscape of our hearts and our experience in the world, and then because we will discover life at its best if we do.

Joy and the *telos* of life. When ancient Greek philosophers thought of the ultimate object or aim of something, they used the word *telos*, which literally means "an end." When they spoke of our *telos* as human beings, they were talking about the point of human life, or the meaning or purpose of our existence. To pursue our final end, to fulfill our great purpose (which, for instance, Aristotle saw as living according to reason and virtue) is to live well and to flourish in life (which, according to Aristotle, is another way of describing happiness).

The people of the ancient Jewish Scriptures envisioned life differently. To them, life is like a journey. Living is like walking.[49] If we take a journey we must choose a path. The path we choose depends on the destination we hope to reach. The path one takes in the journey of life (as opposed to a trip to a neighboring village) is the "path of life." In many ways it comes to the same thing as the Greek's *telos*: It is about direction and a destination. Its concern is the meaning, purpose, and goal of life. Unlike the Greeks, however, Jewish people believed that the path of life is revealed. Reason doesn't discover it; we don't stumble upon it; God makes it known. The path of life is not about human potential and achievement. It isn't about happiness as the Greek philosophers understood it. It is about a relationship with God and the life-encompassing joy we discover there:

> You show to me the path of life.
> In your presence there is fullness of joy;
>> in your right hand are pleasures forevermore. (Psalm 16:11, NRSV)

In this vision of life, joy is our final end, our *telos*, the meaning of our existence.[50]   People who live well enjoy God and the good gifts he bestows.

Joy and the *summum bonum* of life. Another way of talking about the good life frames the issue in terms of our *summum bonum*, or our greatest good. There are many goods in the world: food, clothing, friends, knowledge, and health. A good is anything that has positive value for human life. What is it that distinguishes our greatest good from other goods? Aristotle taught that a final good is one that is desired for its own sake, and not for the sake of anything else. Other things may be related to it as means, but it will never be a means to anything else because there is nothing higher or better.[51] The only thing that meets this requirement, according to Aristotle, is happiness. All other goods are means to this end.

Christians say that God is the Greatest Good. There are two sides to this coin, however. Objectively, God is the greatest good in this world, and must be in any world that he creates. But if we are talking about the greatest good *for us*, it must engage us as subjects. It must involve us in an enjoyment of this good.[52] God is *the* Greatest Good; enjoying him is *our* greatest good. Seeking this is the good life; finding it is life at its very best.

The glory of God and our joy. The Westminster Shorter Catechism approaches the good life by asking the question, "What is the chief end of man?" and then answering, "Man's chief end is to glorify God, and to enjoy him forever." We glorify God as *the* Greatest Good when we enjoy him as *our* greatest good.[53]

What is the link between God's glory and our joy, and how does it help us understand and pursue the good life? Although the word *glory* can be used of the revelation of God's presence in the world, in its primary theological sense glory characterizes God-as-he-is-in-himself.[54] It is his majesty, his magnificence, his infinite worth, and unlimited power. It is all that God is in his transcendence over his creation. Like the holiness of God, the glory of God is not a single attribute, but his very essence. It is his nature in its totality. In all that he is he is glorious. The Biblical writers tried to capture something of this when they called him "the King of glory,"[55] "the God of glory,"[56] the "Father of glory,"[57] and "the Majestic Glory."[58]

The fitting response to the glory of God is reverence, wonder, and awe: a shudder at our own smallness, a shivering sense of the magnitude of God, and a trembling delight in his unbounded greatness and grandeur. Hearts that have been gripped by glory know the tremulous joy that so great a Being exists, and astonishment-that-takes-one's-breath-away that so great a God would invite us to know and enjoy him. It is a pleasure that is at once dread and delight, fear and fascination, amazement and adoration. To glorify God is to acknowledge, confess, celebrate, and live our lives in light of God's glory. This is joy's native habitat, its indigenous environment.

The supremacy of love. No vision of the good life can claim to be Christian unless it centers on what Jesus saw as God's chief concern for our lives. He summed it up this way:

> You shall love the Lord your God with all your heart and with all your soul and with all your mind. This is the great and first commandment. And a second is like it: You shall love your

neighbor as yourself. On these two commandments depend all the
Law and the Prophets. (Matthew 22:37-40)

This is not something different from what we have already learned about the good life. It is another way of talking about the same thing. In fact, the best way to understand these love commands is to retrace our steps. Loving God is a path of life, a way of living in the world. It is finding the meaning and purpose of our existence in relation to God and in a relationship with him, gratefully embracing the joy of his presence and the pleasures he bestows. It is regarding God as the Greatest Good, and reveling in him as our greatest good. It is cherishing him in his infinite worth, putting him first in our thoughts, first in our loves and affections, first in our values and priorities, first in our interests and concerns, and first in all that we hope for and aspire to in life. Loving God is exulting in his glory, exalting him in his majesty, and making our way of life a fitting response so that others see and are inspired to join us in giving him praise.[59]

It might be tempting to stop there, but Jesus did not. For him, loving God includes loving the people he places in our lives. We love them by affirming their value and developing relational virtues, such as kindness, generosity, humility, and forbearance that enable us to live together robustly in God's world. It is more than this, however. We love others when we include them in our fulfillment of the cultural mandate and our calling to steward the earth. Both are world-affirming and life-shaping. Both are meant to be expressions of love. Both are essential to our joy and theirs.

This is the Tale worth telling. This is the Story I will gladly defend.

QUESTIONS FOR THOUGHT AND DISCUSSION

1. What do you think about the relationship between our joy and a joyful God?

2. What do you think about the author's treatment of joy as the central theme of Creation, the Fall, and Redemption?

3. What implications does the "cultural mandate" have for your understanding of the "human project?"

4. How do you see our stewardship of the earth and its implications for joy?

5. What is the significance of joy for your understanding of the good life?

CHAPTER 12

LAY OF THE LAND & FIRST DEFENSE
DIVINE OMNIPOTENCE

N ow you know something of joy's Story. In this chapter and the next I
will respond to its critics: not their criticism of details in the narrative,
but its major premise and central theme: the existence of a good, all-powerful
God who created and governs the world. This critique is known as the
problem of evil, a collection of arguments against the existence of such a God
from the presence of evil in the world. Its centerpiece is a claim that there is a
contradiction in this package of propositions:

(1) God exists.
(2) God is all-powerful.
(3) God is good.
(4) Evil exists.

If there is a contradiction here, it doesn't lie on the surface. None of these
claims contradicts another. True, critics say, but the second and third

assertions have implications that make the contradiction clear. We can restate the problem this way:

(1) God exists.
(2) God is all-powerful.
  (2.1) An all-powerful God could eliminate evil.
(3) God is good.
  (3.1) A good God would eliminate evil.
(4) Evil exists.

This is the logical problem of evil: If evil exists (4), and it is true that an all-powerful God could eliminate evil (2.1), and that a good God would eliminate evil (3.1), then it cannot also be true that God exists (1), or if he does, that he is all-powerful (2) or good (3). Though many claim that this argument vanquishes Christian faith, we will see that for every thrust of its sharp blade there is a successful parry. As a deductive proof, the problem of evil is daunting but not ultimately dangerous to belief in a good, all-powerful God.

Even if that proof fails, however, the problem of evil cannot be dismissed so easily. In an earlier chapter I commented that an argument can fail as a strict logical proof and still be a strong argument. I used this observation to persuade you that there is a strong case for the existence of God, even if the outcome is not logically certain. Turnabout is fair play, which leads us to a second version of the case against God known as the evidential problem of evil. One argument looks like this, with a theological premise, followed by a factual claim and a conclusion.

(1) If a good, all-powerful God exists, then no gratuitous evil exists;
(2) Gratuitous evil exists;
(3) Therefore, a good, all-powerful God does not exist.

When we look at our world, critics say, the magnitude of evil and the horrendous and apparent gratuitous character of much of it makes the existence of a good, all-powerful God less probable than his non-existence. I will endeavor to persuade you that though it seems compelling to many, this argument fails, as well.

Finally, there is the emotional or existential problem of evil. Some people are haunted by the questions, "Why do the wicked prosper?"[1] And "Why do the righteous suffer?"[2] They cannot bring themselves to believe in a good, all-powerful God because they have been victimized by injustice or traumatized by suffering and pain. They have endured hardship, someone they love has suffered, or they have just seen too much evil in the world. The question "Why?" overwhelms their ability or inclination to believe. If that describes you, I can sit with you in your pain, but I can't give you reasons, specific to you, that God has for allowing these things in your experience. I am only a fellow traveler on the path of life. If you walk with me, however, I can tell you how many have experienced joy in the midst of suffering and pain, and invite you to join our company. If there is good news in your bad news, it is that joy is meant for just such times.[3]

EVIL

Since we are exploring evil and the existence of God, we should begin by getting clear about the notion of evil. The word can be used with moral and non-moral meanings. In a Christian vision of life, *moral* evil refers to a character trait or the property of an action (or inaction) for which a moral agent is responsible, that is incompatible with God's character and will, and that directly or indirectly brings harm into his world. Human violence is an example of moral evil. *Natural* evil, in contrast, refers to pain and suffering that happens not as a result of human agency, but of natural forces under the governance of the Creator. Earthquakes, hurricanes, tornadoes, floods, and disease are examples of this kind of evil (though we will qualify this below).

The peculiar nature of moral evil. Some people think of good and evil as if they were equal but opposite traits, as if they were diametrically opposed in moral status, but the same in ontological status (that is, as if they had equal standing with respect to their existence in the world). Picture two mounted knights side by side, identical in every way except the color of their steeds and standards, one light and the other dark, and the causes to which they are committed, one benevolent, the other bent on harm.[4]

Does evil exist in the same way that good does? It does not.

Goodness is eternal because it is an attribute of the everlasting God; evil, on the other hand, is temporal. It began at a point in the history of the cosmos. This is where the path takes a surprising turn. Evil had a beginning, but not as a creation of God. How can this be? How can something begin to exist in God's universe and not be his creation? We must start here: If everything created by God is good, as Christians affirm, then whatever evil is, it cannot be a creation of God.[5]

It is a popular mistake to think of evil as a being, or an entity. It is not. Moral evil is a character trait and the property of an action for which moral agents are responsible. When we speak of evil people or evil beings, they are evil in the sense that they have developed a twisted disposition that results in twisted actions. God takes responsibility for creating moral agents who, in their freedom, can do evil and become evil, and for sovereignly permitting their warped character and misdeeds, but evil is their own making, not God's.[6]

Evil exists, but not properly or natively as a being, an entity, or a thing in itself. It is a corruption of something good. A perversion. C.S. Lewis wrote, "Evil is a parasite, not an original thing. The powers which enable evil to carry on are powers given it by goodness. All the things which enable a bad man to be effectively bad are in themselves good things – resolution, cleverness, good looks, existence itself."[7] Evil is an interloper. A thief. It has nothing of its own.   It must borrow or steal from God's good world to accomplish its ends.

Demonic evil.   From a Christian perspective, humans aren't the only finite moral agents who are responsible for evil in God's world.   At least some, and perhaps much, of what we perceive to be natural evil because it is unrelated to human agency is moral evil on a higher plane. In another book, I wrote:

> If we could part the curtains that hide the unseen spiritual realm and see what is behind the woes of our world, we would see a rejection of God and his ways. And behind that we would see his ancient adversary blinding eyes, hardening hearts, and stirring a pot of malice that spills into our world. He is known by many names in the Scriptures: Lucifer, Satan, the devil, the evil one, the tempter, the accuser, the dragon, the father of lies, the god of this world. With legions of angelic beings who followed him in a primordial rebellion against God, he is bent on deflecting worship from God, defying the will of God, and destroying God's world.
>
> His kingdom is dark; his reign, sinister. His power is great; his rage, greater. In a hymn for the ages, Luther wrote of him: "For still our ancient foe doth seek to work us woe; his craft and power are great, and armed with cruel hate, on earth is not his equal."[8]

In the biblical narrative, Satan and demons are causal agents in the world, bringing about catastrophe, human sickness, and even animal pain and death.[9] In our limitations we are not in a position to quantify evil in the world that can be traced to malevolent spiritual beings; nevertheless, this must be factored into a Christian understanding of evil in the world.[10]

Evil and the Fall. In a Christian vision of life, we are not what we were created to be, and so the world in which we live is not what God created it to be. Theologians describe the primordial turn of events that led to this as "the Fall."[11] Like our first parents, we have fallen from the high purposes of our Creator and have been seriously injured from the fall. The Bible uses the word "death" to describe this condition: alienation from God, from each other, from our environment, and a disintegration and dysfunction within ourselves that impacts both our bodies and our souls.[12] Much of what we consider natural evil is fall-out from the solidarity of the human race in a sinful condition: sickness, disease, infirmity, and, ultimately, the demise of our bodies.[13]

You might reject and even ridicule such notions, but that is irrelevant in this context, since it is the Christian who is being charged with contradictory beliefs. I did not create the doctrine of the Fall to maneuver around charges in the problem of evil. It is part of a rich tradition that Christians have embraced for centuries. We believe that it helps explain the world better than any other point of view. It is a more powerful, illuminating story than any other. You may not share this belief with us, but when it is brought to the problem of evil, it is a significant factor in defeating the claim that our beliefs are mutually exclusive.

Evil and our cultural mandate. We can imagine a world inhabited by creatures that seek only their own good or the good of their own brood or herd. That is not God's plan for our world, with creatures made in his image its crest. The Creator has commissioned us to be his representative, governing his world in his stead. He has entrusted us with a world-shaping project. He has called us to make something of his world from the resources of his world for the good of all people in his world. Guided by goodness, beauty, and truth, we are called to build civilizations, create cultures and institutions, and engage in enterprises that honor our Creator and bring about a world in which all people flourish in joy.

Great good can come from this. Great evil exists in the world because we have failed to deliver on this mandate. This is where we should locate structural evil, violence, and injustice. It is evil that arises from, and is perpetuated by, social institutions. The social configuration may be a family, a clan, a corporation, or a government. It may involve domestic abuse, racism, sexism, terrorism, oppression of the poor, slavery, drug and human trafficking, and even genocide. Because sin permeates all human beings,[14] it pervades all human institutions and impacts all who participate in them. Joy that could be ours has been lost.

Evil and our stewardship of the earth. The earth is host to an intricate network of ecosystems in which we play a pivotal role. In this finely tuned arrangement, we are psychosomatic beings who relate to our world in psychosomatic ways. Physical and spiritual dimensions are thread and strand in the fabric of human nature and our interaction with the world. They can and do affect each other. In our own case, if we mishandle stress (a spiritual issue), it can impact our physical health. If we cultivate bitterness, resentment, suspicion, mistrust, or anxiety (spiritual issues), it will diminish our physical well-being. It is also true that prayer and meditation have physical benefits. Joy contributes to the health of our bodies.[15] The Creator designed us this way.

If this is so, it should not be surprising that our interface with the world is both physical and spiritual. Our joy and the wellness of the world are connected.[16] There is a nexus between our sin and the world's malaise.[17] It is not only what we do in our greed (exploiting others and natural resources), but greed itself, that tears the fabric of the world. It is not only what we do in our quest for pleasure (which results in a culture of consumption, massive landfills, and ground and water pollution) that injures the earth, that false spiritual quest itself rends the intricate web of life on our planet. It is not only what we do in our arrogance that harms the world, arrogance itself causes the world to limp.[18]

We are the ones who have introduced toxins in our environment. We have ravaged and exploited the resources of the earth, and destroyed delicate ecosystems that are essential to our environment and our well-being. In ways that we must rue, we have failed in our stewardship of the earth. Evil is the result.[19]

Evil and the good life. Our understanding of the good life is critically important here. If we see pleasure as our highest good, then pain is a big problem! If God is committed to a hedonistic vision of life for us, either his plan is a poor fit for our world (He is not wise.), or he does a poor job implementing it (He is not omnipotent.). If we think that happiness is our highest good and see it in the superficial way that many do, we end up with a theological vision described by C.S. Lewis:

> What would really satisfy us would be a God who said of anything we happened to like doing, "What does it matter so long as they are contented?" We want, in fact, not so much a Father in Heaven as a grandfather in heaven - a senile benevolence who, as they say, "liked to see young people enjoying themselves" and whose plan for the universe was simply that it might be truly said at the end of each day, "a good time was had by all".[20]

Joy is the *telos* of human existence, or our chief end. It is the centerpiece and crown of the good life. Life as God designed it is a quest to discover this highest and best of all pleasures.[21] God is *the* Greatest Good. He becomes *our* greatest good when we enjoy him and value him above everything else (including an untroubled life). Our greatest joy comes as we seek the glory of God in all that we do and in all that comes our way (including troubles).

This puts evil into a different framework. It invites other questions and suggests different answers than we would find with other versions of the good life. We should see evil as anything that frustrates the realization of our greatest good. It is anything that keeps us, or others, from joy.[22] If this is so, then some things that we may not have regarded as evil *per se* (good things misplaced in our values) are, because they block our path to joy. Some things that we have regarded as evil (pain and suffering), are not inherently so because they may lead us into greater experiences of joy.

MORAL FREEDOM

When I say that God created us with free will, I mean, first, that we can choose one thing and not another without anything but our own agency determining our decision, and second, that in any decision we have made, given the same conditions, we could have done otherwise.[23] In biblical narratives, God holds people accountable for their decisions and judges them for their misdeeds. The implication is that they were responsible for their decisions, and that they could and should have chosen differently.

I can imagine a world in which all creatures were programmed, as we might devise robots to do tasks we assign to them. Some of these creatures might be designed to build cities and bridges and roads. Some might even play musical instruments, draw, paint, sculpt, develop civilizations, and simulate cultures. But robots are not moral agents. In a world of automata, God alone would be responsible. You might wish for a world without freedom (though I find that hard to believe), but that isn't our world. God had something higher and nobler for us in mind.

This kind of freedom is essential to relationships of love, whether it is our relationship with God or with each other. Coerced love is a contradiction in terms. Love must be freely given, and if this is so, it can also be withheld. Love must be freely received, and if this is so, it can also be rejected. You might wish for a loveless world (again, I find that hard to believe), but that isn't our world. God had something far better for us in mind.[24]

AN ALL-POWERFUL GOD

Christians assert that the one God is infinite in power. An omnipotent God brought the universe with its billions of galaxies into being. An omnipotent God sustains this vast expanse – billions of light years from one side to another – in every moment and in every place. An omnipotent God is guiding the course of history to an end that he has determined will come to pass.

An omnipotent God could eliminate evil, critics say. Because evil exists, an omnipotent God does not. In response, we should start by getting clear about the meaning of omnipotence. The Bible affirms that God is omnipotent and that there are things an omnipotent God cannot do. He cannot lie; [25] he cannot change; [26] he cannot deny himself. [27] These observations have led theologians from Aquinas on to refine the meaning of omnipotence from the ability to do anything, to the ability to do anything that is possible.[28] God cannot not exist.[29] He cannot become dependent upon something else for his existence.[30] He cannot become more or less than he is.[31] He cannot cease being Triune.[32] These are absolute impossibilities and imply nothing about a measurement of power.[33] Nor can God do what is logically impossible. He cannot create a universe that has no beginning. He cannot draw a four-sided triangle, or a square circle, or make the statement 2+2=5 true. These are not tests of power, but tomfoolery with words.

FIRST DEFENSE: DIVINE OMNIPOTENCE AND EVIL

Moral evil. Critics contend that an all-powerful God could eliminate evil in the world. But if an omnipotent God cannot do what is logically impossible, then he cannot eliminate evil that results directly or indirectly from moral agency that is free in the way that I have described it. God cannot create moral agents who are free to choose good or evil and at the same time infallibly guarantee (or otherwise bring it about) that they will always choose good and never evil. C.S. Lewis put it this way:

> [God's] Omnipotence means power to do all that is intrinsically possible, not to do the intrinsically impossible. You may attribute miracles to Him, but not nonsense. There is no limit to His power.

> If you choose to say, 'God can give a creature free will and at the same time withhold free will from it,' you have not succeeded in saying anything about God: meaningless combinations of words do not suddenly acquire meaning simply because we prefix to them the two other words, 'God can.'

> It remains true that all things are possible with God: the intrinsic impossibilities are not things but nonentities. It is no more possible for God than for the weakest of His creatures to carry out both of two mutually exclusive alternatives; not because His power meets an obstacle, but because nonsense remains nonsense even when we talk it about God.[34]

This accounts for moral evil, and for some (possibly much) of what we call natural evil if it can be traced to human factors, such as the impact of human activity on our natural environment. It includes a wide array of harm, from unkind words to terrorism, from petty theft to weapons of mass destruction, from frivolous lawsuits to genocide. It includes pain and suffering brought about by toxins in our food, hazardous chemicals in our soil and water, pollution in our air, the widespread destruction of jungles and forests, and the warming of the earth's climates.[35] Illnesses that result from lifestyle choices and psychosomatic maladies belong in this category, as well. Wittingly or not, we do these things to ourselves. Christians lament all of these evils, rejoice that God is omnipotent and good, and maintain that there is no contradiction in doing both.

The debate doesn't end there, however. Another version of the argument takes us into the rarefied air of logically possible worlds. It begins with a modest claim: It is logically possible for a free-willed moral agent to choose good once. Now, if it is logically possible for a morally free agent to choose good once, then it is logically possible for that same agent to choose good every time. We aren't talking about the likelihood of this happening, and not at all about a guarantee beforehand that it will. It is a logical possibility. Critics say that we should take this a step further. If it is logically possible for one moral agent with free will to do this, then it is logically possible for a world to be populated solely with moral agents with free will and a perfect record of choosing good. An omnipotent God, critics say, could create such a logically possible world, and a good God would.[36] That we have our world instead is proof that an omnipotent, good God does not exist.

This argument has two serious flaws. First, if it is logically possible that there is a world inhabited only by morally free creatures who always choose good, it is also logically possible that there is no such world.[37] (If S is the set of logically possible moral agents with free will who always choose good and never evil, S may have members and may have none. There is no contradiction in affirming either.) It is logically possible that all moral agents who have the property of being free also have the property of choosing evil, and that this is so in every logically possible world in which they exist. If this is so, then it is possible that God cannot create a world inhabited exclusively by morally free agents with a perfect record of always choosing good and never evil.[38] The contest of logical possibilities ends in a draw (which is a win for Christian faith because this attempt to defeat it has failed).[39]

Second, critics have set the bar too low in their insistence that God should have created a better world than ours. God is not merely strong; he is omnipotent. He is not merely good; he is supremely good. An omnipotent, supremely good God must create the best of all possible worlds if it is logically possible to do so. That possibility does not exist, however, even for a God with unlimited power:

(1) An all-powerful God can create the best of all possible worlds if it is logically possible to do so;

(2) It is not logically possible to create the best of all possible worlds;

(3) Therefore, an all-powerful God cannot create the best of all possible worlds.[40]

It is not logically possible to create the best of all possible worlds, because there is a contradiction embedded in the notion. A possible world can always be improved by the addition of one more logically possible, morally free agent who always chooses good, *ad infinitum*, and this will be true of any candidate for the best of all possible worlds. Thus, if X is the best of all possible worlds, then X is not (and cannot be) the best of all possible worlds.[41] Therein lies the contradiction.

In sum, it is possible that God cannot create a world populated solely by free moral agents with a perfect record of choosing good and never evil, because it is logically possible that no such world exists. Nor is it a slight to God to say that he cannot create the best of all possible worlds. Even an omnipotent God cannot do what is logically impossible. This should put an end to such nonsense, as Lewis would have put it.

Finally, let's return to the critic's notion of a logically possible world in which all inhabitants are free-willed moral agents who always choose good and never evil. The one thing we know is that ours is not that world. If such a world was possible and you could ask God to substitute it for ours, would you? Before you do, keep in mind that you, with your lifetime of decisions – some good, some bad – would not be included. Neither would anyone else you know. None of your friends. None of your family. No one in the world as we know it. If I could ask God to replace our world with that possible world, I wouldn't do it. I might be wrong, but I don't think that you would either. That is an implicit endorsement of the world God created, whatever critics may say.

Natural evil. Since we have defined natural evil as pain and suffering that happens as a result of natural forces, and is not directly or indirectly related to the volition of anyone but God, who is sovereign over the natural world, it follows that an omnipotent God can eliminate such evil. That he does not always do so shifts the argument to the goodness of God, which we will explore in the next two chapters.

QUESTIONS FOR THOUGHT AND DISCUSSION

1. Summarize the three kinds of argument against God from the existence of evil. Which connects with you the most? In what ways?

2. Discuss the differences between moral and natural evil. Which seems like more of a problem to you?

3. Do you believe in demonic evil? If so, what difference does it make for your understanding of the problem of evil? If not, are you open to that possibility?

4. How do you understand the omnipotence of God? After reading this chapter, what do you think its implications are for the problem of evil?

5. How do you understand the nature of moral freedom? What difference does it make for the problem of evil?

CHAPTER 13

SECOND DEFENSE
DIVINE GOODNESS

Christians believe that God is good. We affirm that He is infinitely worthy, supremely valuable, surpassingly desirable, and unrivaled in moral beauty. In this belief we also affirm that God is the Source of everything good in the universe, and that he is benevolent toward us and generous in his gifts. We teach our children to pray, "God is great, God is good, and we thank him for our food."[1] This belief lies at the heart of our worship:

> Oh, taste and see that the LORD is good! (Psalm 34:8)

> Praise the LORD!
> Oh give thanks to the LORD, for he is good,
>   for his steadfast love endures forever! (Psalm 106:1)

If you affirm the goodness of God, should you accept the critic's claim that a good God would eliminate evil?   Or, if you accept the conclusion I reached about omnipotence in the last chapter, should you concede that a good God would eliminate all the evil he possibly can? I wouldn't if I were you.

Let's start with what we know from family life. Good parents sometimes allow their children to go through painful situations. It requires careful discernment, but if they choose not to prevent such experiences, it is because they believe that these ordeals may bring about a greater good, such as the development of character, endurance, or wisdom in facing the challenges of life. Or consider this: I still have memories of carrying a frightened, tearful child into a doctor's office for an immunization shot. I permitted a small pain in order to prevent greater pain and suffering from childhood diseases. In the language of philosophers, justifications like these constitute "morally sufficient reasons" for permitting evil. They create possibilities of greater good or prevent possibilities of greater evil.

The question before us is whether God has morally sufficient reasons for permitting evil in the world. Believers say that he does. We contend that a good, omniscient, and all-powerful God knows that a world laden with possibilities of good and evil brought about by creatures with free will is better than a world without moral freedom. In itself it is a greater good, and it creates possibilities of greater good. Though evil followed, and God knew that it would, this is the morally sufficient reason behind the creation narrative, "Then God said, "Let us make humankind in our image, according to our likeness.""[2] Not surprisingly, this claim is contested.

Philosophers say that evil is gratuitous if there is no morally sufficient reason for permitting it. It is gratuitous if it does not serve a greater good that would not otherwise come about, or prevent a greater evil that would otherwise take place.[3] The critic's argument is not that there are no instances of evil in which a greater good might result, or a greater evil might be averted, but that there are many (too many, critics say) instances of evil in which this is not the case. What possible good, they ask, can come from the torture of an infant, or the raping and killing a young girl? What greater evil is prevented?[4] A good God would not allow these things in his world.

Any response to such pain and suffering risks making light of the problem. We should weep with those who weep.[5] When we have finished weeping, however, there is an intellectual challenge to be met. There is a charge that must be answered.

THE PROBLEM OF GRATUITOUS EVIL

Now that the notion of gratuitous evil has been introduced, we can state the problem this way:

(1) If a good, all-powerful God exists, then no gratuitous evil exists;
(2) Gratuitous evil exists;
(3) Therefore, a good, all-powerful God does not exist.

I grant that this proof is formally valid, and acknowledge that many find it persuasive. I suggest, however, if the truth were fully known, that the argument is compelling to many for reasons that have nothing to do with logic.

Earlier in this book I explored the relationship between emotions and beliefs, and the way they influence each other in our understanding of the world. There is no way to avoid this, nor should we want to. It is true to who we are as affective-rational beings. This is nowhere clearer than when we talk about suffering and pain, whether it is our own or the experience of another. Our emotions are engaged, often in powerful ways. Whether it is "Man's inhumanity to man," as Robert Burns put it, congenital leukemia, a slow, painful death from pancreatic cancer, or the aftermath of a tsunami or an earthquake, the first response of most people to suffering is a strong desire to see it end. If it doesn't, their next response is likely to be sorrow, followed by anger. The questions may be mute, but they stir deep within: "What did she do to deserve this?" "What good can possibly come from that?"[6]

Even if we bring reason into the discussion, the conversation began with our emotions. Whatever reason may suggest for understanding suffering and pain, it will have to deal with emotions already in play. I understand that. I embrace it. I believe that it is largely what makes this argument seem compelling.[7] I offer this not as a critique, but as an observation in the interests of intellectual honesty.

Another reason this argument seems compelling is that it has a common-sense plausibility. It fits what many people perceive about the world and expect to be the case. We see evil. We may not be able to see a greater good that has come from it, or a greater evil that has been prevented.[8] The evil we see trumps the possibilities we cannot see. The first is often regarded as the *real world*, the second as nothing more than wishful thinking. In hundreds of ways this belief is reinforced in the way many are taught to manage the circumstances of life.

Now, even if my appraisal of the compelling nature of this argument is accurate, I grant that you are rational in your belief that an instance of evil is gratuitous if you look carefully but cannot see a greater good that has come from it, or a greater evil that has been prevented by it. That is a significant concession, but don't make too much of it. To return to a point made earlier in this book, it is possible to be rational in a belief that is false.[9] I will argue that this is the case.

DISTINCTIONS THAT MAKE A DIFFERENCE

Does gratuitous evil exist? I admit that some evil appears to be gratuitous, and that some evil is gratuitous in a qualified sense, but I deny the existence of evil that is categorically gratuitous. Let me explain.

When evil appears to be gratuitous but is not. Evil often seems to be gratuitous. Something bad happens, and in its aftermath we cannot see a greater good that has come or a greater evil that has been prevented. It is gratuitous as far as we can see. What seems to be gratuitous, however, may turn out not to be. Later developments may require a revision of an earlier conclusion. For Christians, there is no greater example of this than the crucifixion of Jesus. For three days following that horrific event, those who knew about it and cared would have been rational in their belief that it was gratuitous. It was senseless, pointless evil. The resurrection and all that followed in its wake were new developments that required a rethinking of their initial assessment.

Or consider the imprisonment of Nelson Mandela under the policy of institutional racism in South Africa. For twenty-seven years, his freedom was unjustly taken from him, and he endured other injustices during his incarceration. For twenty-seven years his followers would have been rational in their belief that this was gratuitous evil. But the story did not end there. There were ways in which Mandela was prepared by his prison experience to lead a nation-changing movement, and there were developments in the social and political world of South Africa that made that movement possible. His eventual release, leadership, and strategic role in ending apartheid brought greater goods that would not, as far as we know, have come about apart from his unjust captivity.

In its opening clause, the first premise of this argument posits a God who is omnipotent and good: "If a good, all-powerful God exists, then no gratuitous evil exists." If you grant this provisionally in the first premise, it has implications for evaluating the second premise that gratuitous evil exists. If we live in a world created and governed by a such a God, Christians say, evil may appear to be gratuitous because:

- The evil is physical and the greater good that comes from it, or the greater evil that is prevented, is spiritual.

- The greater good that comes from it, or the greater evil that is prevented, is for someone other than the one who suffered the evil (that is, it is redemptive in nature).

- The greater good that comes from it, or the greater evil that is prevented, occurs (or is prevented) in another place and another time.

- The greater good that comes from it, or the greater evil that is prevented, will be in an afterlife.

This is not special pleading. It just is the nature of the case, if, for the sake of argument, you grant that a Christian vision of the world is true.[10] Evil may seem gratuitous, but that does not make it so.[11]

When gratuitous evil exists in a qualified sense. Some evil is gratuitous because the greater good that is possible in a situation is contingent upon the actions of morally free agents that do not happen.[12] Suppose that Fred Wilson steals $100 from Stephanie Smith after she leaves an Automated Teller Machine, and that God permitted this to happen. Greater goods that could come in consequence of this evil include the following:

- Mr. Wilson will be overcome with guilt, confess his crime, and become a model citizen who is known for good deeds to people in need.

- Ms. Smith will re-think her values and the inordinate status she has given to money, with an appropriate change of heart and a commitment to a simpler lifestyle.

- Ms. Smith will trust God with her finances from that point forward.

- Jennifer Matson, who witnessed the theft, will be moved to give Ms. Smith $100, and the two women will strike up a friendship that enriches both.

It is possible that none of these greater goods will come about because they are contingent upon the actions of morally free agents that do not occur. If so, gratuitous evil of a qualified sort results. An omnipotent God cannot eliminate such a state of affairs without also revoking the gift of moral freedom that makes it possible. A good God would not.

This is also true if the evil in question is not the act of a moral agent, but the result of natural forces. Let's say that Ms. Smith loses her house in a flood, and that the greater goods that could come from this include the following:

- Ms. Smith will move to another town where flooding is less likely, and will regard her new situation as a significant improvement.

- The local community will rally behind Ms. Smith, help her rebuild her house, and meet her physical and financial needs until life returns to normal.

- Ms. Smith, who previously had only a nominal belief in God, will come to believe that a relationship with God is of greater value than material possessions.

- Debbie Johnson, who reads about Ms. Smith's plight in the local newspaper, will volunteer to take care of the Smith children for the next month, and the two women will become friends for the rest of their lives.

It may be that none of these greater goods will come about because they are contingent upon actions of morally free agents that do not take place. In this case, again, gratuitous evil of a qualified sort results. An omnipotent God cannot eliminate such a state of affairs without also revoking the gift of moral freedom that makes it possible. A good God would not.

When morally free agents are involved, the critical issue is not whether a greater good resulted from an evil, or a greater evil was prevented (though both outcomes are possible), but whether a world in which there is moral freedom and the possibility of evil is better than a world without moral freedom. Christians say that it is, and that this is a morally sufficient reason for a good God to permit evil.[13]

Categorically gratuitous evil. I concede that gratuitous evil exists in appearance and in a contingent relationship with human freedom. I deny the existence of categorically gratuitous evil. If this sort of evil existed, its gratuitous nature would be simple, unqualified, and absolute. It would not serve a greater good or prevent a greater evil in any logically possible world in which it exists. (While the moral agents in our two stories did not bring about a greater good, there are logically possible worlds in which they do, which is another way of saying that they could have chosen otherwise).[14] We can give this evil a name and a definition, but it does not exist in our world.

Evil may appear to be gratuitous because we aren't in a position to see a greater good that has or will come from it or a greater evil that has been or will be prevented. It may be contingently gratuitous because it is related to God's gift of moral freedom. Categorically gratuitous evil, however, does not exist. The evil may be painfully real, but its unqualified gratuitous character is not. We can imagine it, but there is no such thing. Critics may assert that it exists and even protest loudly that it does. As we will see below, however, their arguments do not make good on their claims.

Before we get to those arguments, let's take a brief pause. If you disagree with me, it raises a very important question: Who is qualified to settle our disagreement? Who is in a position to determine when the standard of a morally sufficient reason has been met, or when it has not? Who is qualified to know if it will be met in the future or never will be? It would have to be someone with exhaustive and infallible knowledge of what constitutes a greater good or a greater evil in every instance in which evil occurs. It would have to be someone with complete and perfect knowledge of our world, including all morally free agents, from their first breath to their last, and whatever existence they may have in an afterlife. It would have to be someone with unlimited and unerring knowledge of all logically possible worlds, including all possible greater goods and evils that could come about from, or be prevented by, the existence of evil in our world.

Sounds like a task for an omniscient being.[15]

Either the set of omniscient beings has no members, if atheists are right, or it has one member, if Christians and other monotheists are right. If atheists are right, no one knows whether an evil in the past or the present will result in a greater good or the prevention of a greater evil in the future. We are left with a rhetorical contest without resolution. If Christians (and other monotheists) are right, the only one who knows these things and can render an infallible judgment on them is the God who created the world and permits evil in it.[16]

TWO ARGUMENTS

In conclusion, let's look at two versions of the argument from gratuitous evil. We have already seen the stronger of the two:

(1) If a good, all-powerful God exists, gratuitous evil does not exist.
(2) Gratuitous evil exists.
(3) Therefore, a good, all-powerful God does not exist.

Atheists claim that there is gratuitous evil in the world and insist that believers must prove otherwise. I object. The burden of proof lies with the proponents of the argument. Since it is their claim that gratuitous evil exists, they must demonstrate that it does. I don't believe that they can.

First, their claim requires a leap that logic cannot make. There is a hidden premise in their assertion. It becomes apparent when we recall that evil is gratuitous if there is no morally sufficient reason for its existence. If E is an instance of evil, this is the tacit premise: "We can't see a morally sufficient reason for E." This is the inference drawn from it: "There are no morally sufficient reasons for E." The inference is a *non sequitur*. It does not logically follow. It does not follow from the fact that we cannot see something that it does not exist.[17] That I cannot see you as I write this implies nothing about your existence. That you cannot see me implies nothing about mine.

Second, saying that one cannot see something is not a statement of positive evidence, but an admission of ignorance. Atheists may be faulted for claiming to know more than they do; they should not be blamed for not knowing what they cannot know. They are not in a position to say that any instance of evil in the world is, in fact, gratuitous, and there is nothing they can do to change that. It is the human situation.[18] Our epistemic limitations are too great, our knowledge, too scant.

Perhaps a more modest version of the argument will succeed:

(1) If a good, all-powerful God exists, gratuitous evil does not exist.
(2) Gratuitous evil probably exists.
(3) Therefore, a good, all-powerful God probably does not exist.

Claiming a probable rather than an actual state of affairs in the second premise and the conclusion may seem to make the argument more reasonable and tenable. In fact, however, it fails on those very terms.

First, it still involves a *non sequitur.* If we say again that *E* is an instance of evil, there is a chasm in the logic between "We can't see a morally sufficient reason for *E*." and "There probably are no morally sufficient reasons for *E*." One does not follow from the other. The fact that we cannot see something tells us nothing about the probability of its existence. From the mere fact that I cannot see a solution to a physics problem, nothing can be inferred about the probability that a solution exists.[19] From the fact that I cannot see the Northern Lights from my home in Colorado, nothing can be inferred about the likelihood that there is such a polar light display.

Second, we still don't know enough. If we are not in a position to see future goods that may come or future evils that may be averted in consequence of a past or present evil, we cannot establish probability in the matter. Suppose that we watch two runners in a ten-mile race crest a hill at the quarter-mile mark and disappear from our sight. There isn't any way to know which runner will win the race, or even which runner will probably win. We are not in a position to know, and there is nothing more that we can say about it. You might cheer Runner A, and I, Runner B. You may have reasons for believing that your runner will win; I may have reasons for believing that mine will prevail. You might say, "My runner was faster to the top of that hill!" I might respond, "Yes, but have you never heard the story of the tortoise and the hare? They still have most of the race to go." The only one who knows the outcome is someone standing at the finish line, and that isn't either of us. So it is when we are asked to evaluate the status of something – in this case whether an instance of evil is gratuitous or not – when that status can only be determined by unknown states of affairs in the future.

Third, there isn't an objective way to determine whose claim of probability has won and whose has been defeated. If we were using a statistical notion of probability, an outcome could be measured. In principle we might come to an agreement. In this argument, however, both sides must appeal to a qualitative property of likelihood in a comparison of rival points of view. There isn't a way to measure this.

Fourth, because we are dealing with a qualitative notion, subjective factors come into play. There is great value in discussion and debate. You might convince me that your argument is stronger; I might persuade you of the strength of mine. We might both come away with greater clarity in our thinking. At the end of the day, however, there isn't an objective, neutral position from which the probability of our points of view can be judged.

Finally, this argument is either unpersuasive or it commits the fallacy of ambiguity, and so fails. The second premise and the conclusion use the word "probably." For the argument to succeed, the word must have the same meaning in both instances. In the second premise, the critic says, in effect, that he cannot see a greater good that has come from an instance of suffering, or a greater evil that has been averted, and so concludes that the evil in question is probably gratuitous. We might call this *as-far-as-we-can-see* probability. Now, if this meaning is also used in the conclusion – *As far as we can see,* a good, all-powerful God probably does not exist – the argument may tell us something about our limited vantage point, but it says nothing convincing about the probable existence or non-existence of God.

Now consider the conclusion of the argument. The probability of the existence of God cannot be decided on the basis of any single issue, including evil. The broadest possible range of evidence must be taken into account. Let's call this *all-things-considered* probability. This is a different notion than we began the argument with. If critics import this meaning of probability into the conclusion to give it greater strength, they commit the fallacy of ambiguity, and the argument fails.

CONCLUDING ARGUMENT

With the understanding that I am referring to evil that is categorically gratuitous, let me conclude with my own argument:

(1) If a good, all-powerful God exists, gratuitous evil does not exist.
(2) A good, all-powerful God exists;
(3) Therefore, gratuitous evil does not exist.[20]

The strength of this argument depends on the strength of the premise that a good, all-powerful God exists. Such a God would not permit such evil (which is implied in the first premise). Even if I don't know why God permits one evil or another, there are good reasons for believing in God, who does know.[21] This is not an arbitrary move. It arises suitably from a humble recognition that an omniscient God knows things that we don't, and a confidence that we are on sturdy ground in affirming that an omniscient, good, all-powerful God exists. Even if logical certainty is beyond our reach (and it is), and we acknowledge subjective factors in our beliefs (and we must), this is where the issue must be decided.[22]

POSTSCRIPT: GRATUITOUS EVIL AND THE CROSS

How odd that an instrument of torture and death should become the centerpiece of worship and faith for nearly two and a half billion people around the world today! Yet it is true. The instrument is a cross, the one who hung upon it was Jesus of Nazareth, and the billions who embrace this in faith are Christians.

The cross is an invitation to rethink our understanding of God. John Stott captured its significance in these words:

> I could never myself believe in God, if it were not for the cross. The only God I believe in is the One Nietzsche ridiculed as 'God on the

cross.' In the real world of pain, how could one worship a God who was immune to it? I have entered many Buddhist temples in different Asian countries and stood respectfully before the statue of the Buddha, his legs crossed, arms folded, eyes closed, the ghost of a smile playing round his mouth, a remote look on his face, detached from the agonies of the world. But each time after a while I have had to turn away. And in imagination I have turned instead to that lonely, twisted, tortured figure on the cross, nails through hands and feet, back lacerated, limbs wrenched, brow bleeding from thorn-pricks, mouth dry and intolerably thirsty, plunged in Godforsaken darkness. That is the God for me![23]

The startling claim of Christians is that in Jesus the God who created and sustains the universe has drawn near to us, so near that he became one of us. The God who governs history is so intimately involved in human life that he made it his own. If that were not enough, the more astonishing claim is that in Jesus God submitted himself fully to the conditions of our humanity, lived without wrongdoing, and then, on a cross, offered his sinless life as full payment for the sins of the world.

> Have this mind among yourselves, which is yours in Christ Jesus, who, though he was in the form of God, did not count equality with God a thing to be grasped, but emptied himself, by taking the form of a servant, being born in the likeness of men. And being found in human form, he humbled himself by becoming obedient to the point of death, even death on a cross. (Philippians 2:5-8)

> God shows his love for us in that while we were still sinners, Christ died for us. (Romans 5:8)

> In Christ God was reconciling the world to himself. (2 Corinthians 5:19)

The cross is also an invitation to see evil differently.[24] There is no way to euphemize it: Death by crucifixion is horrendous evil. In the case of Christ, however, it was also redemptive, because God was in Christ, on the cross, reconciling the world to himself. In a powerful paradox, great evil has brought great good. What destroyed now saves. What brought death now brings life. What seemed senseless turns out to be the most significant thing that has happened in the world.

We are invited to see our troubled world in light of the cross. Suffering, pain, and evil may seem pointless, but they are not what they seem, or need not be, because they point to what God has done for us in Christ. And that changes everything.

QUESTIONS FOR THOUGHT AND DISCUSSION

1. "A morally sufficient reason for permitting evil includes bringing about a greater good that would not otherwise happen, or preventing a greater evil that otherwise would." What do you think of this principle? Can you think of examples of each?

2. Discuss the author's understanding of apparent and contingent gratuitous evil. Is it convincing?

3. Discuss the author's understanding of categorically gratuitous evil. Is it convincing?

4. What do you think of the three versions of arguments on gratuitous evil and God? Which argument to you agree with, and why?

5. Discuss the Postscript on the Cross and Gratuitous Evil. Do you agree or disagree? Why?

CHAPTER 14

THIS WORLD AND THE NEXT
A THEODICY

There is good reason to believe that gratuitous evil does not exist in our world, not only because we sometimes see a greater good that would not otherwise happen, and sometimes become aware of a greater evil that has been prevented, but because there are good reasons to believe in a good, all-powerful God who would not allow it.[1]

A world designed for morally free creatures is better than a world without them. If God were to prevent all natural evil so that there was no possibility of sickness or calamity, it would also eliminate many acts of kindness, compassion, cooperation, generosity, courage, and heroism – all of which are grounded in moral freedom. If God were to remove our freedom in order to eliminate the possibility of moral evil, it would also remove the possibility of joy and the good life he intends for us. Neither of these possible worlds would be a better world, and that is a morally sufficient reason for God's permission of evil in ours.[2]

In this chapter we will explore morally sufficient reasons for God's permission of evil in his world. This is sometimes called a *theodicy*, or an attempt to vindicate God and his ways.[3] I offer this with hesitation, first, because I cannot imagine God asking me to defend him. It would be like the sun asking a candle to help illumine the earth, or a hurricane asking a handheld fan to help blow water across the sea. I hesitate, secondly, because I know so little. There is much that is a mystery to me. I am mindful of words like these:

> For my thoughts are not your thoughts,
>   neither are your ways my ways, declares the LORD.
> For as the heavens are higher than the earth,
>   so are my ways higher than your ways
>   and my thoughts than your thoughts. (Isaiah 55:8-9)
> O, the depth of the riches and wisdom and knowledge of God!
> How unsearchable are his judgments and how inscrutable his ways!
>
> "For who has known the mind of the Lord,
>   or who has been his counselor?" (Romans 11:33-34)

I know less of the wisdom and knowledge of God than a tiny crustacean on an ocean floor knows of a ship on the surface miles above. You might think that such a confession would (or should) mark an early end to this chapter. One of the central affirmations of Christian faith, however, is that God has revealed truth about himself and his ways. He has disclosed what would otherwise be closed to us. Not enough or clearly enough to satisfy our curiosity, but enough to help us navigate our way through life with joy.[4] My offering is a reflection upon what God has made known in the Scriptures he has given.

QUESTIONS OF VALUE

The problem of evil has led us to notions of greater good and greater evil. Much of the disagreement between believers and their critics lies here. Whether you agree with them or not, these judgments of value are essential to a Christian vision of life:

- A virtuous character is a greater good than freedom from suffering and pain.

- A misshapen character is a greater evil than suffering and pain.

- An eternal good is a greater good than freedom from temporal suffering and pain.

- Eternal suffering and pain are greater evils than temporal suffering and pain.

- The undimmed, unending enjoyment of God in heaven is an immeasurably greater good than any temporal suffering and pain on the earth.

If you start here, Christians say, the world begins to make sense. If you don't, it never will.

GREATER EVILS

A Misshapen Character. I understand that what I am about to say is so far removed from the values of our culture that it will seem preposterous to many. Nevertheless, Christians believe that God permits and uses pain in our lives because one of its possibilities (possible because our morally free response is required) is averting the greater evil of a misshapen character.[5]

C.S. Lewis put this way:

> The human spirit will not even begin to try to surrender self will as long as all seems to be well with it. Now error and sin both have this property, that the deeper they are the less their victim suspects their existence; they are masked evil. Pain is unmasked, unmistakable evil; every man knows that something is wrong when he is being hurt . . . . pain is not only immediately recognisable evil, but evil impossible to ignore. We can rest contentedly in our sins and in our stupidities; and anyone who has watched gluttons shovelling down the most exquisite foods as if they did not know what they were eating, will admit that we can ignore even pleasure. But pain insists upon being attended to. God whispers to us in our pleasures, speaks in our conscience, but shouts in our pains: it is His megaphone to rouse a deaf world.[6]

Even if we do not, God takes the development of our character seriously. He permits and uses pain and suffering in our lives because he knows that if he does not rouse us with such a warning we will live comfortably in our sin until we are in a hellish place where we cannot do otherwise.[7]

Hell.[8] Pleasure in God is our greatest good. There is nothing better for us. The pure, undimmed, and unbroken enjoyment of God is another way of describing heaven. The pain of separation and alienation from God is our greatest evil, whether we experience it as disquietude, despondence, depression, or despair, or it is the ultimate, unending sorrow of those who reject God, which is what we mean by hell.[9]

If pleasure is an invitation to something far greater, pain is a warning of something far worse. Temporal pleasures point to the goodness of the Creator and beckon us to draw near, where we will discover "fullness of joy" and "pleasures forevermore."[10] Temporal pain and suffering point to the brokenness of a world in rebellion against God, and warn us of the dire, eternal consequences of continuing in that state. God does not wish that for anyone, and will take extreme measures, if necessary, to keep them from it.[11]

GREATER GOODS

The glory of God. In the largest possible frame of reference, Christians say that everything in the universe is teleologically related to the glory of God.[12] His glory is displayed in his creative wisdom and power, from quarks to black holes, from protons and photons to galaxies beyond our count. It is disclosed in his goodness, in the creation of a world that is beneficial to us, that meets our needs and fulfills our desires. His glory is revealed in his justice when he punishes evil or comes to the aid of its victims.[13] It is shown in his mercy when he withholds punishment from those who deserve it, and in his grace when he is generous to the undeserving.

Even if we don't know how something might serve the glory of God, believers say that God's glory is the Greater Good in everything that happens, and say, further, that our joy (which is a greater good for us) is fullest when we embrace this. This is true even when we go through ordeals in life. It is a fruitful paradox, and joy is its fruit. Believers don't expect those who do not live out this paradox to understand or appreciate it, but we would not trade this greater good, this joy, for health, wealth, or the applause of many.

The good life. God's glory and our joy are linked because glory and joy are united in God and he offers himself to us. Karl Barth wrote:

> God's glory is the indwelling joy of His divine being which as such shines out from Him, which overflows in its richness, which in its super-abundance . . . communicates itself.

> God's glory is His overflowing self-communicating joy. By its very nature it is that which gives joy.

> But we cannot overlook the fact that God is glorious in such a way that He radiates joy.[14]

We are invited into a fellowship of this glory and this joy. This is the good life. This is the greater good that God is pursuing for us. He takes action to bring us into a relationship with him and to transform us so that we become the kind of people who seek his glory and joy, and who, in their seeking and finding, flourish in life. This is the morally sufficient reason behind God's permission of evil. It is the "complex good" that God seeks to bring from the "simple evil" of human rebellion and consequent suffering.[15] To the extent that we can fathom his purposes, this is what God is up to in the ordeals of life.

Soul-making. God's joy and his moral perfections are united in an eternal, unbreakable bond. He delights in his righteousness, rejoices in his justice, and takes pleasure in his steadfast love.[16] Our joy is linked to this as his image-bearers. As our character reflects his, God shares his joy with us (or, put another way, we enter into his joy).[17] In the first chapter of the human story this reflection and sharing were perfect, unbroken, and effortless. Not so in our chapter. We participate in God's joy only as he renews his moral likeness in us.[18] For that to happen, sin must be forgiven, a relationship must be restored, hearts must be transformed, and lives must be changed. This is what God offers and accomplishes in redemption.[19]

When God's purposes of redemption are fully realized there will be "new heavens and a new earth in which righteousness dwells."[20] Short of that, and in preparation for that world, joy demands a "soul-making" environment.[21] It requires a habitat in which there can be growth in virtue. It mandates a world in which there are moral heroes – men and women whose character has been forged in the fire of life's challenges – and others who seek to be like them. Short of joy's consummation in the world to come, a world in which joy is our greatest good will feature challenges to meet, obstacles to move, opportunities to seize, possibilities to pursue, risks to take, dangers to embrace, and fears to defeat. It will champion courage, compassion, sacrifice, generosity, resilience, and resolve. Jesus and his followers believed that they lived in such a world. If we are clear-sighted, it looks very much like ours.

The moral freedom that makes joy possible is most significant (that is, we are most virtuous in our exercise of God's gift of moral freedom) when the stakes are high and the risks are great.[22] The stakes are highest and the risks seem greatest when the signs of God's presence and the evidence of his handiwork curl into question marks.[23] Whether we like it or not, God draws near and sometimes he withdraws. He discloses and sometimes conceals. He shouts and sometimes whispers. Sometimes he points without a whisper. Sometimes he doesn't even point. Sometimes he waits for us to cry out to him.

> Yes, if you cry out for insight
>   and raise your voice for understanding;
> if you seek it like silver
>   and search for it as for hidden treasures;
> then you will understand the fear of the LORD
>   and find the knowledge of God. (Proverbs 2:3-5, RSV)

Joy comes when, in the freedom he has granted us, we say "Yes" to God, even when the stakes are high, the peril is great, and the path before us seems uncertain. This is never truer than when we face suffering and pain and encounter evil in the world:

> More than that, we rejoice in our sufferings, knowing that suffering produces endurance. (Romans 5:3, RSV)

You joyfully accepted the plundering of your property, since you knew that you yourselves had a better possession and an abiding one. (Hebrews 10:34, RSV)

Count it all joy, my brothers, when you meet trials of various kinds, for you know that the testing of your faith produces steadfastness. (James 1:2-3, RSV)

In the crucible of life's ordeals, hearts are formed and joy is refined. In a fallen world, joy requires this. Joy mandates a world in which character-quests are possible and we become the kind of people who embrace them. You might wish for a different world, or to be exempt from God's soul-shaping purposes for this one, but neither is an option he has given us.

AN ETERNAL GOOD

Living in light of eternity. Although many in our day seem to have forgotten, Christians through the ages have believed and taught that we begin to make sense of this life only as we see it in light of eternity. God's plans for us include this life, and stretch beyond it for ages without end. It would be a mistake to call that an *afterlife*. If anything, ours now is a *pre-life*. It is preparation for Real Life, which is yet to come. Jesus used the word *joy* to describe it: "Well done, good and faithful servant. . . . Enter into the joy of your master."[24] The apostle Paul used the word *glory*: "For this light momentary affliction is preparing for us an eternal weight of glory beyond all comparison."[25]

Imagine a great set of balanced scales. If we could put all the pain, suffering, and evil in the history of the world on one side, and the glory and joy of a single moment in heaven on the other, the scale would break under the weight of glory and joy, and the ground beneath would shudder and sink into oblivion. The glory and joy of heaven are incommensurable goods.[26] They are so great that nothing in our world can measure them. No model can compare them. No computer can calculate them. No lab can assess them. In our world we know their smallest part in traces of glory and moments of joy.

The best is yet to come! In the early 18th century, philosopher and mathematician, Gottfried Leibnitz, crafted a response to the problem of evil centered on the idea of the "best of all possible worlds." His argument was not that this is a perfect world (which is refuted by cursory observation), but that of all the worlds God could have created, this world, with its balance of good and evil, is the best of them.[27]

Apart from problems with the notion of the best of all possible worlds, the belief that our world has that status does not fit the eschatological focus in the teaching of Jesus and his early followers.[28] For them, the best is yet to come.

This eschatological orientation can be seen in the relationship between joy and hope in the Christian Scriptures. They are thread and strand in the weave of a Godward life.[29] The apostle Paul put it this way in a prayer: "May the God of *hope* fill you with all *joy* and peace in believing, so that by the power of the Holy Spirit you may abound in *hope*."[30] Joy is drawn to the future.[31] It longs to find its fulfillment in the ultimate realization of God's purposes, when his Kingdom comes and his will is done on earth as it is in heaven.[32] This is hope's joy. This is joy's hope.

Hope embraces the *already* and *not-yet* dimensions of joy because both are true to the nature of God's Kingdom, joy's native environment. Because it is true to the Kingdom, however, there is more to joy than present and future tenses. Joy in our present experience, even in our suffering and pain, is the joy of the future Kingdom penetrating the present in advance of its final consummation.[33] It "rends indeed the very web" of history and "lets a gleam come through."[34] It is a foretaste of the new heavens and the new earth. An installment. The first fruits of our future joy in God's undimmed presence. Joy is the closest thing to heaven that we can know in our present state, because it is a bit of heaven itself. It is a brand from heaven's fire. A spark from heaven's blazing glory. A breath of heaven's air. A fragrance from its orchards. A bar of its music. A beam of its light cast into the shadows of our world.

This is not the best of all possible worlds. It is related to the best world, which is yet to come, as a chrysalis is related to a butterfly. One is gloriously transformed into the other. This eschatological good, anticipated in experiences of joy, is the ultimate morally sufficient reason for God creating moral agents who can choose good and evil, and who have chosen evil and brought pain and suffering into our world.

POSTSCRIPT: FINDING JOY IN THE ORDEALS OF LIFE

In this final section we will leave philosophical debates behind and re-enter the world of personal experience. This is my response to what I referred to at the outset as the existential or emotional problem of evil.

We might wish that it were otherwise, but God doesn't offer answers to all of our questions. He offers himself to us in our questions. He doesn't offer life without suffering and pain. In a powerful paradox, he offers joy that comes in and through these things. It is an offer with conditions.[35] There is nothing artificial or arbitrary about this. C.S. Lewis wrote:

> Good things as well as bad, you know, are caught by a kind of infection. If you want to get warm you must stand near the fire: if you want to be wet you must get into the water. If you want joy, power, peace, eternal life, you must get close to, or even into, the thing that has them. They are not a sort of prize which God could,

if He chose, just hand out to anyone. They are a great fountain of energy and beauty spurting up at the very centre of reality. If you are close to it, the spray will wet you: if you are not, you will remain dry.[36]

Because joy is a connection with God, it is possible only as we get close to him. We position ourselves for joy, even in times of suffering and pain, when we draw near to God.

There are three kinds of nearness for us to consider. The first is the nearness of measurable space. If two things are close to each other in this way, the distance between them is small. The smaller the space, the nearer they are. Because God is *omnipresent*, he is always near in this way. The apostle Paul told his audience in Athens that God is never far from us, for "in him we live and move and have our being."[37] As you read these words, God is to your right and to your left. He is above you, below you, before you, and behind. God not only surrounds you at all times, he is nearer to you than the breath in your lungs, the blood in your veins, the thoughts of your mind, and the affections of your heart. In Augustine's words: God is "more intimately present to me than my innermost being."[38]

We may be unaware of his presence, but we can never be nearer to God in the events and situations of our lives than we already are, because he is everywhere present at the same time. There is no escaping God's presence,[39] but we can ignore it. We can be out of touch with it. We can miss it. The awareness of his presence begins in meditation, as we focus our thoughts and affections on this life-shaping truth.[40] There is comfort, strength, peace, and joy as we cultivate an awareness of God's presence with us. We can keep the Lord always before us. Always at our right hand.[41] Always in our "mind's eye."[42] Like a radio that has been tuned to receive unseen sound waves that surround us at all times (even if we are unaware of them), our hearts can be tuned to God's company and the music of his presence.

Spatial nearness is one thing; relational nearness is another. Two people sitting next to each other on a crowded city bus might be close in the first sense (measurable space) but far from each other in this second sense (relational proximity). They might not know each other at all. When we talk about "close friends," this is the nearness we have in mind. It isn't possible to be nearer or farther from God in the first sense, but it is possible to be near or far from God in this way:

> The Lord says: 'These people come near to me with their mouth and honor me with their lips, but their hearts are far from me. (Isaiah 29:13, NIV)

> The LORD is near to the brokenhearted. (Psalm 34:18)

> The haughty he knows from afar. (Psalm 138:6)

> Draw near to God, and he will draw near to you. (James 4:8)

This nearness to God is a nearness of hearts. It is a relational closeness that comes from common interests and concerns. It is an intimacy that comes from sharing life. This is what the Psalmist had in mind when he wrote, "For me it is good to be near God."[43]

Relational nearness to God is a cultivated way of living in the world. It is a congeniality of hearts. It is a nearness that is nurtured and grows when our hearts are aligned with God's, when he is often in our thoughts and treasured in our affections, when our wills beat in rhythm with his. Habituate your thoughts here. Make it a Godward focus in prayer, and then begin acting in appropriate, fitting ways. (The Bible calls this "walking in the truth."[44]) There is joy here, even in times of suffering and pain.

The third kind of nearness I would call the nearness of similitude or likeness. If a painter captures a landscape on a canvas, we say that the painting is "close" to the original. It is near to it in its likeness. We were created in the image of God. In our fallenness, sin has sullied and distorted that likeness. God's image is restored in us in redemption as the Spirit of God re-shapes our hearts so that we become more like Christ.[45] If we draw near to God in times of suffering and pain, he uses these things, as a Potter uses clay, water, and a turning wheel, to make us more like his Son. Little by little in a life-long process, his character is mirrored in ours. His way of living in the world becomes ours.

Jesus is the self-portrait of God in human form. He is the perfect image of God in humanity.[46] The more like him we become, the closer to God we will be, the greater our joy even as we go through ordeals of suffering and pain. "That my joy may be in you," Jesus said, "that your joy may be full."[47]

Questions for Thought and Discussion

1. Looking at the list of value judgments about greater evils and greater goods, do you agree with them? What difference does this make for the problem of evil?

2. What do you think of the author's understanding of heaven and hell? (See also endnote 6.) Do you agree? Disagree?

3. What do you think about the author's treatment of God's glory and our joy?

4. Do you agree or disagree with the author about this world as a "soul-making environment?" What difference does this make for the problem of evil?

5. What are the three types of nearness to God, and how are they relevant to joy?

CHAPTER 15

JOY AND THE KINGDOM OF GOD

THE WORLD'S TRAVAIL

At the end of the day evil is not an intellectual problem to be solved, but a destructive force that must be overcome.[1] God permits evil in his sovereign purposes for our world, but he regards it as a usurper that must be removed, and an enemy that must be banished from his realm. Much of this he intends to do through us.

Sadly, many who should believe this don't seem to. The very people you would expect to find venturing into the world to make it a better place are preoccupied with other things. Lesser things. It is not that they have forsaken the world in a religious sense; they have chosen to neglect the world, to become obsessed with personal interests and concerns, which they dress in religious garb. Hard words, but too often true.[2]

Joy is the highest and best pleasure we can know. My one fear in writing about this is that the cultural hermeneutic of the day will see joy as a subjective experience to be sought in a private inner sanctum isolated from and irrelevant to the world and its travail.[3]   That would be a mistake of enormous proportions!   Archbishop Temple said it well: "Christian joy and hope do not arise from an ignoring of the evil in the world, but from facing it at its worst."[4]

Joy cannot be divorced from the kind of people we are becoming in our pursuit of moral excellence. It cannot be separated from our call to live lovingly, justly, and responsibly in God's world. Those who think that they can flee the world and its problems to gain joy will be disappointed, because it cannot be found that way. Joy is not a grail whose quest takes us away from a world in need; it is more like a magnetic force that draws us into its plight.[5]

Joy does not look away from suffering in the world.[6] It faces it head-on, without flinching, and then looks through it. Suffering is not entirely opaque. There is much that we cannot see, but we can see enough for joy. Joy looks through the lens of suffering to see what God is seeking to do, and exults in this:

> More than that, we rejoice in our sufferings, knowing that suffering produces endurance. (Romans 5:3, RSV)

> You joyfully accepted the plundering of your property, since you knew that you yourselves had a better possession and an abiding one. (Hebrews 10:34, RSV)

> Count it all joy, my brothers, when you meet trials of various kinds, for you know that the testing of your faith produces steadfastness. (James 1:2-3, RSV)

Joy is ruthlessly realistic about the world we live in, but refuses to reach the same conclusions drawn by pessimists and fatalists. Because joy is illumined by a Light they do not have, it envisions possibilities for the world that they do not see and cannot entertain.

JESUS ON THE KINGDOM OF GOD

What is God doing to defeat evil in his world? We see a glimpse of this in what Jesus and his early followers said about the Kingdom of God.

When Jesus began his public ministry, he stirred the air with the dramatic announcement: "The time has come; the kingdom of God is upon you; repent and believe in the gospel."[7] A new era dawned with the coming of the Christ. A new epoch began. History skidded around this turning point and moved in a new direction.

Ancient prophecies sprang to life on the lips of Jesus:

> The Spirit of the Lord is upon me,
> because he has anointed me
> to preach good news to the poor.
> He has sent me to proclaim release to the captives
> and recovering of sight to the blind,
> to set at liberty those who are oppressed,
> to proclaim the acceptable year of the Lord. (Luke 4:18-21)[8]

In the words and deeds of Jesus the Supernatural and natural realms met. In that meeting lives were transformed, wounded hearts were mended, and broken bodies were healed. It was an incursion of the Kingdom of God. Yet to be acknowledged, the rightful King was staking his claim.

Jesus taught his followers to make this Kingdom prayer centermost in the way they lived in the world:

Our Father in heaven,
    hallowed be your name.
Your kingdom come,
    your will be done,
    on earth as it is in heaven.
Give us this day our daily bread,
    and forgive us our debts,
    as we also have forgiven our debtors.
And lead us not into temptation,
    but deliver us from evil.
For yours is the Kingdom, the power and glory, forever. Amen.
(Matthew 6:9-13)[9]

When Jesus preached it was to proclaim the Kingdom.[10] When he taught it was to expound the Kingdom.[11] When he spoke in parables it was to illustrate the Kingdom.[12] When he cast out demons it was warfare for the Kingdom.[13] When he healed it was to display the power of the Kingdom.[14] When he dispatched his disciples throughout the land, it was as emissaries of the Kingdom.[15] When he commissioned them before his departure, it was to take the Gospel of the Kingdom to the ends of the earth.[16] When he promised to build the Church, he gave it the authority of the Kingdom.[17] In the forty days between his resurrection and his ascension he spoke with his disciples about the Kingdom of God.[18]

What is the Kingdom of God? As Jesus and early Christians saw it, it is the dynamic reign of God breaking into history, bringing righteousness, peace, and joy – the boon of his empire.[19] Its fullness lies in the future.[20] One day "every knee will bow, and every tongue will confess that Jesus Christ is Lord, to the glory of God the Father."[21] When that happens, no one will pray for the Kingdom to come, for it will surround us on every side and govern all of life.

The Gospel of the Kingdom is a declaration that the Kingdom of God has entered the world in the life, death, and resurrection of Jesus Christ.[22] It has arrived in advance of its final realization, conquering evil, bringing forgiveness of sin and reconciliation with God, restoring relationships, healing brokenness and disease, and bestowing the blessings of God's reign.[23] It transforms people who will change the world.

ENTERING THE KINGDOM

The Kingdom of God isn't a place, but we must still enter it.[24] Jesus said so, and he knows better than anyone. The gateway to the Kingdom is repentance and faith. Again, Jesus said so, and he should know: "Now after John was arrested, Jesus came into Galilee, proclaiming the gospel of God, and saying, 'The time is fulfilled, and the kingdom of God is at hand; repent and believe in the gospel.'"[25]

To enter the Kingdom we must cross a threshold. The first step is repentance: embracing radically different ways of thinking about God and ourselves.[26] We have falsely imagined God. We have believed that he is indifferent to our sin, and that he will indulge us in our sinfulness. In truth, he is altogether righteous and burns with a pure and wholesome hatred of all that is not. Because we have misunderstood God, we have also nurtured false views of ourselves. The ease with which we accommodate our wrongdoing leads us to believe that our condition is natural, normal, and acceptable. Not so! In the highest and fullest sense of the word, God is holy; in the starkest contrast imaginable, we are not. We are crooked. Bent. Polluted. Stained. Guilty. Worthy of condemnation. Repentance lets truth about God and our condition pierce our hearts with sorrow – not feeling sorry for ourselves, but lamenting the sin that is a monumental affront to God.

Our false understanding of God not only underestimates his righteousness and its unrelenting demands, it understates his boundless love and desire to bless. In our distorted vision, we see him as grudging, stinting, loath to part with his hoard. Our false god is utterly unlike God as Jesus understood him. The true God is like the father whose prodigal son returns in repentance, who sees his son from a distance, is moved with compassion, runs to embrace and kiss his boy, and celebrates his return with a music, dancing, and a great feast.[27]

In repentance we turn from sinful thoughts, affections, words, and deeds that alienate us from God and create a world filled with idols – false gods, every one. In faith, our second step into the Kingdom, we turn to the living and true God.[28] The bad news (for us) is that God is implacably hostile to all that is antithetical to his character and incompatible with his purposes. The good news (for us) is that his hostility is "not to the sinner but to the sin."[29] He loves sinners. He forgives repentant sinners. He welcomes them as friends. He invites them into a fellowship of love. He relates to them in grace and mercy, and gifts them with righteousness, peace, and unspeakable joy. This is the good news of the Kingdom. This is the favor of the King. Faith is the heart that is open and the hand that receives all that God is prepared to give.

Repentance and faith are the first steps into the Kingdom and then a way of living in the Kingdom.[30] They orient us to God and his purposes. They are relational dispositions, tuning our hearts to God's. They are transformative practices, breaking the power of sin and creating an inner environment in which the fruit of God's Spirit can grow.[31] They keep us humble with the recognition of our own fallenness and need, grateful for the gracious riches of God's love in Christ, and joyful in an undeserved life under God's beneficent reign.

AGENTS OF THE KINGDOM

If we respond to the invitation to live in the Kingdom and to act on its behalf, what does that mean in practical terms? The apostle Paul gives us a clue: "The kingdom of God is not food and drink but righteousness and peace and joy in the Holy Spirit,"[32] We are called to pursue righteousness, peace, and joy in the Holy Spirit. This is not embracing an ideology, advancing the agenda of a political party, or protecting or expanding the interests of a nation. God is not a partisan.[33] His Kingdom rules over all. It is meant for all. Righteousness, peace, and joy in the Holy Spirit are supernatural forces that can work in and through us to transform the world and bring the will of God to the earth as it now governs in heaven.

Righteousness, peace, and joy describe the culture of God's Kingdom. They shape the foreign and domestic policies of the Kingdom. They represent the Kingdom-in-action, empowered by God's Spirit. They are not what we hope to find when we look within; they are what we should expect to find when we see people living together – in the power of the Spirit – as representatives of God's Kingdom in the world. They are spheres of service, as Paul says next: "For the one who serves Christ in this is pleasing to God and approved by men."[34] People of the Kingdom are called to be agents of righteousness, brokers of peace, and catalysts of joy in the world. If they do this well, Christ is served, God is pleased, and those who receive the benefit of their action will respond with approval.

Righteousness in this context is "righteous action"[35] or what biblical writers referred to as "doing righteousness."[36] It is action taken to promote and protect the well-being of others.[37] The righteousness of the Kingdom is what the Psalmist thought of when he said of God, "Righteousness and justice are the foundation of his throne."[38] God is committed to a world in which his creatures truly thrive. Ancient people of faith often praised God for his commitment to those who were least likely to flourish in a fallen, sinful world. We practice the righteousness of the Kingdom when our hearts align with God's, and, on his behalf and in partnership with him we seek the good of others – especially those who need our help if they are to prosper in life:[39]

He executes justice for the fatherless and the widow, and loves the sojourner, giving him food and clothing. (Deuteronomy 10:18)

The LORD works righteousness
and justice for all who are oppressed. (Psalm 103:6)

Happy is he whose help is the God of Jacob,
   whose hope is in the LORD his God,
  who made heaven and earth,
    the sea, and all that is in them;
  who keeps faith for ever;
     who executes justice for the oppressed;
  who gives food to the hungry.
The LORD sets the prisoners free;
  the LORD opens the eyes of the blind,
  the LORD lifts up those who are bowed down;
  the LORD loves the righteous.
The LORD watches over the sojourners,
  he upholds the widow and the fatherless;
  but the way of the wicked he brings to ruin.
The LORD will reign for ever,
  thy God, O Zion, to all generations.
Praise the LORD! (Psalm 146:5-10)[40]

Those who have been brought into a right relationship with God long to see others join them. They yearn to see others flourish in God's will.[41] They eagerly share with all whose hearts are open, but seek the oppressed, the hungry, the poor, the fettered, the crippled, the deaf, and the blind, because they know that God is committed to them and their plight. They long to see them discover their help in the God of Jacob and their hope in the LORD their God. They take great pleasure in joining God in what he is doing, becoming the voice through which he speaks and the hands with which he touches people in need. This is the righteousness of the Kingdom.[42] It must be important to followers of Jesus, because it was important to him.[43] He saw it as the heart of his mission, fulfilling Isaiah's prophetic words:

> The Spirit of the Lord is upon me,
> because he has anointed me to preach good news to the poor.
> He has sent me to proclaim release to the captives
> and recovering of sight to the blind,
> to set at liberty those who are oppressed,
> to proclaim the acceptable year of the Lord. (Luke 4:18-19, RSV)[44]

What about Kingdom peace? It is tempting to see this as an experience of inner tranquility, but that moves us further from Paul's thought in this context. There are times when the apostle does have personal peace in mind.[45] Those who know this experience treasure it above all earthly possessions. There are times when he is thinking about peace between people. Sometimes it is peace between fellow believers.[46] Sometimes it includes all who enter the circle of our lives: "If possible, so far as it depends on you, live peaceably with all."[47] When peace is put into the context of God's Kingdom, however, its boundaries are as broad as his reign. It is global in its design and intent. It is a harmony in the world that emerges from right relationships – with God, our neighbor, and the created order in which we have been placed. Because they have been introduced to this peace, people of the Kingdom are peacemakers. They seek to resolve conflict, to end strife, and to guide others into relational health. Before a world that is always watching, they model the possibilities of flourishing in life together.

Kingdom peace is the fulfillment of what the prophets called *shalom*: life at its best under God. Shalom describes health, well-being, fulfillment, harmony, and an environment of joy for all.[48] Cornelius Plantinga writes:

> The webbing together of God, humans, and all creation in justice, fulfillment, and delight is what the Hebrew prophets call *shalom*. We call it peace but it means far more than mere peace of mind or a cease-fire between enemies. In the Bible, shalom means *universal flourishing, wholeness and delight* – a rich state of affairs in which natural needs are satisfied and natural gifts fruitfully employed, a state of affairs that inspires joyful wonder as its Creator and Savior opens doors and welcomes the creatures in whom he delights. Shalom, in other words, is the way things ought to be.[49]

There is a reason why joy follows righteousness and peace in this Kingdom triumvirate. How could we rejoice in a world without them? Such joy would be "insulted and undone."[50] If we are living in right relationships with God and with others, peace is the harmony that results,[51] and joy is our pleasure in that concord.[52] This is healthy joy. This is the joy God seeks for us.[53] One day it will fill the earth.

When the Kingdom comes in its fullness, and the King takes his rightful place in the world, all of creation will respond in joy:

> Let the heavens be glad, and let the earth rejoice;
> let the sea roar, and all that fills it;
> let the field exult, and everything in it!

Then shall all the trees of the wood sing for joy
  before the LORD, for he comes . . . . (Psalm 96:11-12)

Let the sea roar, and all that fills it;
  the world and those who dwell in it!
Let the floods clap their hands;
  let the hills sing for joy together
  before the LORD, for he comes . . . . (Psalm 98:7-8)

For you shall go out in joy,
  and be led forth in peace;
the mountains and the hills before you
  shall break forth into singing,
  and all the trees of the field shall clap their hands . . . . (Isaiah 55:12)

Should we truly imagine the whole realm of nature rejoicing in its Creator? Is this how we are to take these passages? Those of us who would feel at home in Lewis' Narnia or Tolkien's Middle Earth would love to live in such a world. At the very least these prophetic cameos tell us our joy and the joy of creation are linked, that an environment of joy is the ideal for all of creation, and that one day this will be realized.[54] (This should be the ultimate aim of our stewardship of the earth.)   When the ancient harmony of Eden is restored, and raised to even greater heights in God's work of redemption, all creatures – in ways suited to their creaturehood – will reflect the glory of God, and, in that mirrored glory, will experience their share in the joy that binds all creation together with its Creator, Redeemer, and King.[55] At its fullest, our joy will be a fellowship in this cosmic joy.

Emil Brunner wrote, "A Christian is a person who not only hopes for the Kingdom of God, but one who, because he hopes for it, also does something in this world already, which he who has not this hope does not do."[56] Knowing what awaits them in the fullness of God's reign, citizens of the Kingdom give themselves to a quest for global righteousness, peace, and joy even now – with all of its implications for human relationships, their environment, and the creatures with which they share God's world.

God is not limited to our participation in his plans. He does far more apart from us than we will ever know. Nevertheless, the Kingdom is his primary answer to the problem of evil. It awaits your response and mine. Not somewhere else in a world of daydreams; here, where our actions make a difference. Not later, which becomes later, and then later; now, in this moment, and then in the next. Not through grit and determination, but in full reliance on the action of the Holy Spirit in and through us. This is the human side of how God's Kingdom will come. This is how righteousness, peace, and joy will transform our world in its great need.

QUESTIONS FOR THOUGHT AND DISCUSSION

1. Discuss this quote: "Joy is ruthlessly realistic about the world we live in, but refuses to reach the same conclusions drawn by pessimists and fatalists. Because joy is illumined by a Light they do not have, it envisions possibilities for the world that they do not see and cannot entertain." How does this compare with notions of joy that you may have had?

2. Discuss the section on Jesus and the Kingdom. How does this challenge and change your understanding of Jesus, his life, and his message?

3. Discuss this quote: "What is the Kingdom of God? As Jesus and early Christians saw it, it is the dynamic reign of God breaking into history, bringing righteousness, peace, and joy – the boon of his empire." How does this challenge or change your understanding of the Kingdom of God?

4. Discuss this quote: "The Kingdom of God is not a place, but we must still enter it. Jesus said so, and he knows better than anyone. The gateway to the Kingdom is repentance and faith." Does this get much attention in Christian circles that you know of?

5. Discuss the author's understanding of Kingdom righteousness, peace, and joy. What difference would it make if contemporary Christians understood and pursued this?

CONCLUSION

Pascal said that there are two extremes in the quest for truth: to exclude reason and to admit reason alone.[1]   If you believe that rational arguments are irrelevant or irreverent, or you demand strict proofs with logical certainty, you will be disappointed as you come to the end of this book. I have chosen a middle path: to admit reason, but not reason alone. I have attempted to give you an argument from the heart that will satisfy your mind.

Put another way, my argument seeks to engage the mind, but begins and ends with the heart. Not only does reason not have the first word, it does not have the last. Reason is a useful guide, and one whose tracking skills only a fool would neglect, but it is an unworthy magistrate. It is unqualified to be the final arbiter of truth. It swaggers in those robes. It is a usurper and a pretender in that role. Whatever the boasts and pretensions of reason, all of the important decisions in life, in the end, are made by the heart. After reason sorts things out it is the heart and its disposition and desires that will settle the matter. I urge you to weigh the claims and counter-claims in this book with great rigor. When you have done that, whatever your response, your heart will have the final say.

Check its longings. The aspirations that stir in deep and quiet places. The hunger that remains when you have had your fill of the world. The thirst that nothing seems to slake. The nightingale song that sounds in the silent hours of the darkest night. If you listen with your heart, you will hear the beckoning call of joy. If you hear it, you will never be more rational than when you heed its call and follow it Home.

ABOUT THE AUTHOR

In 1983 Rick and Sue Howe moved to Boulder, Colorado, where they raised three children – Amberle, Lorien, and Jamison – and have devoted more than thirty years to campus ministry at the University of Colorado. In addition to writing and speaking, Rick now leads University Ministries, whose mission is to "inspire and nurture a thoughtful pursuit of Christ, one student, one professor, one university at a time." To learn more about Rick, visit his website at www.rickhowe.org. You can also follow him on Facebook at Rick Howe on Joy, or on Twitter @rickhoweonjoy. To learn more about University Ministries, see www.university-ministries.org.

ENDNOTES

CHAPTER 1: GETTING OUR BEARINGS

[1] For evangelical Christian perspectives on Postmodernism, see the following:

> David S. Dockery, ed., *The Challenge of Postmodernism: An Evangelical Engagement* (Grand Rapids, MI: Baker Academic, 2001).

> Millard Erickson, *Truth or Consequences: The Promise & Perils of Postmodernism* (Downers Gove, IL: InterVarsity Press, 2001).

> Stanley J. Grenz, A Primer on Postmodernism (Grand Rapids, MI: Wm. B. Eerdmans Publishing Co., 1996).

> Douglas Groothuis, *Truth Decay: Defending Christianity Against the Challenges of Postmodernism* (Downers Grove, IL: InterVarsity Press, 2000).

> Timothy R. Phillips, Dennis L. Okholm, eds., Christian Apologetics in the Postmodern World (Downers Gove, IL: InterVarsity Press, 1995).

> James K.A. Smith *Who's Afraid of Postmodernism?: Taking Derrida, Lyotard, and Foucault to Church* (Grand Rapids, MI: Baker Publishing Group, 2006).

> R. Scott Smith, *Truth and the New Kind of Christian: The Emerging Effects of Postmodernism in the Church* (Wheaton, IL: Crossway, 2005).

[2] I am using the term "Rationalism" not to refer to a theory of knowledge that contrastswith empiricism, another theory of knowledge, but more broadly to the view known as "classic foundationalism," the idea that knowledge can and must be built upon a strong, sure foundation of beliefs that are self-evident, incorrigible, or evident to our senses. In one form or another, this was the dominant view in the Enlightenment period.

[3] For the case that classic foundationalism is self-defeating, see, e.g., Alvin Plantinga, *Warranted Christian Belief* (New York, Oxford: Oxford University Press, 2000), pp. 94-97, and Alvin Plantinga, "Reason and Belief in God" in *Faith and Rationality*, eds., Alvin Plantinga and Nicholas Wolterstorff (Notre Dame, Indiana: University of Notre Dame Press, 1983), pp. 59-61.

[4] C.S. Lewis, *The World's Last Night and Other Essays* (New York, NY: Mariner Books, 2002) p. 94.

[5] This position is known as "realism," the belief that an objective reality exists independently of us. Postmodernist thought is "anti-realist," that is, it holds either that the world does not exist apart from our engagement with it, or that we have no verifiable connection with it.

[6] There are factors other than reason that shape our beliefs, such as our historic, geographical, cultural, social, economic, and emotional situations, and the language we use to conceptualize our beliefs.

[7] Broadly speaking, I agree with theologians who advocate *critical realism*, described here by New Testament scholar, N.T. Wright:

> I propose a form of *critical realism*. This is a way of describing the process of 'knowing' that acknowledges the *reality of the thing known, as something other than*

the knower (hence 'realism'), while fully acknowledging that the only access we have to this reality lies along the spiralling path of *appropriate dialogue or conversation between the knower and the thing known* (hence 'critical'). This path leads to critical reflection on the products of our enquiry into 'reality', so that our assertions about 'reality' acknowledge their own provisionality. Knowledge, in other words, although in principle concerning realities independent of the knower, is never itself independent of the knower.

N.T. Wright, *The New Testament and the People of God* (Minneapolis, MN: Fortress Press, 1992), p. 35.

Alister McGrath describes his approach to epistemology this way:

Epistemologically, it is held that this reality or realities can be known, however approximately, and that statements which are made concerning it cannot be regarded totally or simply as subjective assertions concerning personal attitudes or feelings. It is possible to gain at least some degree of epistemic access to a reality which exists 'objectively', while at the same time conceding that the manner in which this is apprehended or conceptualized may, to some extent, be conditioned by cultural, social and personal factors.

Alister McGrath, *A Scientific Theology*, Volume 1 (London: T&T Clark, Grand Rapids, MI, Wm. B. Eerdmans, 2001), p. 75.

See also Millard Erickson, *Truth or Consequences: The Promise & Perils of Postmodernism* (Downers Gove, IL: InterVarsity Press, 2001), Chapter 13: "Assessing the Truth."

For a seminal work, see Thomas F. Torrance, *Theological Science*, first published December 31st 1969 by Oxford University Press. See also the paperback version published November 14, 2000 by Bloomsbury T&T Clark.

For a recent survey and analysis, see Andrew Wright, *Christianity and Critical Realism: Ambiguity, truth and theological literacy* (London and New York: Routledge, Taylor & Francis Group, 2013).

[8] We have all learned to live with epistemic limitations without despairing that our limitations bar the gates of knowledge to us. We acknowledge that we don't know the future, that we don't remember all of our past, and that there are many things in our world that we don't know at all.

If we refuse to limit knowledge to what is based upon sense experience or self-evident truths, we will learn, as Shakespeare put it in *Hamlet*: "There are more things in Heaven and Earth, Horatio, than are dreamt of in your philosophy."

[9] This fits well with my beliefs as a Christian. I see myself living in God's world. ("The earth is the LORD's, and the fullness thereof." Psalm 24:1) It is his world, known fully to him apart from my brief existence in it and beliefs about it. (However you read Genesis, the world existed before we appeared in it and had our first thoughts about it.) Though potentially significant, my knowledge of his world is limited and fallible. (As the apostle Paul put it, "For we know in part." 1 Corinthians 13:9) Because of this, I should not accept anything naively or uncritically. ("Test all things; hold fast what is good." 1Thessalonians 5:21, RSV). And I should seek truth in a truth-seeking community (the biblical tradition of "two or three witnesses" to establish a truth-claim. See, for example, Deuteronomy 19:15; Matthew 18:16; 2 Corinthians 13:1; 1 Timothy 5:19).

10   Found at http://bertrandrussell.org/archives/BRSpapers/2012/agnostic.php.

11   Quoted in The New Internationalist Magazine. Found at:
https://newint.org/columns/speechmarks/2008/11/01/bertrand-russell/

12   This is known as a *moral argument for the existence of God*. For more on this, see C. Stephen Evans, "Moral Arguments for the Existence of God," in the Stanford Encyclopedia of Philosophy, found at http://plato.stanford.edu/entries/moral-arguments-god/.

It is noteworthy that Russell's daughter, Katharine Tait, raised an atheist, became a Christian as an adult. See Katharine Tait, *My Father: Bertrand Russell* (U.S.A.: Harcourt Brace Jovanovich, 1975).

13   C.S. Lewis, *The Last Battle*, (New York, NY: Macmillan Books, eleventh printing, 1974), p. 147.

14   Ibid., p. 148.

15   This characterizes much of what is known today as *The New Atheism*, with its strident, adversarial spirit and hostility toward anything that has to do with God and religion.

16   See René Descartes, *Meditations and Selections from the Principles of Philosophy*, trans. John Veitch (La Salle, IL: The Open Court Publishing Company, 1966).

17   From W.K. Clifford, *The Ethics of Belief*, found at http://people.brandeis.edu/~teuber/Clifford_ethics.pdf.

18   Rational people believe many things that don't meet the standards of Descartes or Clifford. You probably believe that the world did not come into existence five minutes ago, replete with appearances of age and people with fictitious memories of a world that did not exist six minutes ago. You likely believe that other minds exist, that your senses are reliable, and that your memories connect with events that have happened in the past. Rational people (including Descartes and Clifford) believe these things and much more.

Alvin Plantinga quotes Cardinal Newman:

> Nor is the assent which we give to facts limited to the range of self-consciousness. We are sure beyond all hazard of a mistake, that our own self is not the only being existing; that there is an external world; that it is a system with parts and a whole, a universe carried on by laws; and that the future is affected by the past. We accept and hold with an unqualified assent, that the earth, considered as a phenomenon, is a globe; that all its regions see the sun by turns; that there are vast tracts on it of land and water; that there are really existing cities on definite sites, which go by the names of London, Paris, Florence and Madrid.

He then goes on to say:

> But how much of this can be seen to be probable with respect to what is certain for us? How much meets the classical conditions for being properly basic? Not much, if any. I believe that I had cornflakes for breakfast, that my wife was amused at some little stupidity of mine, that there really are such 'external objects' as trees and squirrels, and that the world was not created ten minutes ago with all its dusty books, apparent memories, crumbling mountains, and deeply carved canyons.

Alvin Plantinga, *Warranted Christian Belief* (New York, Oxford: Oxford University Press, 2000) pp. 97-98.

19   Some of these are moral beliefs. I am a moral realist; that is, I hold the view that there are objective moral facts and properties, and that our beliefs about them can be true or false. Like other beliefs about the world, however, moral beliefs are corrigible and provisional. Some may be highly plausible and uncontroversial ("It is always wrong to torture babies."), but all carry some degree of uncertainty that we must embrace as moral agents. (That does not make moral standards relative. It is a commentary on our epistemic limitations, and not on the binding status of moral principles themselves. As a Christian I affirm that God has revealed essential moral standards that are true to his character and purposes, and true to the world and his designs for it. They form the basis of many of my moral beliefs, but are distinct from them.)

20   Sheldon Vanauken, *A Severe Mercy* (San Francisco: Harper and Row Publishers, 1977).

21   Ibid., p. 100.

22   The essence of faith, according to Paul Tillich. See Paul Tillich, *Dynamics of Faith* (New York, NY: Harper Colophon Books, 1957).

23   The concept of a leap of faith is most often associated with Søren Kierkegaard. See his *Fear and Trembling* (New York: Penguin, 1986). I am not suggesting that belief in God is a leap into the unknown with no supporting evidence. That isn't a fitting description of robust faith. Nevertheless, there are leaps that no one can avoid.

24   Blaise Pascal, *Pascal's Pensées*, trans. W.F. Trotter (New York: E.P. Dutton & Co., Inc., 1958), #253.

25   Ibid. #277

26   James 2:19

27   This is true of any field of inquiry, but especially true in spiritual matters.

28   Pascal, *Pensées*, #430. Also: "God has set up . . .visible signs to make Himself known to those who should seek Him sincerely, and that He has nevertheless so disguised them that He will only be perceived by those who seek Him with all their heart." Ibid. #194.

CHAPTER 2: ON SECOND THOUGHT

1   The eighteenth century German philosopher, Immanuel Kant, is someone who thought this way. Justin Oakley comments:

> It is not surprising that Kant made such claims, since his view seems to be based on a simple sensation model of emotions as non-cognitive phenomena over which we have little if any control. Kant regarded emotions (other than respect for the moral law) as belonging to a causally determined empirical world of sense, and, as such, amenable to natural scientific description and explanation.

Justin Oakley, *Morality and the Emotions* (London and New York: Routledge, 1992), p. 94.

2   I am not denying that physical factors are involved in our emotions. They can be positive or negative. In some situations the physical dimension of our emotions (chemical, hormonal) takes a dominant position and gives rise to unhealthy emotional states. When that happens it is unlikely that we will be able to change beliefs and desires without also changing physical states that are part of our emotional life.

3   Oakley, *Morality and the Emotions*, pp. 6ff.

4   Love begins with the affirmation, "It is *good* that you exist; how wonderful that you are!" Josef Pieper, *About Love* (Chicago: Franciscan Herald Press, 1974), p. 27.

5   Fear and anger can be reflective and deliberative, however. The more I think about a perceived wrong, the angrier I can get. The more I think about a looming crisis, the more fearful I may become. But this simply underscores my point, that our emotions – whether they emerge quickly, or "simmer" over a period of time – are part of our thought life.

This is the foundational premise of cognitive therapy. Daniel Goleman makes a distinction between a "first impulse" in an emotional situation, and a slower emotional reaction in which "there is a more extended appraisal; our thoughts – cognition – play the key role in determining what emotions will be roused." Daniel Goleman, *Emotional Intelligence* (New York: Bantam Books, 1995), p. 293. See also pp. 13ff. Not in the same way, perhaps, but cognition plays a key role even in our "first impulses."

6   William Alston writes:

> Thus we are not afraid of x unless we take x to be dangerous; we are not angry at x unless we take x to be acting contrary to something we want; we do not have remorse over having done x unless we regard it as unfortunate that we did x; we are not grief-stricken over x unless we see x as the loss of something we wanted very much; we do not have pity for x unless we take x to be in an undesirable state; and so on.

William P. Alston, "Emotion and Feeling," in *The Encyclopedia of Philosophy*, ed., Paul Edwards (New York: Macmillan Publishing Co., 1967), Vol. II, pp. 479ff.

7   Louis Pojman has written, "All experiencing takes place within the framework of a world view. . . . What we see depends to some degree on our background beliefs and our expectations. The farmer, the real estate agent, and the artist looking at the "same" field do not see the *same* field." See his article, "A Critique of Gutting's Argument from Religious Experience" in Louis P. Pojman, ed., *Philosophy of Religion: An Anthology* (Belmont, CA: Wadsworth Publishing Co., 1987), pp. 139-140.

8   Robert C. Roberts, *Spirituality and Human Emotion*, (Grand Rapids: Williams B. Eerdmans Publishing Co., 1982), p. 26. According to Roberts, "The Christian emotions . . . (e.g., love, joy, peace) are ways of 'seeing' which are determined by the peculiar Christian concepts and the scheme of beliefs which give rise to those concepts." Ibid., p. 10. And, "They are "concerned ways of viewing things through the 'lenses' of Christian teaching." Ibid., p. 25.

9   For Descartes, that we are thinking beings is the one thing we cannot doubt: I think, therefore I am! See René Descartes, *Meditations and Selections from the Principles of Philosophy*, trans. John Veitch (La Salle, IL: The Open Court Publishing Company, 1966).

10   See Immanuel Kant, *Religion within the Limits of Reason Alone* (New York: Harper & Brothers, 1960).

11 When we talk about intellectual pleasures, we are really talking about emotional pleasures that accompany intellectual pursuits. The pleasures that come with learning, discovery, mastering a body of information, or solving a problem, are powerful forces that motivate and shape our intellectual life.

12 You might wonder why I am talking about beliefs when the subject is rethinking reason. This gives us an opportunity for clarification. In a philosophical sense, beliefs are about propositions. If I believe that it is snowing outside, I believe that the proposition, "It is snowing outside" is true. Philosophers say that knowledge is justified, true belief. In other words, I can be said to have knowledge if I believe a proposition to be true, it is true, and I have justification for believing it to be true. For instance, I can be said to know that it is snowing if 1) I believe that the proposition "It is snowing" is true; 2) The proposition is true: It is snowing; and 3) I see clouds overhead, neighborhood children building snowmen, sidewalks being shoveled, and when I step outside I am cold and wet from frozen moisture falling from the sky. Even though the language of belief is used, it is the domain of reason as we normally think of it.

13 Bertrand Russell, mentioned in the last chapter, captured the implications of a godless universe:

> That man is the product of causes which had no prevision of the end they were achieving; that his origin, his growth, his hopes and fears, his loves and his beliefs, are but the outcome of accidental collocations of atoms; that no fire, no heroism, no intensity of thought and feeling, can preserve an individual life beyond the grave; that all the labors of the ages, all the devotion, all the inspiration, all the noonday brightness of human genius, are destined to extinction in the vast death of the solar system, and that the whole temple of man's achievement must inevitably be buried beneath the debris of a universe in ruins — all these things, if not quite beyond dispute, are yet so nearly certain that no philosophy which rejects them can hope to stand. Only within the scaffolding of these truths, only on the firm foundation of unyielding despair, can the soul's salvation henceforth be safely built.

Bertrand Russell, "A Free Man's Worship" in Bertrand Russell, *Why I Am Not a Christian and Other Essays on Religion and Related Subjects* (New York: Simon and Schuster, 1957), p. 107.

14 A noetic structure is the "sum total of everything that (a) person believes." Ronald H. Nash, *Faith and Reason: Searching for a Rational Faith* (Grand Rapids: Zondervan Publishing House, 1988), p. 21. See also Alvin Plantinga, "Reason and Belief in God" in *Faith and Rationality*, eds., Alvin Plantiga and Nicholas Wolterstorff (Notre Dame, Indiana: University of Notre Dame Press, 1983), pp. 48-63.

15 See Nicholas Wolterstorff, *Reason within the Bounds of Religion* (Grand Rapids: Eerdmans Publishing Co., 1976), pp. 63-66.

16 Of course, the emotional factors in judging sufficient evidence can be positive. I may be overly generous in giving the benefit of the doubt to a friend because of emotions I attach to that relationship. Religious devotees are notorious for claiming sufficient evidence for arguments that support their beliefs because of the positive emotions they associate with their religious community.

17 This is not specific to gender. It is characteristically true of all human beings.

18 Literally, *to the man.* Here criticism is directed to personal factors rather than to the merits of evidence and arguments.

[19] Literally, *of* or *from the man.*

[20] For instance, it is possible to make a distinction between certainty and certitude. Certainty, philosophers say, is about the warrant for believing something whether you believe it or not; certitude is about the emotions you have if you do believe it. Certainty has to do with the evidential or logical strength of a proposition; certitude is the emotional state of being convinced or persuaded. Certainty involves freedom from error; certitude involves freedom from doubt. Because we can make a distinction between certainty and certitude does not mean that they exist apart from each other in our actual beliefs. In fact, I would say that they are intimate associates.

We are often quick to see emotional factors involved in the beliefs of others, and slow to see the same things at play in our own. This is exemplified by Bertrand Russell, mentioned in the last chapter. Russell was quick to charge that fear is the basis of religion:

> Religion is based, I think, primarily and mainly upon fear. It is partly the terror of the unknown and partly, as I have said, the wish to feel that you have a kind of elder brother who will stand by you in all your troubles and disputes. Fear is the basis of the whole thing – fear of the mysterious, fear of defeat, fear of death.

Russell, *Why I Am Not a Christian*, p. 20. If you read Russell on religion, his disdain for Christianity opens a Pandora's box of emotional issues in play. Freud asked the question, "If there is no God, why is there religion?" It can just as easily be asked, "If God exists, why are there atheists?" Dr. Paul C. Vitz, Emeritus Professor of Psychology at New York University, created a four-part video series entitled "The Psychology of Atheism." See his article, "The Psychology of Atheism," found at: http://www.leaderu.com/truth/1truth12.html. See also the audio series by R.C. Sproul, "The Psychology of Atheism," found at: http://www.ligonier.org/store/the-psychology-of-atheism-cd/.

[21] Jonathan Edwards, "On Religious Affections" in *The Works of Jonathan Edwards,* Perry Miller, Gen. ed., (New Haven: Yale University Press, 1959), Vol. 2, p. 272.

Although nuanced differently, Pascal made a similar distinction between reason and the heart, or the intellect and intuition.

[22] The heart, *lev*, "functions in all dimensions of human existence and is used as a term for all the aspects of the person: vital, affective, noetic, and voluntative." See *Theological Dictionary of the Old Testament*, ed., G. Johannes Botterweck, Helmer Ringgren, and Heiz-Josef Fabry (Grand Rapids, MI: William B. Eerdmans Publishing Company, 1995), Volume 7, p. 412. *Lev* is "the innermost part of man." It is the "seat of rational functions" as well as planning and volition, religious and moral conduct. See *Theological Dictionary of the New Testament,* ed., Gerhard Kittle, trans., and ed., Geoffrey Bromiley, (Grand Rapids, MI: Wm. B. Eerdmans Publishing Company, 1965) Volume 3, pp. 606-607. *Lev* is the "seat of man's spiritual and intellectual life, the inner nature of man." It is the "seat of emotions," the "seat of understanding and of knowledge." See *The New International Dictionary of New Testament Theology*, ed., Colin Brown (Grand Rapids, MI: Zondervan Publishing House, 1971), Volume 2, page 181.

[23] In an ideal state (pre-fallen or fully redeemed) the intellectual, affective, and volitional dimensions of our hearts would always act in harmony. In our current state they are often at odds with each other. Their voices speak over each other. Wisdom teaches us how to listen to each voice, and virtue inclines us to act appropriately.

[24] Proverbs 4:23

CHAPTER 3: A THEOLOGICAL PRIMER ON JOY, PART 1

1   Most of the content of this chapter and the next is taken from the first three chapters of Rick Howe, *Path of Life: Finding the Joy You've Always Longed For* (Boulder, CO: University Ministries Press, 2017) and from "Enjoying God" in Rick Howe, *River of Delights: Quenching Your Thirst for Joy, Volume 1* (Boulder, CO: University Ministries Press, 2017).

2   NRSV

3   Psalm 4:7. See also Zechariah 10:7.

4   Pascal was right when he said that Christians "give up pleasures only for greater pleasures"! Quoted by Donald Bloesch, *Freedom for Obedience* (San Francisco: Harper & Row, 1987), p. 37.

5   See Psalm 63:5.

6   See Psalm 119:14 and Isaiah 9:3.

7   See Isaiah 61:10; 62:5.

8   See Matthew 13:44.

9   See Matthew 22:1-10 and Luke 14:15-24.

10 For the series of parables, see Luke 15.

11 For an excellent treatment of the New Testament vocabulary of joy, see William Morrice, *Joy in the New Testament* (Grand Rapids, Michigan: William B. Eerdmans Publishing Co., 1984), especially Part One.

12 The writers of the New Testament cautiously avoided any positive use of the word *hedone,* the classic term for sensual pleasure, no doubt because of its keystone position in hedonism – a pagan philosophy which they rightly considered a serious rival to the true Gospel. The noun *hedone* does occur five times in the New Testament, but always negatively, of passions and pleasures pursued in defiance of God, e.g., Luke 8:14; Titus 3:3; James 4:1, 3 and 2 Peter 2:13.

Even with that note of caution, however, some writers used its adverbial forms, *hedeos* and *hedista,* in a positive sense to describe joy. The former is used of the gladness with which a great throng heard Jesus (Mark 12:37), and the latter is used of Paul's pleasure in experiencing the power of Christ in the midst of difficulties (2 Corinthians 12:9), and of his joy in spending himself on behalf of those whom he had led to Christ (2 Corinthians 12:15). There is something almost sensual about this Christ-centered joy! Something tangible. Concrete.

There were other terms that were more congenial to the early Christian description of joy, but they focus no less on joy's pleasure. The words used most frequently in the New Testament are *chara* and *chairo,* a noun and verb related to a Sanskrit word meaning "to take pleasure in." *The New International Dictionary of New Testament Theology,* Gen. ed., Colin Brown (Grand Rapids: Zondervan, 1976) Vol. II, p. 352. *Chara* expresses joy, delight, or pleasure (Liddell and Scott, *Greek-English Lexicon,* Abridged Edition: [Oxford: Oxford University Press, Impression, 1980], p. 777), and *chairo* the action of rejoicing, being glad, delighted, or pleased (Ibid., p. 774.). These were not "sacred "words. Their native home was not the religious world but the world of common pleasures. One scholar calls them, in fact, "intrinsically secular terms" (Morrice, *Joy in the New Testament*, p. 69).

Two other words in the early church's vocabulary of joy were *agalliaomai* and its cognate noun *agalliasis*. The verb appears 11 times in the New Testament (e.g., Matthew 5:12; Luke 1:47; Acts 2:26; 16:34), and the noun five times (e.g., Hebrews 1:9; 1 Peter 1:6, 8; and Jude 24). They were apparently coined by the translators of the Septuagint, and were then used by Jewish and Christian writers who were dependent upon that translation for their reading of Scripture. They were derived from the Greek *agallo* and *agallomai*, which were used of the rapture and ecstasy of the devotees of Dionysus, the Greek god of wine (Morrice, *Joy in the New Testament*, p. 19). Although they felt compelled to alter these words slightly in order to remove them from a context of debauchery and the worship of a false god, the writers of the Greek Bible clearly felt that these words captured an important dimension of joy in God.

Finally, there are the terms *euphraino* and *euphrosyne*. In classical Greek these were words used of the pleasures of food and drink particularly in the context of a banquet or festivity. They are used that way even in the New Testament: negatively, as in the case of the rich fool in Luke 12:19, and the rich man in Luke 16:19, and positively, as in the case of the banquet held in honor of the prodigal son upon his return (Luke 15:23, 32), and of the gift of gladness bestowed by God even upon the pagan world (Acts 14:17). They are also used of joy in God! Peter used the noun in his citation of Psalm 16:11 in Acts 2:28 – "You have made known to me the ways of life; you will make me full of gladness with your presence." The apostle Paul used the verb of Gentiles who have been included in the promises of salvation (Romans 15:10), and of the cheer experienced in fellowship with other believers (2 Corinthians 2:2). The verbs appear again in Revelation 12:12 and 18:20, referring to the joy of those in heaven.

13   See, for example, Psalm 5:11 and Psalm 31:7.

14   See Song of Solomon. 1:4.

15   See Proverbs 5:18-19.

16   See Ecclesiastes 11:9.

17   See Ecclesiastes 3:22.

18   See Ecclesiastes 5:19.

19   See Deuteronomy 12:7.

20   See Deuteronomy 26:11.

       A cognate noun, *simchah*, illustrates the same truth. It is used of the believer's joy in God (e.g., Psalm 16:11), but also of exultation in military victory (1 Samuel 18:6; 2 Chronicles 20:27), the festive gaiety of a coronation (1 Kings 1:40), delight in sensual pleasure and wealth (Ecclesiastes 2:10), and in the pleasures of food and drink (1 Chronicles. 12:38-40; Ecclesiastes 9:7).

21   See 1 Timothy 4:3-5.

22   See also: Deuteronomy 16:13-14,RSV; 1 Chronicles 12:38-40, RSV; 1 Chronicles 29:20-22, RSV; Ecclesiastes 9:7, RSV.

23   Arthur Holmes wrote, "The Old Testament writers rejoice in physical beauty and are awed by its grandeur. They delight in food, drink, sight, sound, sexuality." Arthur F. Holmes, *Contours of a World View* (Grand Rapids, MI: William B. Eerdmans Publishing Co., 1983), p. 111.

24   Thomas á Kempis, *The Imitation of Christ* (New York: Grosset & Dunlap, n.d.), p 104.

25   C.S. Lewis, *The Four Loves* (New York: Harcourt, Brace, Jovanovich, 1960).

26   So Aquinas taught: "If . . . spiritual pleasures be compared with sensible bodily pleasures, then, in themselves and absolutely speaking, spiritual pleasures are greater." *Summa Theologica,* I, II, Q. 31, A. 5. See also Q. 34, A. 3, where Aquinas responds to the question of whether any pleasure can be the greatest good:

> Happiness is the greatest good: since it is the end of man's life. But Happiness is not without pleasure: for it is written (and here he quotes Psalm 16:11, which speaks of the believer's joy in God): Thou shalt fill me with joy with Thy countenance; at Thy right hand are delights (i.e., pleasures) even to the end . . . Accordingly, man's last end may be said to be either God Who is the Supreme Good simply; or the enjoyment of God, which implies a certain pleasure in the last end. And in this sense a certain pleasure of man may be said to be the greatest among human goods.

27   "Lectures on Galatians," *Luther's Work,* Jaroslav Pelikan, ed., (Saint Louis: Concordia Publishing House, 1963), Vol. 26, p. 230.

Aquinas had something similar to say (Aquinas, *Summa*, I, II, Q. 5, A. 2):

> But as to the attainment or enjoyment of this Good, one man can be happier than another; because the more a man enjoys this Good the happier he is. Now, that one man enjoys God more than another, happens through his being better disposed or ordered to the enjoyment of Him. And in this sense one man can be happier than another.

28   See Philippians 4:10.

29   See Psalm 43:4.

30   See Matthew 2:10, KJV.

31   See Psalm 16:11 and John 15:11.

32   See 2 Corinthians 7:4.

33   See Psalm 137:6, NIV.

34   See 1 Peter 1:8.

35   See Psalm 16:11.

36   Aristotle, *The Nicomachean Ethics,* trans. J.A.K. Thompson (Penguin Books, 1976), pp. 66-67.

37   St. Augustine, "The Trinity," in *Augustine: Later Works*, p. 95.

38 According to Aristotle, "The good for man is *an activity of the soul* in accordance with virtue." (Emphasis added.) Aristotle, *Nicomachean Ethics*, p. 76.

According to one ancient commentator on Aristotle," Happiness is activity (*energeia*) in accordance with virtue . . . happiness is life, and life is the fulfillment . . . of activity." Quoted in Julia Annas, *The Morality of Happiness* (New York: Oxford University Press, 1993), p. 45.

39 Although the Stoics could, with Aristotle, speak of happiness consisting in the active exercise of virtue, they also viewed it as an *"inner state* which, once achieved, cannot be increased," and "a *desirable state* that one would reasonably want to be in." See Annas, Ibid., pp. 408, 409. Emphasis added.

See the article "Stoicism" in *The Encyclopedia of Philosophy*, ed., Paul Edwards (New York: Macmillan Publishing Co., 1967) Vol. 8, p. 21:

> The consequence of such a life (living according to the benevolence and orderliness of the universe) is *apatheia*, or *euthymia*, spiritual peace and well-being; another term for this ultimate desideratum was *eudaimonia*, the happy condition of the daimon, or soul, when it resembles the deity.

The Stoic philosopher, Seneca, wrote, "What is the happy life? Self-sufficiency and abiding tranquility. This is the gift of greatness of soul." Quoted in *The Stoic Philosophy of Seneca, Essays and Letters*, trans. Moses Hadas, (New York: The Norton Library, 1958), p. 239.

While the Stoics viewed happiness as an inner state, it would be a mistake to say that they equated it with feelings. See F.H. Sandbach, *The Stoics* (Indianapolis: Hackett Publishing Company, second edition, 1989), pp. 40-41.

40 Aristotle, *Nicomachean Ethics*, p. 75.

41 Following Aristotle, Aquinas called it the pleasure which "follows reason." Thomas Aquinas, *Summa Theologica*, trans. Fathers of the English Dominican Province (London: Burns Oates & Washburn, Ltd., third ed. 1941), I, II, Q. 31, A. 3.

42 For recent literature from a Christian perspective, see J.P. Moreland, *Love Your God With All Your Mind: The Role of Reason In The Life Of The Soul* (Colorado Springs: NavPress, 1997); James W. Sire, *Habits of the Mind: Intellectual Life as a Christian Calling* (Downers Grove: InterVarsity Press, 2000); and W. Jay Wood, *Epistemology: Becoming Intellectually Virtuous* (Downers Grove, Illinois: InterVarsity Press, 1998).

43 Augustine "Teaching Christianity" in *The Works of Saint Augustine*, I/11, p. 144. See Arthur F. Holmes, *All Truth is God's Truth* (Grand Rapids: William B. Eerdmans Publishing Co., 1977).

44 See Annas, *The Morality of Happiness*, p. 59: "Aristotle famously defines virtue as a state involving choice which is 'in a mean relative to us, a mean defined by reason, i.e., the reason by which the intelligent person would define it.'"

45 James Gilman writes, "Joy is what humans experience when the way the world is and the way the world ought to be converge. For Christians joy is love's delight in God and God's promised kingdom, when the way the world is and the way God wills the world converge." James E. Gilman, *Fidelity of Heart: An Ethic of Christian Virtue* (Oxford: Oxford University Press, 2001), p. 54.

46 The distance between Aristotle and the New Testament account of virtue is captured well by Alasdair MacIntyre. After acknowledging some common ground, he comments: "Aristotle would certainly not have admired Jesus Christ and he would have been horrified by St. Paul." See *After Virtue* (London: Duckworth, 1985), p. 172.

47 The active dimension of joy is found in its cognate verbs: *rejoice* and *enjoy*.

48 One commentator describes Aristotle's view in these words: "Happiness is thus thought of as active rather than passive, and as something that involves the agent's activity, and thus as being . . . up to the agent." Annas, *Morality of Happiness*, p. 45.

49 "But the fruit of the Spirit is love, joy, peace, patience, kindness, goodness, faithfulness." (Galatians 5:22, ESV)

50 New Testament scholar, Luke T. Johnson, describes the joyful experience of early Christians as one of the "certain states in which they found themselves," and then goes on to put this into the context of a "power with which they had been touched" which "came from God." Luke T. Johnson, *The Writings of the New Testament: An Interpretation* (Philadelphia: Fortress Press, 1986), pp. 94-95.

51 See Annas, *Morality of Happiness*, chapter 19, "Theophrastus and the Stoics: Forcing the Issue."

52 William Barclay, *The Gospel of Matthew*, Revised Edition (Philadelphia: The Westminster Press, 1975) Vol. I, p. 89.

53 Matthew 5:4

54 Augustine: "On Free Will," in *Augustine: Earlier Writings*, p. 150. In stronger language, but to the same point, Jacques Ellul wrote:

> The validity of happiness, including that which might come from the fulfillment of needs and passions or the use of earthly things, rests solely on the recognition that it comes from God and is given by God. All happiness in which man does not recognize that it is God's work and stands in relation to him is rejected and is under condemnation.

Jacques Ellul, *The Ethics of Freedom*, trans. & ed., Geoffrey W. Bromiley (Grand Rapids: Eerdmans, 1976) p. 260.

55 St. Augustine, "The Trinity," in *Augustine: Later Works*, 95. See also Aquinas: "to desire happiness is nothing else than to desire that one's will be satisfied" (*Summa Theologica*, trans. Fathers of the English Dominican Province (London: Burns Oates & Washburn, Ltd., third ed. 1941), I, II, Q. 5, A.8.

56 Augustine's definition of joy is in fact indistinguishable from his definition of happiness. See the previous footnote for his definition of happiness. On joy, he wrote: "For what is desire or joy but an act of will in agreement with what we wish for. . . . We use the term desire when this agreement takes the form of the pursuit of what we wish for, while joy describes our *satisfaction* in the attainment" St. Augustine, *City of God*, trans., Henry Bettenson, ed., David Knowles (Baltimore: Penguin Books, 1972), p. 556. Emphasis added.

57 Karl Barth calls joy "a gratefully perceived and an enjoyed fulfilment." Karl Barth, *Church Dogmatics*, eds., Geoffrey W. Bromiley, T. F. Torrance (Edinburgh: T. & T. Clark, 1968), Vol. III, Part 4, p. 381.

58 Psalm 37:4, NASB.

59 As Aquinas put it, "Joy itself is the consummation of happiness." Aquinas, *Summa*, I, II, Q.3, A.4. An analogy may be helpful: as a finger is a member of the body; so happiness is a species of joy. As a finger finds its fulfillment in its relation to the hand and the rest of the body, so happiness is fulfilled in relation to the many other dimensions of joy. A finger is "meant" for a hand, and the rest of one's body; happiness is "meant" for joy in its fullest sense.

Augustine wrote:

> Is it, perchance, that as one joys in this, and another in that, so do all men agree in their wish for happiness, as they would agree, were they asked, in wishing to have joy – and this joy they call the happy life? Although, then, one pursues joy in this way, and another in that, all have one goal, which they strive to attain, namely, to have joy.

Basic Writings of Saint Augustine, ed., Whitney J. Oates, (Grand Rapids, MI: Baker Book House, 1948, reprint. 1980), Vol. 1, p. 163.

60 See "The Highest and Best of All Pleasures" in Richard R. Howe, *Path of Life: Finding the Joy You've Always Longed For* (Boulder, CO: University Ministries Press, 2017).

61 "With you is the fountain of life; in your light do we see light." (Psalm 36:9, NRSV)

62 Aquinas wrote: "When they desire any good whatsoever, whether by intellective, sensitive, or unconscious appetite, all things desire God as their end, for nothing attracts but for some likeness to God." *St. Thomas Aquinas: Philosophical Texts*, ed. and trans. Thomas Gilby (Durham, North Carolina: The Labyrinth Press, 1982), p. 130.

63 Augustine wrote, "But when you enjoy a human being in God, you are really enjoying God rather than the human being. You will be enjoying the one, after all, in whom you find your bliss." Saint Augustine, "Teaching Christianity" in *Works of Saint Augustine*, p. 122.

64 Augustine, "The Confessions," in *Basic Writings of Saint Augustine*, Vol. I, p. 3. I have modernized the English translation.

65 Blaise Pascal, *Pascal's Pensées*, trans. W.F. Trotter (New York: E.P. Dutton & Co., Inc., 1958), #425.

66 "*Delight yourself in the LORD*, and he will give you the desires of your heart." (Psalm 37:4)

67 Jonathan Edwards wrote: "[True saints] first rejoice in God as glorious and excellent in himself, and then secondarily rejoice in it, that so glorious a God is theirs." Jonathan Edwards, "On Religious Affections," *The Works of Jonathan Edwards*, Perry Miller, Gen. ed., (New Haven: Yale University Press, 1959), Vol. 2, pp. 249-50.

CHAPTER 4: A THEOLOGICAL PRIMER ON JOY, PART 2

1 Justin Oakley describes the experience of joy (without its theological dimensions) as feeling "a certain 'lightness', 'buoyancy', or energy permeating the mind, and affecting the way we see the world, the thoughts and desires we have, and the manner in which we act." Justin Oakley, *Morality and the Emotions*, (London and New York: Routledge, 1992), p. 10.

Dallas Willard describes it as "a pervasive *sense* – not just a thought – of well-being: of overall and ultimate well-being. Its primary feeling component is delight in an encompassing good well-secured." Dallas Willard, *Renovation of the Heart: Putting on the Character of Christ* (Colorado Springs, CO: NavPress, 2002), pp. 132-133. Emphasis original.

[2] St. Augustine, "Confessions," in *The Basic Writings of Saint Augustine*, ed., Whitney J. Oates (New York, NY: Random House Publishers, 1948), Volume 1, p. 180. I have contemporized the King James pronouns and verb endings.

[3] Robert Roberts writes, "'Joy' is less the name of a Christian emotion than a name for a characteristic of many of the Christian emotions. Love, hope, peace, and gratitude are all joyful emotions, and I suspect that when one has said enough about these others, there will be nothing left to say about joy." Robert C. Roberts, *Spirituality and Human Emotion*, (Grand Rapids, MI: William B. Eerdmans Publishing Co., 1982), p. 74.
Dallas Willard writes:

> Of course it is impossible to separate love, joy, peace, faith (confidence), and hope from one another in practice. They lose their true nature when separated. Try imagining love without joy and peace, joy without love and peace, or peace without love and joy, or any combination of them without faith and hope. You will see, upon making a slight effort, that love, joy, and so on without the others just wouldn't be themselves.

Willard, *Renovation*, pp. 135-136.

[4] John 16:33, KJV

[5] PT

[6] NIV, RSV, NEB

[7] NASB

[8] NASB. The Greek words are *tharreo* and *tharseo*, meaning, respectively, "to be confident, courageous," and "be cheerful, be courageous." William F. Arndt & F. Wilbur Gingrich, *A Greek-English Lexicon of the New Testament* (The University of Chicago Press, 1957), p. 352.

[9] See the following: Psalm 30:11; Ecclesiastes 3:4; Job 21:11; Luke 7:32; Exodus 15:20, RSV; Psalm 149:3; Psalm 150:4; Luke 15:25.

[10] 1 Peter 1:8, KJV

[11] Blaise Pascal, *Greater Shorter Works of Pascal*, trans. Emile Cailliet and John C. Blankenagel (Westport, Connecticut: Greenwood Press, Publishers, 1948, reprint. 1974), p. 117. I have changed the King James pronouns and verb endings to their contemporary forms.

[12] C.S. Lewis, *Surprised by Joy* (New York: Harcourt, Brace & World, Inc. 1955), p. 17.

[13] Hebrews 6:5

[14] For two recent works that explore this haunting desire, see Mark Buchanan, *Things Unseen (Living in Light of Forever)* (Sisters, Oregon: Multnomah, 2002) and John Eldridge, *The Journey of Desire: Searching for the Life We've Only Dreamed Of* (Nashville: Thomas Nelson Publishers, 2000).

15 Lesslie Newbigen, *Journey into Joy* (Grand Rapids, MI: William B. Eerdmans Publishing Co., 1972), p. 116.

16 See Philippians 4:4 and 1 Thessalonians 5:16.

Dallas Willard describes what life is like for those who are "well on their way" in the renovation of their hearts: "Finally, here, life in the path of rightness becomes easy and joyous." Dallas Willard, *Renovation of the Heart: Putting on the Character of Christ* (Colorado Springs, CO: NavPress, 2002), p. 227. This is very much what I have in mind when I speak of dispositional joy.

17 For more on this, see the "Postscript" in Chapter 14 on joy and nearness to God. See also Part 3, "The Ethics of Joy" in my book, *Path of Life*, and its Chapters:

    7   The Joyful Heart
    8   Joy and the Theological Virtues
    9   Joy and the Good Life
   10   Joy and the Quest for Pleasure
   11   Joy as an Imperative
   12   Joy and the World's Travail

18 The fact that joy is perspectival does not make it merely subjective. That we can and do experience joy is evidence that the perspective is true. It fits the world that we live in.

19 According to Jonathan Edwards, "Holy affections are not heat without light; but evermore arise from some information of the understanding, some spiritual instruction that the mind receives, some light or actual knowledge." Jonathan Edwards, "On Religious Affections" in *The Works of Jonathan Edwards,* Perry Miller, Gen. ed., (New Haven: Yale University Press, 1959), Vol. 2, p. 281.

Paul Holmer wrote: "Christian beliefs are like the river-bed for one's thoughts and emotions, within which contentment, peace and joy can truly flourish." Paul L. Holmer, "Blessedness" in *Baker's Dictionary of Christian Ethics*, ed., Carl F.H. Henry (Grand Rapids: Baker Book House Co., 1973), p. 66.

Robert Roberts contends that emotions "are no less tied to concepts than arguments and beliefs are." *Spirituality*, pp.10, 21. He also writes that "The Christian emotions . . . (e.g., love, joy, peace) are ways of 'seeing' which are determined by the peculiar Christian concepts and the scheme of beliefs which give rise to those concepts." (Ibid., p. 10.) And, "They are "concerned ways of viewing things through the 'lenses' of Christian teaching." (Ibid., p. 25).

20 Josef Pieper, *About Love,* trans., Richard and Clara Winston (Chicago: Franciscan Herald Press, 1974), p. 73. Before him, Aquinas called joy the "delight which follows reason." Thomas Aquinas, *Summa Theologica,* trans. Fathers of the English Dominican Province (London: Burns Oates & Washburn, Ltd., third ed. 1941), I, II, Q. 31, A. 3. I would only add that joy follows reason when reason is illumined by divine revelation.

21 Greek scholars would tell us that in each of these verses we find a causal use of a participle: "because you know," or "since you know," or "for you know."

22 Faith is one of the "foundational conditions" for joy. Dallas Willard, *Renovation of the Heart: Putting on the Character of Christ* (Colorado Springs, CO: NavPress, 2002), p. 141.

23   Roberts writes, "The gospel message provides people with a distinctive way of construing the world; the maker of the universe is your personal loving Father and has redeemed you from sin and death." Roberts, *Spirituality,* p. 16.

24   Of Paul's view of the Christian mind, Herman Ridderbos wrote: "It is not so much a matter of thinking in an intellectual sense, but of the new moral and religious consciousness, of the new insight into who God is and what his will is according to his revelation in Christ, and of permitting oneself to be determined thereby in the manifestation and circumstances of . . . life." Herman Ridderbos, *Paul: An Outline of His Theology,* trans. John Richard De Witt (Grand Rapids, MI: William B. Eerdmans Publishing Co., 1975), p. 228.

25   I explore how beliefs change from a notional understanding to a sense of the heart in Rick Howe, *River of Delights: Quenching Your Thirst For Joy,* Volume 1 (Boulder, CO: University Ministries Press, 2017), Chapters 5 and 6.

26   Robert Roberts has written:

> Whatever else Christianity may be, it is a set of emotions. It is love of God and neighbor, grief about one's waywardness, joy in the merciful salvation of our God, gratitude, hope and peace. So if I don't love God and my neighbor, abhor my sins, and rejoice in my redemption, if I am not grateful, hopeful and at peace with God and myself, then it follows that I am alienated from Christianity.

Roberts, *Spirituality,* p. 1.

27   Although I am not prepared to say that it gives a full accounting of how we gain and validate claims to knowledge, a Christian version of "virtue epistemology" is a fruitful way of approaching this very important issue. Not only are intellectual virtues (good dispositions and habits of the mind) such as curiosity, open-mindedness, honesty, humility, courage, and perseverance, essential to our acquisition of knowledge, they cannot ultimately be separated from moral virtues. All are character traits. All put us in a position to flourish in life, including our pursuit of knowledge. As you might imagine, I see joy in a central place in all of this. In the next chapter I will say:

> Joy has very much to do with functioning and flourishing in life. It is a sign that our hearts are working the way God intends them to. Joy results from a harmony between our desires, decisions, and deeds, and the congeniality of our hearts with God's. When it is ours, we live robustly in God's world. We flourish in life beneath his good hand.

This includes our pursuit of knowledge.

To learn more about virtue epistemology from a Christian perspective, see the following:

> Robert C. Roberts and W. Jay Wood "Proper Function, Emotion, and Virtues of the Intellect" in *Faith and Philosophy* Volume 21, Issue (2004: pp. 3-24) found at https://www.pdcnet.org/pdc/bvdb.nsf/purchase?openform&fp=faithphil&id=faith phil_2004_0021_0001_0003_0024
> W. Jay Wood, *Epistemology: Becoming Intellectually Virtuous* (Downers Grove, IL: InterVarsity Press, 1998)
>
> Linda Zagzebski, *Virtues of the Mind: An Inquiry into the Nature of Virtue and the Ethical Foundations of Knowledge* (Cambridge, UK: Cambridge University Press, 1996)

28 This approach to moral philosophy is known as *aretaic* or virtue ethics. Unlike deontological ethics, with its focus on the intrinsic rightness or wrongness of an action, or consequentialism, which focuses on the outcome of actions, virtue ethics places its primary emphasis on moral agents and their character traits. In my own view, a complete accounting of the moral life includes virtue, commands, and outcomes, in that order. With respect to moral guidance, virtues provide a general wisdom (what a virtuous person would do, e.g., Jesus); commands inform virtues and give guidance when virtue might allow multiple courses of action; outcomes provide "tie-breakers," i.e., all other things being equal, one ought to seek the best outcome possible.

29 See Deuteronomy 6:5 and 30:2.

30 Joy is the reward of virtue (even our smallest steps and our slightest growth). It is God's way of saying, "Well done, good and faithful servant!" God does not bribe us to pursue his will with money, sensual pleasure, or anything else that might capture our hearts apart from actually doing his will. The pleasure of joy-as-a-reward arises, and only arises, from wholehearted obedience itself. It is one and the same as delighting in obedience and enjoying God's reward for doing so. See Matthew 25:21, 23: "His master said to him, 'Well done, good and faithful servant. You have been faithful over a little; I will set you over much. Enter into the joy of your master.'"

31 According to Justin Oakley, Aristotle's view of virtue includes "having the right emotions in the right way towards the appropriate objects and to the right degree." Justin Oakley, *Morality*, p. 2.

Rosalind Hursthouse writes, "The emotions are morally significant. . . . The virtues . . . are all dispositions not only to act, but to feel emotions as reactions as well as impulses to action. (Aristotle says again and again that the virtues are concerned with actions and feelings.") Rosalind Hursthouse, *On Virtue Ethics* (Oxford: Oxford University Press, 1999), p. 108.

Linda Zagzebski writes that "the primary bearers of moral properties are emotions." See Linda Zagzebski, "The Virtues of God and the Foundations of Ethics," in Kelley James Clark, ed., *Readings in the Philosophy of Religion* (Canada: Broadview Press, 2000), p. 80.

32 For Aristotle, pleasure in virtue is the mark of true virtue: "Just acts give pleasure to a lover of justice." And, "In the same way just acts give pleasure to a lover of justice, and virtuous conduct generally to the lover of virtue." Aristotle, *The Nicomachean Ethics*, trans. J.A.K. Thompson (Penguin Books, 1976), p. 79.

For Kant, such pleasure is morally irrelevant:

> To be beneficent when we can is a duty; and besides this, there are many minds so sympathetically constituted that, without any other motive of vanity or self-interest, they find a pleasure in spreading joy around them, and can take delight in the satisfaction of others so far as it is their own work. But I maintain that in such a case an action of this kind, however proper, however amiable it may be, has nevertheless no true moral worth.

Immanuel Kant, *Fundamental Principles of the Metaphysics of Morals*, trans., Thomas K. Abbott (New York: The Liberal Arts Press, 1949), pp. 15-16.

Aristotle was right; Kant was wrong. If there is no pleasure in moral action, there is no virtue. Sheer grit and determination to do what is right is better than nothing, but that's about all that can be said for it. Its true moral worth is very small in the economy of heaven. In fact in heaven it can't be found at all!

33   Augustine, "The Spirit and the Letter" in *Augustine: Later Works*, ed., John Burnaby (Philadelphia: The Westminster Press, 1955), p. 197.

34   Jonathan Edwards, "On Religious Affections," p. 97.

CHAPTER 5: IMPORTANT DISTINCTIONS

1   This distinction is used by William Lane Craig in his work, *Reasonable Faith: Christian Truth and Apologetics* (Wheaton: Crossway Book, 1994), pp. 31ff. Another helpful distinction is George Mavrodes' "having a reason" and "giving a reason." See George I. Mavrodes, *Belief in God* (New York: Random House, 1970), pp. 11ff.

2   They are arrow and target, path and destination. The aim of rationality is the acquisition of truth. A claim to rationality is therefore at least implicitly a claim to truth. See J.P. Moreland and Kai Nielsen, *Does God Exist? The Great Debate* (Nashville: Thomas Nelson Publishers, 1990), pp. 221-223.

3   The distinction, summing up Aristotle's thought, is made by Paul Holmer in *Baker's Dictionary of Christian Ethics*, ed., Carl F.H. Henry (Grand Rapids: Baker Book House, 1973), pp. 512-513.

4   See John Piper, *A Godward Life: Savoring the Supremacy of God in All of Life* (Colorado Springs, Colorado: Multnomah, First Edition 1997; New Edition 2001; New Hardcover 2015).

5   See Mark 8:31-33.

6   There is another interesting dimension to joy as a taking-pleasure-in. Although the emphasis in this kind of pleasure may seem to be on the subject (his values, her interests) it has an important objective dimension, as well. The statement, "I take pleasure in being a family man," tells you something about me, but also something more than that – namely, that I have a family. It would present a serious problem if I made such a claim but you knew that I was a bachelor! Indeed, the very words (Here grammar mirrors life.) "I take pleasure in" point to an object, and demand it. In the chapters that follow, I will argue that some of the experiences of joy not only seem to come from God, but seem to be about God, that God not only seems to be the Source of the experience, but its Object, and that the existence of God best explains this.

7   C.S. Lewis, *The Four Loves* (New York: Harcourt, Brace, Jovanovich, 1960), pp. 25ff.

8   Naturalism is the view that the world and everything in it derives from and consists of nothing more than physical properties and natural forces.

9   The psalmist wrote of God: "In your presence there is fullness of joy." (Psalm 16:11)

10   The two arguments involve what are known as "perceptual" and "explanatory" models of religious experience, the former focusing on experiences in which God seems to be the Object of the experience, and the latter in which God seems to be the Source. I agree with William Hasker and J.P. Moreland that these are not rival models and arguments, but are compatible, and may be combined in fruitful ways. See, e.g., J.P. Moreland, *Scaling the Secular City* (Grand Rapids: Baker Book House, 1987), p. 231ff., and William Hasker, "The Epistemic Value of Religious Experience: Perceptual and Explanatory Models" in *The*

Rationality of Belief and the Plurality of Faith: Essays in Honor of William P. Alston, Thomas D. Senor, ed., (Ithaca and London: Cornell University Press, 1995), p. 150ff.

[11]   C.S. Lewis, *The Problem of Pain* (New York: Macmillan Press, 1962), pp. 16-17.

[12]   Rudolf Otto, *The Idea of the Holy,* trans. J.W. Harvey, second ed. (New York: Oxford University Press, 1950), pp. 12-13.   In this context Otto is describing a component of numinous experience that he calls *mysterium tremendum.*

[13]   According to the *Oxford Latin Dictionary* {ed., P.G.W. Glare (Oxford: The Clarendon Press, 1982) p. 755}, *numen* refers to: "1. A motion of the head . . . 2. Divine or supernatural power or influence . . . 3. Divine power as controlling events or activities . . . 4. Divine nature or majesty, divinity, godhead . . . 5. A supernatural force in a place, divine presence . . . 6. a deity, god."

Numinous experience is not limited to God.   There are other spiritual beings with whom mortals have encounters, such as angels and demons.

[14]   C.S. Lewis described this experience this way:

> We can't – or I can't – hear the song of a bird simply as a sound. Its meaning or message ("That's a bird") comes with it inevitably – just as one can't see a familiar word in print as a merely visual pattern.   The reading is as involuntary as the seeing.   When the wind roars I don't just hear the roar; I "hear the wind."   In the same way it is possible to "read" as well as to "have" a pleasure. Or not even "as well as."   The distinction ought to become, and sometimes is, impossible; to receive it and to recognise its divine source are a single experience. This heavenly fruit is instantly redolant of the orchard where it grew.   This sweet air whispers of the country from whence it blows.   It is a message. We know we are being touched by a finger of that right hand at which there are pleasures for evermore.   There need be no question of thanks or praise as a separate event, something done afterwards. To experience the tiny theophany is itself to adore.

C.S. Lewis, *Letters to Malcolm: Chiefly on Prayer* (New York: Harcourt, Brace & World, Inc.: 1964), pp. 89-90.

[15]   In the Bible there is a continuum of joy: simple joy   (Galatians 5:22), rejoicing greatly (Philippians 4:10, ESV), an exceeding joy (Psalm 43:4, ESV), an exceeding great joy (Matthew 2:10, KJV), fullness of joy (Psalm 16:11, ESV), overflowing with joy   (2 Corinthians 7:4, ESV), one's highest joy, (Psalm 137:6, NIV), and an "unutterable and exalted joy" (1 Peter 1:8, RSV).

I can illustrate nuances of the numinous from daily life.   Consider the sun. We rarely see it directly.   Our eyes cannot withstand its brilliance. More often than not we see it obliquely, on the edge of our field of vision.   Most often we simply live in its light.   As I do not always see the sun, but sense its presence, feel its warmth, and see the world in its light, so I may not always be keenly and clearly aware of God in an experience of joy (which is another way of describing its numinous dimensions), but may sense and enjoy his presence as it illumines the path of my life.   In the words of this ancient hymn of praise:

> How precious is your steadfast love, O God!
>   The children of mankind take refuge in the shadow of your wings.
> They feast on the abundance of your house,
>   and you give them drink from *the river of your delights.*

For with you is the fountain of life;
in your light do we see light. (Psalm 36:7-9).

My visual experience of the sun differs at sunrise, noon, and sunset. Nothing about the sun changes at those times. It is the earth's relation to the sun and my position on the earth that have changed. Similarly, God never changes, but we do, and that changes the ways in which we experience him.

16 We may miss the numinous dimensions of joy because we think of the interface between the natural and the Supernatural realms as something that must be unusual, ostentatious, or uncanny in an obvious way, or perhaps something distant and remote. C.S. Lewis wrote, "The Supernatural is not remote and abstruse: it is a matter of daily and hourly experience, as intimate as breathing. Denial of it depends on a certain absent-mindedness." C.S. Lewis, *Miracles: A Preliminary Study*, Chapter 6: "Answers to Misgivings," found at: http://pdbooks.ca/pdbooks/english/L/Lewis-C-S--Miracles/cjyaqv_files/text/part0007.html.

17 Perhaps a cheerful mood, feelings of elation, or a buoyant sense of well-being.

18 Richard Swinburne, *The Existence of God* (New York: Oxford University Press, 1979), pp. 249ff.

19 Luke 24:41 – "And while they still disbelieved for joy and were marveling, he said to them, 'Have you anything here to eat?'"

20 See word studies my *Path of Life: Finding the Joy You've Always Longed For* (WestBow Press: Bloomington, IN, 2015), Chapter 1.

21 Blaise Pascal, *Greater Shorter Works of Pascal*, trans. Emile Cailliet and John C. Blankenagel (Westport,Connecticut: Greenwood Press, Publishers, 1948, reprint. 1974), p. 117.

CHAPTER 6: JOY AND THE RATIONALITY OF FAITH

1 See, for example:

> J.P. Moreland, *Scaling the Secular City: A Defense of Christianity* (Grand Rapids, MI: Baker Book House, 1987)

> Richard Swinburne, *The Existence of God*, Second Edition (Oxford: Oxford University Press, 2004.)

> William Lane Craig, *Reasonable Faith: Christian Truth and Apologetics,* Third Edition (Wheaton, IL: Crossway Books, 2008)

> Keith Ward, *The Evidence for God: The Case for the Existence of a Spiritual Dimension,* (London: Darton, Longman & Todd, 2014).

2 Pascal wrote, "The heart has its reasons, which reason does not know." And "We feel it in a thousand things. It is the heart which experiences God, and not the reason. This, then, is faith: God felt by the heart, not by the reason." Blaise Pascal, Pascal's Pensées, trans. W.F. Trotter (New York: E.P. Dutton & Co., Inc., 1958), #277 and #278.

3 Since the aim of rationality is the acquisition of truth, I recognize that a claim to rationality is also at least implicitly a claim to truth. J.P. Moreland makes insightful comments about

this. See J.P. Moreland and Kai Nielsen, *Does God Exist? The Great Debate* (Nashville: Thomas Nelson Publishers, 1990), pp. 221-223.

[4]   John Hick, *Arguments for the Existence of God* (New York: Herder and Herder, 1971), p. 109.

[5]   Ibid., p. 112. Emphasis original.

[6]   Speaking of the justification of belief from religious experience, William Alston recommends the strategy of "taking only what is based on the experience in question as *prima facie* justified by the experience. . . ." William P. Alston, *Perceiving God: The Epistemology of Religious Experience* (Ithaca and London: Cornell University Press, 1991), p. 260. Emphasis added.

Alvin Plantinga affirms the same kind of qualification: ". . . justification conferring conditions . . . must be seen as conferring *prima facie* rather than *ultima facie* or all-things-considered justification." Alvin Plantinga, "Reason and Belief in God" in *Faith and Rationality*, eds., Alvin Plantinga and Nicholas Wolterstorff (Notre Dame, Indiana: University of Notre Dame Press, 1983), p. 83. Emphasis original.

[7]   Richard Swinburne, *The Existence of God* (New York: Oxford University Press, 1979), p. 254. See his *Is There A God?* (Oxford: Oxford University Press, 1996), pp. 131ff., for an application of this principle to religious experience.

[8]   The Jewish philosopher, Abraham Heschel claims that in all joy, "joy itself attaches not to the subject but to the object ...." See Abraham Joshua Heschel, *God in Search of Man* (New York: Farrar, Straus & Giroux: 1955), p. 386.

[9]   Thomas à Kempis, *The Imitation of Christ* (New York: Grosset & Dunlap), pp. 109-110.

[10]   Many have made the attempt, but no one has succeeded in proving that God does not exist. The last section of this book will address arguments against the existence of God from the presence of evil in the world.

[11]   Even if you were able to demonstrate an emotional imbalance independently of alleged encounters with God, it could still be the case that experiences of joy are moments of lucidity!

[12]   This is a term used by Keith Yandell in his discussion of numinous experience in Keith E. Yandell, *Christianity and Philosophy* (Grand Rapids: Eerdmans, 1984), pp. 4-44.

[13]   This is a term used by William Alston in his discussion of religious experience in *Perceiving God*, pp. 14ff.

[14]   The experience of God reported in the Scriptures was so vivid to hearts that poets used the language of perception to describe it. See, for example, Psalm 17:15; 25:15; 26:3; 27:4.

[15]   J.P. Moreland lists seven features of "normal acts of sensory perception," and argues that some religious experiences include all seven. See J.P. Moreland, *Does God Exist?*, p. 235 ff.

[16]   See Alston, *Perceiving God*, chapter one: "The Experience of God: A Perceptual Model."

[17]   Ed. L. Miller, *God and Reason: A Historical Approach to Philosophical Theology* (New York: Macmillan Press, 1972), p. 115.

[18]   George I. Mavrodes, *Belief in God* (New York: Random House, 1970), p. 76.

CHAPTER 7: ON THE THRESHOLD OF JOY

[1]   I still have the text for that class in my library. The author, Helena Curtis, wrote:

> The flower is a device by which plants induce animals to make these movements [involved in sexual reproduction] for them. . . . The more attractive the plants were to the beetles, the more frequently they would be visited and the more seeds they would produce. . . . Most of the distinctive features of modern flowers are special adaptations that encourage constancy of particular pollinators. The varied colors and odors are "brand names" for guiding pollinators.

Helena Curtis, *Invitation to Biology* (New York, NY: Worth Publishers, Inc., 1972), p. 263.

[2]   Adaptation and change in an ever-unfolding world have been features of life on our planet since the dawn of creation. They display the wisdom of God and the way he has ordered his world. I deny, however, that this is, or possibly can be, a blind, unwitting force without a Creator. All things are his servants. (See Psalm 119:91.)

[3]   Genesis 2:9

[4]   The fact that the fragrance and color of flowers aids their survival adds another layer of utility that is even more amazing!

[5]   In a Christian vision of the world, creation is a work of art, and God's creative activity, the work of an Artist. The Genesis story tells us that the earth was *without form and void*. God gave form, structure, shape, and content to this formless void and made something beautiful from it. He invented colors and then painted the heavens and the earth with them.

Augustine put it this way:

> Question the beauty of the earth, question the beauty of the sea, question the beauty of the air, amply spread around everywhere, question the beauty of the sky, question the serried ranks of the stars, question the sun making the day glorious with is bright beams, question the moon tempering the darkness of the following night with its shining rays, question the animals that move in the waters, that amble about on dry land, that fly in the air . . . . They all answer you, 'Here we are, look; we're beautiful." Their beauty is their confession. Who made these beautiful changeable things, if not one who is beautiful and unchangeable?

St. Augustine, "Sermon 241," in *The Works of Saint Augustine: A Translation for the 21ˢᵗ Century*, ed. John E. Rotelle, O.S.A., trans. Edmund Hill, O.P. (New York: New City Press, 1996), III/7, p. 71.

Beauty in the world, Christians believe, connects us with the beauty of the World's Maker. To behold one is to encounter the Other, even if we are heedless of the meeting; even if we are not fully in touch with the deep longing in our hearts for a beauty greater than we have beheld with our eyes.

In a Christian perspective, the beauty of this world is a foretaste of the world to come. N.T. Wright tells the story of the discovery of a musical manuscript that turned out to be part of a larger masterpiece written later by the famous composer, Mozart:

The point of the story is that the masterpiece already exists – in the mind of the composer. At the moment, neither the instruments nor the players are ready to perform it. But when they are, the manuscript we already have – the present world with all its beauty and all its puzzlement – will turn out to be truly part of it. . . . Just as, in one of the New Testament's greatest claims, the kingdoms of this world are to become the kingdom of God, so the beauty of this world will be enfolded in the beauty of God – and not just the beauty of God himself, but the beauty which, because God is the creator par excellence, he will create when the present world is rescued, healed, restored, and completed.

N.T. Wright, *Simply Christian: Why Christianity Makes Sense* (U.S.A.: HarperSanFrancisco, 2006), p. 47.

If Christians are right, there is more to the beauty of the world than the beauty of the world. It is more significant than our sentience alone can tell us. Beauty in the world points us to the beauty of the Lord.

What do Christians mean when they say that God is beautiful? (Psalm 27:4, RSV) It is not an aesthetic appraisal of color, shape, and texture, since these are not properties of God. Nor, if the Hebrew prophets were right, can we compare God to something else that we believe to be beautiful, and then say that God is like that (See, e.g., Isaiah 40:25). Karl Barth wrote:

We must be careful not to start from any preconceived ideas, especially in this case a preconceived idea of the beautiful . . . God is not beautiful in the sense that he shares in an idea of beauty superior to him, so that to know it is to know him as God. On the contrary, it is as he is God that he is also beautiful, so that he is the basis and standard of everything that is beautiful and of all ideas of the beautiful.

Karl Barth, *Church Dogmatics*, eds., Geoffrey W. Bromiley, T. F. Torrance (Edinburgh: T. & T. Clark, 1968),Vol. II, Part 1, p. 656.

To those who know it, the enjoyment of God is very much like aesthetic delight. My pleasure in the changing autumn colors of aspen on steep slopes of the Rocky Mountains, and my pleasure in God as I worship, seem similar. My heart knows the affinity, even if I find it difficult to put into words. Both are pleasures of appreciation. Both are delights in beauty. See C.S. Lewis, *The Four Loves* (New York: Harcourt, Brace, Jovanovich, 1960), pp. 25ff.

My pleasure in the beauty of the aspen draws my heart beyond them to God. Joy in the beauty of creation points to, and is fulfilled in, an enjoyment of God, Christians believe, because all creaturely beauty bears a likeness to, and is sourced in, the greater, more powerful beauty of the Creator. In the words of Augustine, "You, my Father . . . are the highest good and the loveliness in all lovely things." Augustine, " Confessions" in *The Works of Saint Augustine*, I/1, p. 81.

This is the way C.S. Lewis saw it: "We do not want merely to see beauty . . . we want something else which can hardly be put into words – to be united with the beauty we see, to pass into it, to receive it into ourselves, to bathe in it, to become part of it." C.S. Lewis, "The Weight of Glory" in *The Weight of Glory: And Other Addresses (New York, NY: HarperCollins, 1980)*, p. 42.

God's beauty, Christians believe, is primal. Primary. Ultimate. We are drawn to his beauty through the beauty of the world he made: To quote Lewis again:

The books or the music in which we thought the beauty was located will betray us if we trust to them; it was not in them, it only came through them, and what came through them was longing. These things—the beauty, the memory of our own past—are good images of what we really desire; but if they are mistaken for the thing itself they turn into dumb idols, breaking the hearts of their worshippers. For they are not the thing itself; they are only the scent of a flower we have not found, the echo of a tune we have not heard, news from a country we have never yet visited.

Ibid., p. 30.

If beauty points us to God, then whatever the beauty of the Lord is, he possesses it in himself. It does not point to anything else. His beauty existed before the foundations of the world. He is, simply, beautiful. As Jürgen Moltmann put it, "The beautiful in God is what makes us rejoice in him." Jürgen Moltmann, *Theology and Joy,* trans. Reinhard Ulrich (London: SCM Press, LTD, 1973), p. 62.

Speaking of joy and the beauty of God, Karl Barth wrote: "He has it as a fact and a power in such a way that He acts as the One who gives pleasure, creates desire and rewards with enjoyment, because He is the One who is pleasant, desirable, full of enjoyment, because first and last He alone is that which is pleasant, desirable and full of enjoyment." Barth, *Church Dogmatics,* Vol. II, Part 1, p. 651.

A.W. Tozer knew this same truth: "The blessed and inviting truth is that God is the most winsome of all beings, and in our worship of Him we should find unspeakable pleasure." A.W. Tozer, *Whatever Happened to Worship?* ed., Gerald B. Smith (Camp Hill, Pennsylvania: Christian Publications, 1985), p. 28.

[6]   Of the notion that pleasure always replenishes a deficiency, Aristotle wrote:

This theory seems to have been derived from the pains and pleasures connected with eating: it is assumed that it is because we have experienced a lack, and felt pain, that we subsequently find pleasure in replenishment. But this does not happen in the case of all pleasures. The pleasures of learning, for instance, have no antecedent pains; neither have some even of the sensuous pleasures, such as those of smell, and many sounds and sights too, and memories and hopes.

Aristotle, *The Nicomachean Ethics,* trans. J.A.K. Thompson (Penguin Books), pp. 316-317.

[7]   The famous atheist, Sigmund Freud, wrote, "Beauty has no obvious use; nor is there any clear cultural necessity for it. Yet civilization could not do without it." Sigmund Freud, *Civilization and Its Discontents* W. W. Norton & Company, New York: NY, 1961) p. 24.

[8]   Peter Kreeft has written that a "joyful spirit inspires joyful feelings and even a more psychosomatically healthy body." He says, for example that "we need less sleep when we have joy and have more resistance to all kinds of diseases from colds to cancers." Peter Kreeft, *Heaven: The Heart's Deepest Longing* (San Francisco: Ignatius Press, Expanded Edition, 1980), 129.

Let's say that this is true. One could, with this observation in hand, make a case that joy serves the interests of survival. But this would only create a greater problem. It would be extremely odd if it were granted that 1) health is conducive to survival, 2) joy is conducive to health, and 3) the experiences of joy involve an awareness of the presence and activity of God, but not also granted that 4) God exists! Remove the fulcrum and the cargo will never get off the ground.

9   Clark H. Pinnock, *Reason Enough: A Case for the Christian Faith* (Downers Grove: InterVarsity Press, 1980) p. 65. Those who are troubled by the magnitude of evil in the world should also take surfeit pleasure in the world into account.

10   Aristotle wrote, "It is generally agreed that pleasure is very closely bound up with human nature." Aristotle, *Ethics*, p. 312.

11   Ibid., p. 321.

12   Edward John Carnell, *A Philosophy of the Christian Religion* (Grand Rapids: Baker Book House, reprint. 1980), p. 58.

13   See Psalm 16:11.

14   C.S. Lewis, *The Pilgrim's Regress* (Grand Rapids: Eerdmans Publishing Co., 1958), pp. 7ff.

15   See a statement of Lewis' argument in "The Weight of Glory," *in The Weight of Glory and Other Addresses* (Grand Rapids: William B. Eerdmans Publishing Co., 1965). See also C. Stephen Evans "The Mystery of Persons" in *Why Believe? Reason and Mystery as Pointers to God* (Revised edition, Grand Rapids, Michigan, William B. Eerdmans Publishing Co., 1996).

16   C.S. Lewis, *Surprised by Joy* (New York: Harcourt, Brace & World, Inc., 1955), p. 230.

17   Kreeft, *Heaven*, pp. 202-203.

18   Seen, for instance in early human burial rites with religious overtones.

19   C.S. Lewis, *Mere Christianity* (New York: Macmillan Publishing Co., 1952), p. 120.

20   Kreeft, *Heaven*, pp. 209-210.

21   Richard L. Purtill, *Reason to Believe* (Grand Rapids: William B. Eerdmans Publishing Co., 1974), p. 104.

CHAPTER 8: JOY AND THE EXISTENCE OF GOD

1   That is to say, the numinous presentation of the experience includes a sense that it has come from God.

2   See Chapter 5: Important Distinctions.

3   Philosophers call this the principle of sufficient reason: For every fact there must be an explanation why it is the case.

4   You may wonder why I make God one causal factor among the possibility of others, and not the sole cause of the experience. When joy has sensory dimensions (i.e., interfaces with the world of our senses), those factors must be included as causal conditions as well. It is more than a sensory or aesthetic pleasure, but it is not less. Even if there are other causal factors involved, God is both the necessary and sufficient cause of joy.

[5]   Joy is likened to the pleasure of wine, the pleasure of a feast, the pleasure of wealth, and to the delight of a bridegroom in his bride. See, for instance, Psalm 4:7; 63:5; 119:14; Isaiah 9:3; 61:10; 62:5; Zechariah 10:7.

[6]   See Acts 2:1-13.

[7]   Even if there are similarities between the pleasure of wine and the presence and activity of God in one's experience, there are significant differences: not only in causality, but in outcomes in one's life. See Ephesians 5:18-19: "And do not get drunk with wine, for that is debauchery, but be filled with the Spirit, addressing one another in psalms and hymns and spiritual songs, singing and making melody to the Lord with your heart."

[8]   You could argue that those who say they experience joy as a gift from God are deceitful or deceived (which we will explore below).

[9]   C.S. Lewis, *The Lion, the Witch and the Wardrobe* (New York: Collier Books, 1950, 22nd Printing, 1977), p. 45.

[10]   Attributed to Abraham Lincoln.

[11]   See John Hick, ed., *The Existence of God* (New York: Macmillan Publishing Co., Inc., 1964), pp. 260-261.

[12]   Which interpretation proves to be veridical depends on what lies at the end of the road.

[13]   Gerard Manley Hopkins, "God's Grandeur," in *Chief Modern Poets of Britain and America*, ed., Gerald DeWitt Sanders, John Herbert Nelson, M.L. Rosenthal (London: The Macmillan Company, 1970), Vol. I, p. 60.

[14]   Joy and suffering are not incompatible. In fact the New Testament sees them closely related. Jesus taught his disciples to face adversity squarely and with joy: "Blessed are you when others revile you and persecute you and utter all kinds of evil against you on my account. Rejoice and be glad." (Matthew 5:11-12) When they faced the persecution that Jesus said would come, his followers rejoiced "that they were counted worthy to suffer dishonor" for the name of Christ (Acts 5:41). The apostle Paul wrote, "I rejoice in my sufferings" (Colossians 1:24). James taught, "Count it all joy, my brothers, when you meet trials of various kinds" (James 1:2). Peter exhorted his reading audience, "Rejoice insofar as you share Christ's sufferings" (1 Peter 4:13).
Christians through the centuries have faced death for embracing Christ. They knew what lay before them, and mocked it with an undaunted and a defiant joy. Let me tell you a few stories.

Ignatius, a disciple of the apostle John was executed just after the turn of the first century. As he was being arrested it was said of him that he "joyfully submitted his limbs to the fetters," and when he was told that he would be fed to the lions, he responded, "I have joy of the beasts that are prepared for me!" (Taken from Cal Samra, *The Joyful Christ: The Healing Power of Humor* (San Francisco: Harper & Row Publishers, 1986), p. 93.)

A few decades later another disciple of John, Polycarp, was arrested for his faith in Christ. When threatened with the pyre, he responded, "Why do you delay? Bring against me what you please." A witness reported that as he spoke "he appeared in a transport of joy and confidence, and his countenance shown with a certain heavenly grace." (Ibid., pp. 93-94.)

With these two men the last link to the eyewitnesses of Christ came to an end, but the heritage of courageous joy lived on. According to Ambrose, St. Agnes was beheaded in A.D. 304 under the persecution of the Roman emperor, Diocletian. Upon learning that this was to be her fate, Agnes was "filled with joy on hearing this sentence, [and] went to the place of execution more cheerfully than others go to their wedding." (Ibid., p. 96.)

A contemporary of hers, Vincent of Saragossa, was tortured for refusing to deny his faith in Christ. He endured the rack, iron hooks tearing into his flesh, salt rubbed into his wounds and finally a gridiron of fire and spikes. Augustine wrote that "the more Vincent suffered, the greater seemed to be the inward joy and consolation of his soul." (Ibid.)

John Huss, the early reformer, met the same kind of fate with the same courageous joy. With hands manacled behind his back, his neck bound to the stake by a chain, and straw and wood heaped up to his chin, Huss refused to recant his understanding of the Gospel. Instead, he exclaimed to his executioners, "I shall die with joy today in the faith of the Gospel which I have preached." (Philip Shaff, *History of the Christian Church* (Grand Rapids: Eerdmans Publishing Co., 1910, reprint. 1974), Vol. VI, p. 382.)

[15] Swinburne writes of religious experience: "If some people do not have these experiences, that suggests that they are blind to religious realities – just as someone's inability to see colours does not show that the many of us who claim to see them are mistaken, only that he is colour blind." Richard Swinburne, *Is There a God?* (Oxford: Oxford University Press, 1996), p. 133.

C.D. Broad similarly writes,

> Let us, then, compare tone-deaf persons to those who have no recognizable religious experience at all; the ordinary followers of a religion to men who have some taste for music but can neither appreciate the more difficult kinds nor compose; highly religious men and women and saints to persons with an exceptionally fine ear for music who may yet be unable to compose it; and the founders of religions to great musical composers, such as Bach and Beethoven.

Quoted in Caroline Franks Davis, *The Evidential Force of Religious Experience* (Oxford: Clarendon Press, 1989), p. 69.

[16] As Caroline Franks Davis notes (ibid., p. 195) : ". . . the empirical evidence for the widespread operation of such pathological factors in religious experience is far from conclusive, and the psychological research dealing with such factors is plagued by empirical and conceptual problems."

[17] Swinburne, *Is There a God?* pp. 133-134. See also Richard Swinburne, *The Existence of God* (New York: Oxford University Press, 1979), pp. 271-272.

[18] David Elton Trueblood wrote of religious experience:
> It is not necessary for the positive believer in God to show that all reporters are trustworthy and sound; without any harm to his position he can admit that some are not. All he needs to show is that any of them are sound and trustworthy. If any man, anywhere, has truly met God and continues to meet him, then God is.

David Elton Trueblood, *Philosophy of Religion* (New York, NY: Harper and Brothers Publishers, 1957) p. 146.

[1] Ed. L. Miller, *God and Reason: A Historical Approach to Philosophical Theology* (New York: Macmillan Press, 1972), p. 114.

[2] Rem B. Edwards, *Reason and Religion: An Introduction to the Philosophy of Religion* (New York, NY: Harcourt, Brace and Jovanovich, 1972), p. 222. He also wrote:

> Often the theistic proofs are criticized on the grounds that one is not required to accept the conclusion unless one first accepts the premises. This is true, but the theistic proofs are not peculiar in this respect. All arguments for everything everywhere are like this. If this is a weakness, it is a weakness of the entire enterprise of rationality and not simply a weakness of the philosophy of religion.

Ibid., pp. 222-223.

[3] Sometimes known as abductive reasoning or inference to the best explanation, this kind of argument moves from an observation to the simplest, most likely explanation.

[4] For an introduction to this kind of argument, see, for example:

> J.P. Moreland, *Scaling the Secular City: A Defense of Christianity* (Grand Rapids, MI: Baker Book House, 1987)

> Richard Swinburne, *The Existence of God*, Second Edition (Oxford: Oxford University Press, 2004.)

> William Lane Craig, *Reasonable Faith: Christian Truth and Apologetics,* Third Edition (Wheaton, IL: Crossway Books, 2008)

> Keith Ward, *The Evidence for God: The Case for the Existence of a Spiritual Dimension*, (London: Darton, Longman & Todd, 2014).

[5] For this argument, see Wayne Proudfoot, *Religious Experience* (Berkeley: University of California Press, 1985).

[6] My first response is that I do not see how this objection is relevant to the problems of beauty, pleasure, and *Sehnsucht*. They bring us to the threshold of joy and all of its theological implications, but it would not be apt to call them religious experiences. Appreciating beauty, in itself, is not a religious experience. Neither is an experience of surfeit pleasure. Nor is the existential paradox of pleasure. If anything, *Sehnsucht* is an absence of religious experience and a longing for it.

[7] Carolyn Franks Davis, *The Evidential Force of Religious Experience* (Oxford: Clarendon Press, 1989), pp. 26-27.

[8] As evidence, I concede that this does not carry the same weight that other experiences do. But it is not insignificant. In a cumulative case for the existence of a God, it adds weight to the overall argument. It is just the kind of thing we would expect if God exists and is involved in the lives of people who are open and responsive to him.

[9] F.R. Tennant wrote: "When a mystic believes he intuits God with sense-like immediacy, he is perhaps but causally interpreting his elation, peace, etc. by aid of a concept already to hand." Quoted in D. Elton Trueblood, *Philosophy of Religion* (Grand Rapids: Baker Book House, reprint. 1973), p. 156.

10 Louis Pojman has written:

> All experiencing takes place within the framework of a world view. Certain features of the world view may gradually or suddenly change in importance, thus producing a different total picture, but there is no such thing as neutral evaluation of the evidence. What we see depends to some degree on our background beliefs and our expectations. The farmer, the real estate agent, and the artist looking at the "same" field do not see the same field.

See his article, "A Critique of Gutting's Argument from Religious Experience" in Louis P. Pojman, ed., *Philosophy of Religion: An Anthology* (Belmont, CA: Wadsworth Publishing Co., 1987), pp. 139-140.

11 Franks Davis, *Evidential Force*, pp. 148ff.

12 Ibid., p. 149. Elsewhere (pp. 27-28) she says that "incorporated interpretation" is an . . .

> . . . interpretation we perform unconsciously to transform the stimuli with which we are constantly bombarded into intelligible experiences of recognizable percepts. It is incorporated without our awareness into an experience and is thus inseparable from it; it is what makes us have *that* experience, see things *that* way. Far from being 'mere interpretation', it is necessary to all perception.

13 C.S. Lewis wrote:

> We can't – or I can't – hear the song of a bird simply as a sound. Its meaning or message ("That's a bird") comes with it inevitably – just as one can't see a familiar word in print as a merely visual pattern. The reading is as involuntary as the seeing. When the wind roars I don't just hear the roar; I "hear the wind." In the same way it is possible to "read" as well as to "have" a pleasure. Or not even "as well as." The distinction ought to become, and sometimes is, impossible; to receive it and to recognise its divine source are a single experience. This heavenly fruit is instantly redolent of the orchard where it grew. This sweet air whispers of the country from whence it blows. It is a message. We know we are being touched by a finger of that right hand at which there are pleasures for evermore. There need be no question of thanks or praise as a separate event, something done afterwards. To experience the tiny theophany is itself to adore.

C.S. Lewis, *Letters to Malcolm: Chiefly on Prayer* (New York: Harcourt Brace Jovanovich, Inc., 1963), pp. 89-90.

14 Psalm 34:8.

15 See Keith Yandell, *Christianity and Philosophy* (Grand Rapids: William B. Eerdmans Publishing Co., 1984), Chapter 1.

16 See Isaiah 6:1-5:

17 Philippians 4:7

18 William James, *The Varieties of Religious Experience* (USA: Mentor Books, 1958), p. 65.

19 Franks Davis writes, "The fact that an experience has been 'interpreted' in terms of a specific conceptual framework or mental model (religious or otherwise) cannot in itself make that

experience evidentially suspect; the skeptic must show that the model or concept was inappropriate in some way." Franks Davis, *Evidential Force*, p. 148.

[20] Richard Swinburne, *The Existence of God* (New York: Oxford University Press, 1979), p. 254. See his *Is There A God?* (Oxford: Oxford University Press, 1996), pp. 131ff., for an application of this principle to religious experience.

[21] This is one place where I disagree with Postmodernism and its belief that there is no way to evaluate worldviews because we are fully trapped within them.

Even if we grant that those who seem to encounter God in experience are rational in their belief that God exists, we are not required to accept the explanation of the experience in terms of its accompanying belief system. For those who have such experiences, this is what keeps the argument from religious experience from being circular – using religious experience to give credibility to a belief system, and using that belief system, in turn, to give credibility to the alleged experience. If the only evidence for a Christian vision of life were experiences in which God seems to be involved, believers would be guilty of circular reasoning. If numinous experience is only one line of evidence among several lines that support a Christian worldview, the circle is broken.

[22] See the following:

> Ronald Nash, *Worldviews in Conflict: Choosing Christianity in a World of Ideas.* (Grand Rapids, MI: Zondervan, 1992).

> James W. Sire, *Naming the Elephant: Worldview as a Concept* (Downers Gove, IL: InterVarsity Press, 2015).

> David L. Wolfe, *Epistemology: The Justification of Belief* (Downers Grove, IL: InterVarsity Press, 1982).

Chapter 10: Answering Objections, Part 2

[1] John Hick suggests that this is the case: "[People] living within other traditions . . . are equally justified (as justified as we are) in trusting their own distinctive religious experience and in forming their beliefs on the basis of it." John Hick, *An Interpretation of Religion* (New Haven: Yale University Press, 1989) p. 235.

[2] Louis P. Pojman, "A Critique of Gutting's Argument from Religious Experience" in Louis P. Pojman, ed., *Philosophy of Religion: An Anthology* (Belmont, CA: Wadsworth Publishing Co., 1987), p. 138. Re-formatted.

[3] The Roman Catholic Church teaches as dogma the Assumption of Mary, a claim that she did not die a normal death, but was transported, body and soul, into heaven to end her earthly existence. I have no reason to believe that this is true, and so I do not include it as an exception to other postmortem encounters. Even if I did, the same considerations would be in play.

[4] For instance, Samuel (1 Samuel 28:1ff); and Moses and Elijah (Matthew 17:1ff).

[5] Here is his account of the encounter with Lewis:

A few days after his death, while I was watching television, he "appeared" sitting in a chair within a few feet of me, and spoke a few works which were particularly relevant to the difficult circumstances through which I was passing. He was ruddier in complexion than ever, grinning all over his face, and, as the old-fashioned saying has it, positively glowing with health. The interesting thing to me was that I had not been thinking about him at all. I was neither alarmed nor surprised nor . . . did I look up to see the hole in the ceiling that he might have made on arrival! He was just *there* – large as life and twice as natural." A week later, this time when I was in bed, reading before going to sleep, he appeared again, even more rosily radiant than before, and repeated to me the same message, which was very important to me at the time. I was a little puzzled by this, and I mentioned it to a certain saintly bishop who was then living in retirement here in Dorset. His reply was, "My dear J-----, this sort of thing is happening all the time."

J.B. Phillips, *Ring of Truth: A Translator's Testimony*, New York: Macmillan Co., 1967), pp. 118-119.

[6] This is not analogous to the resurrection of Jesus in very important respects. First, Jesus foretold both his death and resurrection. It was part of his teaching, so that when it took place, it gave credibility to his claims. Second, a resurrection from the dead is not the same as a postmortem appearance. It had empirical dimensions that could be confirmed or disproved.

[7] He could be rational in his belief, but mistaken. "Yes, but what if he really did see him?" Curiosity might ask the question, but answering would take us beyond the rationality of a belief to its truthfulness, and that is beyond the scope of the principle of credulity.

I don't know how it could be established, but suppose, hypothetically, that the evidence was strong that the monk really did encounter Buddha-post-mortem. As a Christian I might have to make adjustments in my understanding of Buddha, or my beliefs about the after-life, but it would not, in itself, be incompatible with the core beliefs of my faith. Some contemporary Roman Catholics and mainline Protestants accept teachings and practices of Buddhism. See, for example, Paul F. Knitter, *Without Buddha I Could Not Be a Christian* (London: Oneworld Publications, 2009). Knitter is the Paul Tillich Professor of Theology, World Religions and Culture at Union Theological Seminary in New York.

[8] George Mavrodes makes this point in his response to John Hick:

> He argues that 'persons living within other traditions, then, are equally justified [as justified as we are] in trusting their own distinctive religious experience and in forming their beliefs on the basis of it.' And he apparently wants to draw from this the conclusion that we cannot reasonably 'claim that our own form of religious experience, together with that of the tradition of which we are a part, is veridical whilst the others are not.' And so, since we assert the reality of our God, we must also accept the analogous assertions of others. This is fallacious because it confuses the notions of justification and truth or veridicality. Other people may be as justified as I am in relying on what seems to us to be our divergent experience. But that justification is largely independent of the veridicality of those experiences, and of the truth of the beliefs that they generate. As Hick himself says, 'A proposition believed can be true or false: it is the believing of it that is rational or irrational" . . . And the rationality of a belief, unlike the truth of what is believed, is sensitive to the epistemic situation of the believer. So, contrary to what Hick seems to argue, there is nothing unreasonable in a person's asserting that someone else is justified

in relying in a person's asserting that someone else is justified in relying on a certain experience, but that nevertheless the experience is nonveridical.

George Mavrodes, "Polytheism" in *The Rationality of Belief & The Plurality of Faith,* Thomas D. Senor, ed., (Ithaca and London: Cornell University Press, 1995), pp. 277-278.

[9] Even if religious experiences are embedded in belief systems and cannot be extracted from them, belief systems can be evaluated. Given a broader range of evidence, and the greater issue of truth (as opposed to the rationality of holding a belief), I would argue that it is least likely that polytheism is true, more likely that a finite creator-god exists, more likely yet that an infinite (non-trinitarian) God exists, and most likely that the Triune God of Christian faith exists. But that belongs to another discussion.

[10] Ronald Nash, *Faith and Reason: Searching for a Rational Faith* (Grand Rapids: Zondervan Publishing House, 1988), p. 156, n. 33.

[11] Peter Kreeft, *Heaven: The Heart's Deepest Longing* (San Francisco: Ignatius Press, Expanded Edition, 1980), pp. 48-49.

[12] Compare 1 Corinthians 8:4-6 and 10:19-21. In the first passage Paul acknowledges that although there is only one true God, behind the worship of idols there may indeed be "so-called gods in heaven or on earth," and in the second he calls these beings demons – supernatural malevolent beings apparently posing as "gods" and "lords."

[13] George Mavrodes, *Rationality of Belief,* p. 278.

[14] For instance, Michael Martin proposes a "negative principle of credulity: "If it seems (epistemically) to a subject S that x is absent, then probably x is absent" and uses it as an argument against the existence of God. Quoted in Michael Peterson, et al, *Philosophy of Religion: Selected Readings* (Oxford: Oxford University Press, 1996), p. 52.

[15] Carolyn Franks Davis writes:

> Experiences of the apparent absence of an entity (non-occurrence of an event, etc.) are *prima facie* evidence, but only in a very limited respect: they are *prima facie* evidence only for the claim that an entity which is perceptible by the means the subject was using at the time (e.g., vision) was not present in the area to which the subject was directing his attention on that occasion. They are not *prima facie* evidence that the entity does not exist at all; for that, the claim must be added that there is very good reason to believe the subject would have perceived the entity there and then if it had existed anywhere, or that subjects have failed to perceive the entity at all times and places that it should have been perceptible to them if it had existed. Where the very existence of an entity is at issue, then, a failure to perceive it is not by itself *prima facie* evidence for its nonexistence, whereas an experience of its *presence* is itself *prima facie* evidence for the entity's existence.

Carolyn Franks Davis, *The Evidential Force of Religious Experience* (Oxford: Clarendon Press, 1989), p. 98.

Similarly, Richard Swinburne argues:

> Nor, again, does the fact that some of a group of travellers cannot see some object which they cannot reach mean that, if many of the group claim to be able to see it, they are mistaken. The more rational belief -- in the absence of further evidence about the visual powers of the different travellers -- is that the former do not have

good enough sight. If three witnesses in a law court claim (independently) to have seen the suspect in some street at a certain time, and three witnesses who were in the street at that time claim not to have seen him, then -- other things being equal – the court will surely normally take the view that the suspect was there, and that the latter three witnesses simply did not notice him. It is basic to human knowledge of the world that we believe things are as they seem to be in the absence of positive evidence to the contrary.

Richard Swinburne, *Is There A God?* (Oxford: Oxford University Press, 1996), p. 133.

[16] Jürgen Moltmann writes: "Being aware of God is an art and – if the term my be permitted – a noble game." Jürgen Moltmann, *Theology and Joy* (London: SCM, 1973), p. 49. An art is something that must be developed with sensitivity. A game can only be played if the rules for the game are observed.

See the last section of Chapter 4 in this book, "An Epistemology of Joy."

[17] C. Stephen Evans, *Philosophy of Religion: Thinking About Faith* (Downers Grove: InterVarsity Press, 1985), p. 94.

[18] William P. Alston, "Christian Experience and Christian Belief," in *Faith and Rationality,* eds. Alvin Plantinga and Nicholas Wolterstorff (Notre Dame: University of Notre Dame Press, 1983), p. 105.

[19] C.S. Lewis, *Mere Christianity* (New York: Simon & Schuster, Touchstone edition, 1996), p.144. This should not be surprising. It is true of all personal relationships. I can know a fellow human only if he discloses himself to me, only if she reveals herself to me. The same is true in knowing God. He must take the initiative. He must reveal himself.

[20] Acts 14:16-17.

[21] Those who do not see what the signs point to are like the dog that sees his master pointing to a food dish and sees only his master's finger. They have taken on a "doglike mind," as C.S. Lewis put it. They see the signs but miss their significance:

You will have noticed that most dogs cannot understand *pointing*. You point to a bit of food on the floor: the dog, instead of looking at the floor, sniffs at your finger. A finger is a finger to him, and that is all. His world is all fact and no meaning. And in a period when factual realism is dominant we shall find people deliberately inducing upon themselves this doglike mind.

C.S. Lewis, "Transposition" in *The Weight of Glory and Other Addresses* (Grand Rapids: Eerdmans Publishing Co., 1949, reprint. 1974), p. 28:

[22] Hebrews 11:6 – "And without faith it is impossible to please him, for whoever would draw near to God must believe that he exists and that he rewards those who seek him."

[23] C.S. Lewis wrote:

Good things as well as bad, you know, are caught by a kind of infection. If you want to get warm you must stand near the fire: if you want to be wet you must get into the water. If you want joy, power, peace, eternal life, you must get close to, or even into, the thing that has them. They are not a sort of prize which God could, if He chose, just hand out to anyone. They are a great fountain of energy and beauty spurting up at the very centre of reality. If you are close to it, the spray will wet you: if you are not, you will remain dry.

C.S. Lewis, *Mere Christianity*, p. 153.

CHAPTER 11: A TALE WORTH TELLING, A STORY WORTH DEFENDING

[1] St. Augustine, "Confessions," in *The Basic Writings of Saint Augustine,* ed., Whitney J. Oates (Grand Rapids: Baker Book House, 1948, repr. 1980), p. 114.

[2] Aquinas, *Summa Theologica,* trans. Fathers of the English Dominican Province (London: Burns Oates & Washburn, Ltd., third ed. 1941), I, Q. 26, A. 1.

[3] Per Aquinas, "God is happiness by His Essence: for He is happy not by acquisition or participation of something else, but by His Essence." Ibid., I, II, Q. 3., A. 1.

[4] Karl Barth discusses the relationship between the triunity and the joy of God:

> As the triunity – and by this we mean in the strictest and most proper sense, God Himself – is the basis of the power and dignity of the divine being, and therefore, also of His self-declaration, His glory, so this triune being and life (in the strict and proper sense, God Himself) is the basis of what makes this power and dignity enlightening, persuasive and convincing. For this is the particular function of this form. *It is radiant, and what it radiates is joy. It attracts and therefore it conquers. It is, therefore, beautiful. But it is this, as we must affirm, because it reflects the triune being of God.* It does not do this materially, so that a triad is to be found in it. It does it formally, which is the only question that can now concern us. It does this to the extent that in it there is repeated and revealed the unity and distinction of the divine being particular to it as the being of the triune God. To this extent the triunity of God is the secret of His beauty. If we deny this, we at once have a God without radiance and without joy (and without humour!); a God without beauty (emphasis added).

Karl Barth, *Church Dogmatics,* eds., Geoffrey W. Bromiley, T. F. Torrance (New York: Charles Scribner's Sons, 1957), Vol. II, p. 661. Emphasis added.

[5] C.S. Lewis, *Mere Christianity* (New York: Simon & Schuster. Touchstone Edition, 1996), p. 153. The quote in its context is as follows:

> Good things as well as bad, you know, are caught by a kind of infection. If you want to get warm you must stand near the fire: if you want to be wet you must get into the water. If you want joy, power, peace, eternal life, you must get close to, or even into, the thing that has them. They are not a sort of prize which God could, if He chose, just hand out to anyone. They are a great fountain of energy and beauty spurting up at the very centre of reality. If you are close to it, the spray will wet you: if you are not, you will remain dry.

[6] For a development of this theme, see "The Joy of the Lord," "Joy Incarnate," and "The Joyful Spirit" in Rick Howe, *Path of Life: Finding the Joy You've Always Longed For* (Boulder, CO: University Ministries Press, 2017).

223

7   ". . . when the morning stars sang together
    and all the sons of God shouted for joy?" (Job 38:7)

This inspired C.S. Lewis in his story of the creation of Narnia. In *The Magician's Nephew*, Lewis wrote:

> In the darkness something was happening at last. A voice had begun to sing. It was very far away and Digory found it hard to decide from what direction it was coming. Sometimes it seemed to come from all directions at once. Sometimes he almost thought it was coming out of the earth beneath them. Its lower notes were deep enough to be the voice of the earth herself. There were no words. There was hardly even a tune. But it was, beyond comparison, the most beautiful noise he had ever heard. It was so beautiful he could hardly bear it. . . .
>
> Then two wonders happened at the same moment. One was that the voice [of Aslan] was suddenly joined by other voices; more voices than you could possibly count. They were in harmony with it, but far higher up the scale: cold, tingling, silver voices. The second wonder was that the blackness overhead, all at once, was blazing with stars. They didn't come out gently one by one, as they do on a summer evening. One moment there had been nothing but darkness; next moment a thousand, thousand points of light leaped out – single stars, constellations, and planets, brighter and bigger than any in our world. There were no clouds. The new stars and the new voices began at exactly the same time. If you had seen and heard it, as Digory did, you would have felt quite certain that it was the stars themselves which were singing, and that it was the First Voice, the deep one, which had made them appear and made them sing.

C.S. Lewis, *The Magician's Nephew* (New York: NY, HarperTrophy, 1983), pp. 116-117.

8   In Anselmian terms, God is that than which no greater can be conceived. He is supreme in every conceivable way.

9   "God created the world not out of reason or necessity or practicality, but out of sheer joy. It is all gloriously superfluous." Peter Kreeft, *Heaven: The Heart's Deepest Longing* (San Francisco: Ignatius Press, 1989), p. 144.

10   Lewis Smedes, "Theology and the Playful Life," in *God and the Good: Essays in Honor of Henry Stob*, eds., Clifton Orlebeke and Lewis Smedes (Grand Rapids, MI: William B. Eerdmans Publishing Co., 1975), p. 56.

11   We see the Creator's joy in his creative work first in his benedictions over it: "And God saw that it was *good.*" (Genesis 1:10, 12, 18, 21, 25, 31)

12   A literal rendering of the name of the Garden in *The Septuagint*, the ancient Greek translation of the Hebrew Scriptures.

13   Karl Barth wrote of God and creation, "Although he did not create it divine, He did not create it ungodly, or anti-godly, but in harmony and peace with Himself, and therefore, according to His plan, as the theatre and instrument of His acts, an object of His joy and for participation in this joy." Barth, *Church Dogmatics*, Vol. 3.1, p. 102.

14   It may be true, as Shakespeare put it, that "to err is human," but this is only true of us in our fallenness. Christians say that this was not the case with humanity-as-created-by-God.

15   Psalm 16:4, RSV

16   See Jeremiah 2:10-13.

17   See 1 Timothy 6:10.

18   See Ecclesiastes 2:1-10.

19   Peter Kreeft, *Heaven: The Heart's Deepest Longing* (San Francisco: Ignatius Press, Expanded edition, 1980), p. 21.

20   See Genesis 3:5.

21   Ephesians 2:3

22   The wrath of God is more than this. It includes his hatred of sin, his anger towards sin, and his judgment of sin. In Romans 1, however, wrath is God "giving sinners up" to the consequences of their sinfulness. He allows us to reject him, and to live with the ramifications of that rejection. He steps back from us, as it were, to let our sins and their consequences play out, and in that relational distance joy is lost. That is what hell will be with unmitigated finality.

23   Kreeft, *Heaven*, p. 135.

24   See Matthew 8:12.

25   See Psalm 16:11.

26   See 2 Thessalonians 1:9.

27   The sorrow of hell is unending because the sin of choosing another god is ongoing. C.S. Lewis wrote: "I willingly believe that the damned are, in one sense, successful, rebels to the end; that the doors of hell are locked on the inside." C.S. Lewis, *The Problem of Pain* (New York: Macmillan, 1962), p. 127.

28   C.S. Lewis wrote:

> There are only two kinds of people in the end: those who say to God, "Thy will be done," and those to whom God says, in the end, "Thy will be done." All that are in Hell, choose it. Without that self-choice there could be no Hell. No soul that seriously and constantly desires joy will ever miss it. Those who seek find. To those who knock it is opened.

C.S. Lewis, *The Great Divorce* (San Francisco: HarperCollins, 2001), p. 75.

29   ". . . and hope does not put us to shame, because God's love has been poured into our hearts through the Holy Spirit who has been given to us." (Romans 5:5)

30   Robert Kolb and Timothy J. Wenger eds. *The Book of Concord: The Confessions of the Evangelical Lutheran Church*, trans. Charles Arand, et al (Minneapolis: Fortress Press, 2000), p. 23.

31   Jürgen Moltmann asks this question, and finds its answer in the freedom, good will, and love of God. See Jürgen Moltmann, *Theology and Joy*, trans. Reinhard Ulrich (London: SCM Press, 1973), pp. 47ff.

32   Micah 7:18

[33] Luke 12:32. "The Kingdom of God stands as a comprehensive term for all that the messianic salvation included." George Eldon Ladd, *A Theology of the New Testament* (Grand Rapids: William B. Eerdmans Publishing Co., 1974), p. 72.

[34] See Luke 15:7, 23-25, RSV.

[35] Hebrews 12:2, RSV

[36] C.S. Lewis wrote, "For this tangled absurdity of a Need . . . which never fully acknowledges its own neediness, Grace substitutes a full, childlike and delighted acceptance of our Need, a joy in total dependence. We become 'jolly beggars.'" C.S. Lewis, *The Four Loves* (New York: Harcourt, Brace, Jovanovich, 1960), p. 180.

[37] C.S. Lewis, *Mere Christianity*, p. 52.

[38] Luke 1:46-47

[39] C.S. Lewis' way of describing the Trinity. See Chapter 24, "The Three-Personal God" in his *Mere Christianity*.

[40] Josef Pieper wrote, "All love has joy as its natural fruit." Josef Pieper, *About Love* (Chicago: Franciscan Herald Press, 1974), p. 71. David Gill speaks of joy as "love's delight." See David W. Gill, *Becoming Good: Building Moral Character* (Downers Grove, Illinois: InterVarsity Press, 2000), p. 54.

[41] See Psalm 24:1; 89:11.

[42] For instance, in the dialogue, *Phaedo*, Plato has Socrates say, "Nothing makes a thing beautiful but the presence and participation of beauty in whatever way or manner obtained . . . I stoutly contend that by beauty all beautiful things become beautiful. Plato, "Phaedo" in *Five Great Dialogues*, trans. B. Jowett, ed., Louise Ropes Loomis (New York: Walter J. Black, Inc., 1969), p. 138. See also Paul Edwards, ed., *The Encyclopedia of Philosophy* (New York: Macmillan Publishing Co., Inc., & The Free Press, 1967), Volume Six, pp. 320-324.

[43] C.S. Lewis saw them as facets of God's glory: "I was learning the far more secret doctrine that pleasures are shafts of the glory as it strikes our sensibility. As it impinges on our will or our understanding, we give it different names -- goodness or truth or the like." *C.S. Lewis, Letters to Malcolm: Chiefly on Prayer* (New York: Harcourt Brace Jovanovich, Inc., 1963), p. 89.

[44] "Oh, taste and see that the LORD is good!" (Psalm 34:8)

[45] We live out our days enveloped by the *sacramentum mundi* (the sacrament of the world, or the world as sacrament.)

[46] John Walton sees the creation account in Genesis portraying the cosmos as a temple in which God comes to dwell, and through which he makes his glory known. John H. Walton, *The Lost World of Genesis One: Ancient Cosmology and the Origins Debate*, (Downers Grove, IL: InterVarsity Press, 2009).

The world as the theater of God's glory was a significant theme in the thought of John Calvin. See "John Calvin and the World as a Theater of God's Glory" in Belden C. Lane, *Ravished by Beauty: The Surprising Legacy of Reformed Spirituality* (Oxford: Oxford University Press, 2011), pp. 57-85.

For explorations of stewarding the earth in a Christian vision of life, see: Steven Bouma-Prediger, *For the Beauty of the Earth: A Christian Vision for Creation Care* (Grand Rapids, MI: Baker Academic, 2001); Wesley Granberg-Michaelson, ed., *Tending the Garden: Essays on the Gospel and the Earth* (Grand Rapids, MI: Eerdmans, 1987); James A. Nash, *Loving Nature: Ecological Integrity and Christian Responsibility* (Nashville: Abingdon, 1993); Francis A. Schaeffer, *Pollution and the Death of Man: The Christian View of Ecology* (Wheaton, IL: Tyndale House, 1970); Loren Wilkinson, ed., *Earthkeeping in the '90s: Stewardship of Creation* (Grand Rapids, MI: Eerdmans, 1990) .

[47]   With future generations in mind, our responsible use of the world's resources should include renewable energy as much as possible. It is tragic not only when we, through our governments, rack up debts that will crush future generations, but when we deplete the resources of the earth, leaving future generations in peril. We should oppose both economic policies and energy policies that endanger those who come after us.

[48]   See Matthew 22:36-40.

[49]   In ancient Hebrew parlance, the word "way" is a metaphor for life, and the verb *halak*, literally to go or to walk, was used to describe the process of living. See, for instance, entry #2143 in *New International Dictionary of Old Testament Theology and Exegesis*, gen. ed., Willem A. VanGemeren (Grand Rapids, MI: Zondervan Publishing House, 1997), Vol. 1, pp. 1032-1033.

[50]   Jürgen Moltmann writes, "Man is to give glory to the true God and rejoice in God's and his own existence, for this by itself is meaningful enough. Joy is the meaning of human life, joy in thanksgiving and thanksgiving as joy." Moltmann, *Theology and Joy*, p. 42.

[51]   Augustine believed that two conditions must be met for something to be our greatest good: It must be a "good than which there is nothing better," and "it must be something which cannot be lost against the will." Augustine, "Morals," p. 321.

[52]   Augustine put it this way:

> No one can be happy who does not enjoy what is man's chief good, nor is there any one who enjoys this who is not happy. (Ibid.)

> The happy life . . . (occurs) when that which is man's chief good is both loved and possessed. (Ibid.)

> No one is blessed who does not enjoy that which he loves. For even they who love things that ought not to be loved, do not count themselves blessed by loving merely, but by enjoying them. Who, then . . . will deny that he is blessed, who enjoys that which he loves and loves the true and highest good?. . . He who loves God is blessed in the enjoyment of God. (Augustine, *City of God*, Vol. 2, p. 110.)

Similarly, Aquinas wrote, "Man's last end may be said to be either God who is the Supreme Good absolutely; or the enjoyment of God, which denotes a certain pleasure in the last end." (Aquinas, *Summa*, I, II, Q. 3. A. 4.)

[53]   There are two dimensions of our chief end – glorifying God and enjoying him. We do not have two chief ends, but one with two facets (As John Piper observes in his work, *Desiring God: Meditations of a Christian Hedonist* [Portland, Oregon: Multnomah Press, 1986], p. 13. As C.S. Lewis saw it, "Fully to enjoy is to glorify. In commanding us to glorify Him, God is inviting us to enjoy Him." C.S. Lewis, *Reflections on the Psalms* [New York: Harcourt Brace Jovanovich, 1958], p. 97.)

54 Bernard Ramm calls glory "both a modality of the self-revelation of God, and an attribute of God." Bernard Ramm, *Them He Glorified* (Grand Rapids, MI: William B. Eerdmans Publishing Co., 1963), p. 10. Karl Barth wrote: "[God's glory] is God Himself in the truth and capacity and act in which He makes himself known as God." Barth, *Church Dogmatics*, Vol. II, p. 64.

55 See Psalm 24:7.

56 See Acts 7:2.

57 See Ephesians 1:17.

58 See 2 Peter 1:17.

59 See Matthew 5:14-16.

CHAPTER 12: LAY OF THE LAND & FIRST DEFENSE: DIVINE OMNIPOTENCE

1 See Jeremiah 12:1.

2 This is the haunting question behind the book of Job, echoed many times in the Scriptures.

3 I wrote in another volume:

Sometimes joy banishes sorrow:

> They shall obtain joy and gladness,
> and sorrow and sighing shall flee away. (Isaiah 35:10)

> Weeping may tarry for the night,
> but joy comes with the morning. (Psalm 30:5)

> May those who sow in tears
> reap with shouts of joy!
> He that goes forth weeping,
> bearing the seed for sowing,
> shall come home with shouts of joy. (Psalm 126:5-6)

> You will be sorrowful, but your sorrow will turn into joy. (John 16:20)

Other times sorrow remains, but becomes a bittersweet experience when it is touched by joy:

> When the cares of my heart are many, your consolations cheer my soul. (Psalm 94:19)

> Happy are those who mourn: they shall be comforted. (Matthew 5:4, JB)

> We are treated as impostors, and yet are true; as unknown, and yet well known; as dying, and behold we live; as punished, and yet not killed; as sorrowful, yet always rejoicing. (2 Corinthians 6:9-10)

It is not that sorrow and joy come one after the other; they are facets of the same experience. I have known this myself (as you may have) when, in grieving over the death of a loved one, joy comes quietly and gently, not removing sorrow, but transposing the lament into a calm and soothing key. Joy in the midst of sorrow is like a soft light illumining the darkness, or the pleasure of a crying child in the comfort of her mother's loving arms.

See Rick Howe, *Path of Life: Finding the Joy You've Always Longed For* (Boulder, CO: University Ministries Press, 2017), p. 28.

[4]   In the history of religion, there have been traditions that see good and evil as equal, opposite, cosmic forces or deities. Dualistic thought had is origins in the ancient Persian and Middle-Eastern worlds, found in Zoroastrianism and later in Manichaeism.

[5]   See Genesis 1:10, 12, 18, 21, 25, 31, where God pronounces his creation good, and very good.

Depending upon the translation, there are two verses in the Old Testament that seem to say that God does, in fact create evil. The first is Isaiah 45:7. In the King James Version it reads: "I form the light, and create darkness: I make peace, and create evil: I the LORD do all these things." The second is Amos 3:6, which, in the King James Version reads, "Shall a trumpet be blown in the city, and the people not be afraid? Shall there be evil in a city, and the LORD hath not done it?"

In Hebrew, the word translated "evil" in these verses is *rah.* The field of meaning for this word includes moral evil. In the King James Version, however, it is also translated hurt, harm, ill, sorrow, mischief, displeased, adversity, affliction, trouble, calamity, grievous, misery, and trouble. These are all possible translations – even for that version.

Rah can mean something that is not good for us, in the sense that it causes pain. For instance, it is used in Jeremiah 24:2 of "bad" figs. If you eat them, you may get sick! It is also used in Proverbs 15:10 of correction, or discipline. It is evil in the sense that it might involve pain.

Modern translations translate *rah* in Isaiah 45:7 as "calamity," and in Amos 3:6 as "calamity" or "disaster." This is what we would call "natural evil" in our discussion. God takes responsibility for this, but it is not the same as "moral evil."

[6]   Christians regard Satan as chief among the "fallen angels" – angelic beings who were created good, but who fell in a primordial rebellion against God.

[7]   C.S. Lewis, *Mere Christianity* (New York: Macmillan Publishing Co., 1952), p. 45.

[8]   Rick Howe, *River of Delights: Quenching Your Thirst For Joy*, Volume 2 (Boulder, CO: University Ministries Press, 2017), p. 150.

[9]   In the prologue of Job, Satan is responsible for human sickness and death, and the death of animals. He is a causal agent behind "fire from heaven" a deadly "great wind," and human violence in the story. In the Gospels demonic beings are forces behind human sickness and infirmity, and the death of animals. For a treatment of the significance of demonic evil in the larger context of the problem of evil, see Gregory Boyd, *Satan and the Problem of Evil* (Downers Grove, IL: IVP Academic, 2001).

C.S. Lewis wrote "There are two equal and opposite errors into which our race can fall about the devils. One is to disbelieve in their existence. The other is to believe, and to feel an excessive and unhealthy interest in them. They themselves are equally pleased by both errors, and hail a materialist or magician with the same delight." C.S. Lewis, *The Screwtape Letters* (New York: HarperCollins, 1996) p. ix.

11 See, for instance, Genesis 3 and Romans 5:12-21.

12 See Genesis 2:16-17; 3:1ff.

13 The fallen condition of the world is not merely a result of human freedom. It is also God's judgment on human sin. We must not only come to grips with the divine blessing upon our world (Genesis 1), but a divine curse because of our sin (Genesis 3). Together, they provide a general background for our experience in the world – pleasure on the one hand, and pain and suffering on the other – the first an expression of God's goodness toward sinners, and the second, an expression of his judgment upon their sin.

Some (but not all) instances of pain and suffering are judicially related to God. There are times in the Scriptures when God does bring pain and suffering to people as punishment for sin. But not all pain and suffering can be explained this way (as in the famous case of Job). As the state punishes wrongdoers, with the result that their pain and suffering is just, so God magnifies his justice through the punishment of sin, whether it is served indirectly through moral agents or natural forces, or directly by him. The greater good served in such instances is the glory of God. If God does not exercise justice, or frees sinners from the just consequences of their sin, it is God exercising mercy.

14 I take "total depravity" to mean not that we are as bad as we can be, but that sinfulness taints every facet of our humanity.

15 Dallas Willard wrote: "Full joy is our first line of defense against weakness, failure, and disease of mind and body." Dallas Willard, *Renovation of the Heart: Putting on the Character of Christ* (Colorado Springs, CO: NavPress, 2002), p. 133.

Peter Kreeft makes the same point: "A joyful spirit inspires joyful feelings and even a more psychosomatically healthy body. (For example, we need less sleep when we have joy and have more resistance to all kinds of diseases from colds to cancers.)" Peter Kreeft, *Heaven: The Heart's Deepest Longing* (San Francisco: Ignatius Press, Expanded Edition, 1980), p. 129.

16 This is the joy which Madeleine L'Engle sees captured in the Sanskrit word, *ananda*: "that joy in existence, without which the universe will fall apart and collapse." Madeleine L'Engle, *A Swiftly Tilting Planet* (New York, NY: Dell Publishing, 1979), p. 40. It is the joy that binds Being to being, and all created things to each other. It is the aim of creation and redemption alike.

17 In the Garden story, God's curse upon human sin was multi-faceted, and included the relationship between humans and their natural environment. The apostle Paul commented:

> For the creation was subjected to futility, not willingly, but because of him who subjected it, in hope that the creation itself will be set free from its bondage to corruption and obtain the freedom of the glory of the children of God. For we know that the whole creation has been groaning together in the pains of childbirth until now. (Romans 8:20-22)

This will be remedied in what the New Testament calls the Resurrection, or the New Heavens and New Earth:

"For behold, I create new heavens and a new earth, and the former things shall not be remembered or come into mind." (Isaiah 65:17)

But according to his promise we are waiting for new heavens and a new earth in which righteousness dwells. (2 Peter 3:13)
Then I saw a new heaven and a new earth, for the first heaven and the first earth had passed away, and the sea was no more. (Revelation 21:2)

[18] In other words, it is not only what we do individually and as a race that impacts the world. Who we are and who we are becoming, individually and as a race, have repercussions for the health and well-being of our planet.

[19] Whether it involves human negligence or malevolence, many of the evils that we might consider *natural* turn out to be directly or indirectly the result of *moral* evil.

The contemporary issue of global warming helps us understand how humans can use their moral freedom in ways that impact our planet, and even produce phenomena, such as flooding and drought, that earlier generations would have seen as natural evil. They are regarded as *anthropogenic*, that is, they are brought about, directly or indirectly, by the activity of humans.

[20] C.S. Lewis, *The Problem of Pain* (New York, NY: HarperOne, 2001). P. 31.

[21] See Psalm 16:11.

[22] If you think of joy as a private, personal experience that is unrelated to life, you will miss its significance for the problem of evil. For a brief review see Chapters 3, 4, and 11 of this volume. For an in-depth exploration of joy as an integrating motif in all of life, see Rick Howe, *Path of Life: Finding the Joy You've Always Longed For* (Boulder, CO: University Ministries Press, 2017), and Rick Howe, *Rivers of Delight: Quenching Your Thirst for Joy, Volumes 1 and 2* (Boulder, CO: University Ministries Press, 2017).

[23] In my understanding of freedom, we are free if, given the identical antecedents leading to a decision, we could have chosen otherwise. I would add quickly, however, that though we *could* have done otherwise, in most instances we *would* not have. We only think we would have with the benefit of hindsight. But the addition of a retrospective look at the situation and the events that emerged from it means that the set of antecedents which led to the original decision is no longer intact. The antecedents would no longer be identical. Remove all post-decision factors, replay the exact set of antecedents again, and, even though we could have chosen otherwise, we rarely (if ever?) would.

That we *could* have done otherwise is a metaphysical issue; whether we *would* have done otherwise is a moral issue. Facing a similar situation, and choosing to respond differently (especially after processing and evaluating our earlier decision and everything that followed from it), is what it means to grow in wisdom. That is another issue.

While this understanding of freedom best fits the moral reasoning of the Scriptures, it does not mean that we can do anything we want. We are significantly free, but not absolutely free. Ours is a boundaried freedom, with limits determined by God.

The book of Job provides us with this notion of boundaries set by God. Of his work in the realm of nature, God says:

Or who shut in the sea with doors, when it burst forth from the womb; when I made clouds its garment, and thick darkness its swaddling band, and prescribed bounds for it, and set bars and doors, and said, 'Thus far shall you come, and no farther, and here shall your proud waves be stayed'? (38:10-11, RSV. See also Psalm 104:5-9)

The first two chapters of the book of Job show God operating in the same way with moral agents. God gives Satan (an supernatural moral agent, but still a moral agent) freedom to act, but sets the boundaries of his freedom at the same time (1:12; 2:6).

The apostle Paul saw this same pattern to God's relation to human nations: "And he made from one every nation of men to live on all the face of the earth, having determined allotted periods and the boundaries of their habitation" (Acts 17:26, RSV).

When Paul tells believers that God will not allow them to be tested beyond their strength (1 Corinthians 10:13), he is assuring them that God in his sovereign wisdom and loving commitment to them knows where to fix the boundaries in their lives (which includes, in many cases, setting the boundaries of what he will allow other free agents to do to them).

The freedom that God gives always takes place within the boundaries that he has established. They are boundaries of time and place, nature and nurture, and God's own providential acts in the course of life – all of which provide room for a significant degree of freedom, but at the same time protect, preserve and fulfill his sovereign plan.

Although I am wary of some of the ways in which this analogy can be used, there is some merit in seeing similarities between divine providence and a game of chess. God is the Chess Master, and we are on the other side of the board. We have freedom to move our pieces, but it is not absolute. There are limiting factors: the board itself, the chess pieces, the rules of the game, moves that have already been made, moves that will be made by the Master, and our own limitations in the decision-making dynamics of the game. Our freedom has boundaries.

[24] In the inimitable words of C.S. Lewis:

God created things which had free will. That means creatures which can go either wrong or right. Some people think they can imagine a creature which was free but had no possibility of going wrong; I cannot. If a thing is free to be good it is also free to be bad. And free will is what has made evil possible. Why, then, did God give them free will? Because free will, though it makes evil possible, is also the only thing that makes possible any love or goodness or joy worth having. A world of automata – of creatures that worked like machines – would hardly be worth creating. *The happiness which God designs for His higher creatures is the happiness of being freely, voluntarily united to Him and to each other in an ecstasy of love and delight compared with which the most rapturous love between a man and a woman on this earth is mere milk and water. And for that they must be free.*

C.S. Lewis, *Mere Christianity*, p. 52. Emphasis added.

Peter Van Inwagen writes:

Human beings have not been made merely to mouth words of praise or to be passively awash in a pleasant sensation of the presence of God. They have been made to be intimately aware of God and capable of freely acting on this awareness; having seen God, they may either glorify and enjoy what they have seen – the glorification and the enjoyment are separate only by the intellect in an act of severe abstraction – or they may reject what they have seen and attempt to order their own lives and to create their own objects of enjoyment. The choice is theirs and it is a free choice: to choose either way is genuinely open to each human being.

God wishes to be the object of human glorification and enjoyment not out of vanity, but out of love: He is glorious and enjoyable to a degree infinitely greater than that of any other object. He has given us free will in this matter because it is only when a person, having contemplated the properties of something, freely assents to the proposition that that thing is worthy of glory, and then proceeds freely to offer glory to it, that a thing is truly glorified. And it is only when a person, having enjoyed a thing, freely chooses to continue in the enjoyment of that thing that true enjoyment occurs

Peter Van Inwagen, "Non Est Hick" in *The Rationality of Belief & the Plurality of Faith*, Thomas D. Senor, ed., (Ithaca and London: Cornell University Press, 1995), pp. 220-221.

[25]   See Numbers 23:19; Titus 1:2; Hebrews 6:18.

[26]   See Psalm 102:24-27; Malachi 3:6; James 1:17.

[27]   See 2 Timothy 2:13.

[28]   See St. Thomas Aquinas, *Summa Theologica* trans., Fathers of the English Dominican Province, (U.S.A.: Benzinger Brothers 1947), I, I, Q. 25, A. 3.

[29]   This is what it means to say that God is a necessary being.

[30]   Theologians use the word *aseity* for this, which means that God exists in and of himself. He is not dependent upon anything outside himself for his existence.

[31]   If God is the Supreme Being, that is, he is that than which no greater can be conceived (Anselm), it is logically impossible for him to be more or less than he is.

[32]   The Nicene Creed, as given in the First Council of Constantinople (381) speaks of the Son as "begotten from the Father before all time, Light from Light, true God from true God, begotten not created" and of the Spirit as "the Lord and life-giver, Who proceeds from the Father, Who is worshiped and glorified together with the Father and the Son." See John H. Leith, ed., *Creeds of the Churches: A Reader in Christian Doctrine from the Bible to the Present*, third edition, (Louisville: John Knox Press, 1982), p. 33

[33]   Some critics contend that these concessions defeat the claim that God is omnipotent. I disagree. If it comes down to it, however, Christians can frame the power of God in terms of supreme power, or being "almighty," and lose nothing that is essential to the faith. See Chapter 4 of Thomas V. Morris, *Our Idea of God: An Introduction to Philosophical Theology* (Downers Grove, IL: InterVarsity Press, 1991) for other ways of thinking about the power of God.

[34]   C.S. Lewis, *The Problem of Pain*, p. 18.

[35]   Earlier in this chapter I spoke of evil in the natural world that has come about from the Fall of our first parents into sin. Whether one views this as God's punishment upon sin, or a world that has gone awry because of sin, it is possible that many (some would say all) natural evils have their source in moral evil. While it may have seemed far-fetched at one time, it is now commonly accepted in scientific circles that many natural phenomena, such as the melting of glaciers, flooding and drought, and even hurricanes, may be *anthropogenic*, that is brought about by human factors at play in the environment.

Earlier in this chapter I also wrote about demonic evil. Although they may not be able to identify or quantify it, Christians who accept the reality of the demonic nevertheless say that we must also take moral evil on a higher plane into account in the disruption of natural forces at play in the world.

[36] J.L. Mackie wrote:

> If God has made men such that in their free choices they sometimes prefer what is good and sometimes what is evil, why could he not have made men such that they always freely choose the good? If there is no logical impossibility in a man's choosing the good on one, or on several occasions, there cannot be a logical impossibility in his freely choosing the good on every occasion. God was not, then, faced with a choice between making innocent automata and making beings who, in acting freely, would sometimes go wrong: there was open to him the obviously better possibility of making beings who would act freely but always go right. Clearly, his failure to avail himself of this possibility is inconsistent with his being both omnipotent and wholly good.

See J.L. Mackie, "Evil and Omnipotence" in William L. Rowe, ed., *God and the Problem of Evil* (Malden, MA: Blackwell Publishers, 2001), p. 86.

[37] It may seem that the eternal state of the redeemed will be just such a world, inhabited by morally free creatures who always choose good. The inhabitants of the new heavens and earth will not be *de novo* creations, however, but resurrected and redeemed sinners. To our point, they will be morally free agents who have chosen evil. That world will come into being through a total transformation of morally free creatures who were once moral failures. Redemption is predicated upon Creation and the Fall, and brings about possibilities that would not otherwise come about.

[38] It is possible that all possible free creatures suffer from what Plantinga calls "transworld depravity." "What is important about the idea of transworld depravity," Plantinga claims, "is that if a person suffers from it, then it wasn't within God's power to actualize any world in which that person is significantly free but does no wrong – that is, a world in which he produces moral good but no moral evil." See Alvin Plantinga, *God, Freedom, and Evil* (Grand Rapids, MI: Eerdmans, 1977), p. 48.

[39] If there were a way to assess logical possibilities beyond the bare fact that they are logically possible, our experience of moral agents is uniform and without exception: We have experience of moral agents who choose evil, and no experience whatsoever of moral agents who always choose good and never evil.

[40] Christians can avoid the problems that beset the best-of-all-possible-worlds by talking instead about a world that best serves the purposes of an omnipotent, supremely good God. In Christian theology, that will be the new heavens and new earth. This world is a necessary means to that world to come.

[41] A number of philosophers believe that the notion of the best of all possible worlds is incoherent, including Brian Leftow, Alvin Plantinga, Richard Swinburne, Dean Zimmerman, Timothy O'Conner and Michael Almeida. See *the Closer to Truth* video series found at: https://www.closertotruth.com/series/the-best-all-possible-worlds.

CHAPTER 13: SECOND DEFENSE: DIVINE GOODNESS

1 On this issue, there is enough food in the world to feed the entire world. That is God's gift. That is the expression of his goodness. The problem of starvation is one of human stewardship and the management and distribution of resources, whether on a large scale or in a small, local setting.

What about famine and drought? They, too, can be "anthropogenic," that is, can be brought about directly or indirectly by human factors, such as global warming and climate change. They are features of a world that is no longer in harmony with the purposes of the Creator. In the Bible, famine and drought often mirror the spiritual conditions of a people, and are used by God to disrupt a sinful status quo and bring about repentance, faith, and obedience – which, I would argue, is a potential greater good.

2 Genesis 1:26, NRSV.

3 See William L. Rowe, *Philosophy of Religion: An Introduction* (Encino, CA: Dickenson, 1978), p. 89.

4 Critics also cite examples of animal pain as gratuitous evil. The problem of animal pain is important, but would take me too far from my focus on joy and the problem of evil. To explore this issue further, see Chapter IX, "Animal Pain" in C.S. Lewis, *The Problem of Pain* (New York: Macmillan, 1962). For a more recent treatment, see Michael J. Murray, *Nature Red in Tooth and Claw: Theism and the Problem of Animal Suffering* (Oxford University Press, 2009).

5 See Romans 12:15.

6 The more sympathetic, compassionate, or concerned about justice we are, the more powerfully these emotions shape our beliefs. This doesn't mean that if we are sympathetic, compassionate, or concerned about justice, we will deny the existence of God because there is evil in the world. Jesus was all of these things, but did not. When he was told by Mary of the death of his friend, Lazarus, the Gospel of John says: "When Jesus saw her weeping . . . he was deeply moved in his spirit and greatly troubled. . . . Jesus wept." (John 11:33-35) These are emotions of sorrow and indignation in the face of evil. If you grant the high Christology of the Gospel of John, this is God himself railing against evil in his world. For many, these strong emotions animate and shape a belief in God that finds its practical expression in acts of kindness and mercy, and the pursuit of justice.

7 Which is to say that the success of the evidential problem of evil depends largely upon the emotional or existential problem of evil.

8 By the nature of the case, if an evil has been prevented, we will not be able to see it because it did not happen. Sometimes, however, looking back on a situation we have a sense of "what might have been" if other circumstances had played out, and we see how a greater evil did not happen that might have.

9 William Rowe makes this distinction in his case for "friendly atheism," the view that an atheist can acknowledge that theists are rational in their belief that God exists, even if it is the case that he does not. In my view, Christians should extend this same "principle of charity" to atheists, even when we have strong disagreements about what is true. See "The Problem of Evil and Some Varieties of Atheism" in *The Evidential Argument from Evil*, Daniel Howard-Snyder, ed. (Bloomington, IN: Indiana University Press, 1996).

10   Some of these theological considerations are not implied by the existence of a good, all-powerful God. Nevertheless, they are compatible with the existence of such a God, and are part of the rich, Christian theological tradition associated with belief in such a God.

11   C.S. Lewis believed that God brings a complex good from a simple evil:

> In the fallen and partially redeemed universe we may distinguish (1) the simple good descending from God, (2) the simple evil produced by rebellious creatures, and (3) the exploitation of that evil by God for His redemptive purpose, which produces (4) the complex good to which accepted suffering and repented sin contribute.

C.S. Lewis, *The Problem of Pain*, p. 111.

This is illustrated by J.R.R. Tolkien's notion of *eucatastrophe*, or a "good catastrophe." He used this as a literary motif in his stories:

> The eucatastrophic tale is the true form of fairy-tale, and its highest function . . . . It does not deny the existence of *dyscatastrophe*, of sorrow and failure: the possibility of these is necessary to the joy of deliverance; it denies . . . universal final defeat and in so far is *evangelium*, giving a fleeting glimpse of Joy, Joy beyond the walls of the world, poignant as grief . . . . In such stories . . . we get a piercing glimpse of joy, and heart's desire, that for a moment passes outside the frame, rends indeed the very web of story, and lets a gleam come through.

J.R.R. Tolkien, *The Tolkien Reader* (New York: Ballentine Books, 1966), pp. 86-87.

There are *dyscatastrophes* in our world. Sorrow, suffering, and evil are painful realities, but not the final reality. They are darkness in our world. Eucatastrophe is a shaft of light piercing that darkness. It is God bringing a small good from sorrow and failure – often in unexpected and even surprising ways – as a preview of the far greater good that he will bring at the end of time. Until deliverance comes, evil seems gratuitous.

12   Or a greater evil may not be prevented similarly because its prevention depended on acts of morally free agents that do not occur.

13   Alvin Plantinga has written:

> God's creation of persons with morally significant free will is something of tremendous value. God could not eliminate much of the evil and suffering in this world without thereby eliminating the greater good of having created persons with free will with whom he could have relationships and who are able to love one another and do good deeds.

Quoted in the Internet Encyclopedia of Philosophy, "The Logical Problem of Evil," by James R. Beebe, found at: http://www.iep.utm.edu/evil-log/#H4.

14   In the case of our imagined theft, I would say further that God knew beforehand that these moral agents would not act to bring about these greater goods, and that he factored this into a larger plan in which, nevertheless, the theft of $100 ultimately brings about a greater good or prevents a greater evil that is known to him, if not yet to Ms. Smith. Although evil entered the world through Fred Wilson's theft, the will of a good, all-powerful God will prevail. Even if it is not the good that God prepared if we had obeyed him, as Ransom says

in C.S. Lewis's *Perelandra*, "Whatever you do, He will make good of it." C.S. Lewis, *Perelandra* (New York, NY: Scribner, 1996), p. 96.

15 Calvinists traditionally affirm that God knows the future, but deny the kind of moral freedom that I have posited for human beings. An emerging group of Christian philosophers and theologians advocate what is known as "open theism," a view in which libertarian freedom is affirmed, but God's knowledge of the future, insofar as it is contingent on the actions of morally free agents, is denied or highly qualified. I hold a middle position that affirms libertarian freedom and an understanding of the omniscience of God that includes the future actions of moral agents who possess libertarian freedom. For a survey of views on these issues, see *Divine Foreknowledge: Four Views*, edited by James K. Beilby and Paul R. Eddy (Downers Grove, IL: InterVarsity Press, 2001). See also http://www.reasonablefaith.org/scholarly-articles/divine-omniscience for articles by William Lane Craig on divine omniscience and human freedom.

16 Further back, believers say that the very notion of moral evil – even on the lips of atheists – implies the existence of God.

If Christianity is true, our ability to evaluate life in moral categories such as right and wrong, good and evil, just and unjust, is a finite reflection of the moral agency of God. (To say that God is a moral agent is to say that he possesses and exercises powers of moral agency, such as intelligence and volition, and possesses dispositions to act in certain ways and not in others, which he characterizes as good and evil.) If, for the sake of argument, there is no such God, and that we do not bear his image, how is it that we have come to regard some things in the world as "evil?"

This wouldn't be a problem if the word "evil" were just a code word for something that we don't happen to like, or something that frustrates our desires and aspirations. While some people might think that way, there are many who go beyond that in their understanding of evil. Whether they are right or wrong, they regard evil as something that is inherently out of harmony with the "way things should be."

C.S. Lewis put it this way: "My argument against God was that the universe seemed so cruel and unjust. But how had I got this idea of just and unjust? A man does not call a line crooked unless he has some idea of a straight line. What was I comparing this universe with when I called it unjust?" C.S. Lewis, *Mere Christianity*, Simon and Schuster, Touchstone Edition, 1996), p. 45.

If God doesn't exist, how is it that there are creatures in this world who are able to form the moral judgment that there is evil in the world? It is a fact that demands an explanation, and one that fits. This is known as a *moral argument for the existence of God*. For more on this, see the following:

> William Lane Craig, "Five Reasons Why God Exists" in *God: A Debate Between a Christian and an Atheist*, ed., William Lane Craig and Walter Sinnott-Armstrong (New York: Oxford University Press, 2004).
>
> C. Stephen Evans, "Moral Arguments for the Existence of God," in the Stanford Encyclopedia of Philosophy, found at http://plato.stanford.edu/entries/moral-arguments-god/.

17 Stephen Wykstra, calls this a "Noseeum Move," that is, "We no see 'um, so they don't exist." See "Rowe's Noseeum Arguments from Evil" in Howard-Snyder, *Evidential Argument*.

18   Believers fare no better. Even if we say that we know something of God's purposes, broadly speaking, we are not in a position to know what specific greater good might come, or what specific greater evil might be averted, if God permits an evil to occur. This situation arises inevitably from the epistemic distance between God and mortals.   An omniscient God knows things that we do not.   See William P. Alston, "The Inductive Argument from Evil and the Human Cognitive Condition," in Howard-Snyder, *Evidential Argument,* ibid, and Paul Draper, "The Skeptical Theist," ibid.

19   If there were a solution, someone with greater knowledge and skills would be able to see it.

20   This is an example of what is known as a "G.E. Moore shift," standing an opponent's argument on its head by denying the conclusion of the argument and making the denial a premise in one's own.   For more on this, see William L. Rowe, "The Problem of Evil and Some Varieties of Atheism" in Howard-Snyder, *Evidential Argument,* ibid.

21   I have given you reasons for believing that God exists.   There are many others that are beyond the scope of this book. A short list of helpful sources by date includes:

      Does God Exist?: The Debate Between Theists & Atheists
      J. P. Moreland and Kai Nielsen
      Prometheus Books, 1993

      GOD?: A Debate Between a Christian and an Atheist
      William Lane Craig and Walter Sinnott-Armstrong
      Oxford University Press, 2004

      Richard Swinburne
      Is There a God? Revised Edition
      Oxford University Press , 2010

      C. Stephen Evans
      Why Christian Faith Still Makes Sense: A Response to Contemporary Challenges
      Baker Academic, 2015

22   I haven't taken the time or space to address the issue of horrendous evil.   The problem of evil is at its most challenging when it seems horrendous to us, whether this has to do with magnitude, intensity, or both. Horrendous evil, critics say, can involve moral evil or natural evil.   Horrendous evil has a gratuitous element.   Its victims do not appear to be positioned for a greater good or to escape a greater evil.

      Marilyn McCord Adams gives the following examples of horrendous moral evil:

      > I offer the following list of paradigmatic horror: the rape of a woman and axing off of her arms, psycho-physical torture whose ultimate goal is the disintegration of personality, betrayal of one's deepest loyalties, child abuse of the sort described by Ivan Karamazov, child pornography, parental incest, slow death by starvation, the explosion of nuclear bombs over populated areas, having to choose which one of one's children shall live and which will be executed by terrorists, being the accidental and/or unwitting agent of the disfigurement or death of those one loves best.   I regard these as paradigmatic, because I believe most people would find in the doing or suffering of them prima-facie reason to doubt the positive meaning of their lives.

      "Horrendous Evils and the Goodness of God," *The Problem of Evil* (ed., Marilyn McCord Adams and Robert Merrihew Adams (New York: Oxford University Press, 1990, pp. 211-12.

Apart from their gut-wrenching emotional impact, at the end of the day believers say that such evil exists because of human freedom and depravity, and a world impacted and skewed by the evil of its inhabitants. If God bestows the kind of moral freedom that we have stipulated, then free-willed moral agents can use their will for good or evil – even if their choice involves horrendous evil. A world in which free-willed creatures can choose good or evil is better than a world without them.

23 John R. W. Stott, *The Cross of Christ* (Downers Grove, IL: InterVarsity Press, 2006), pp. 326-327.

24 For a robust development of this view, see Marilyn McCord Adams, *Horrendous Evils and the Goodness of God* (Ithaca, NY: Cornell University Press, 1999).

CHAPTER 14: THIS WORLD AND THE NEXT: A THEODICY

1 From the last chapter:

> I concede that gratuitous evil exists in appearance and in a contingent relationship with human freedom. I deny the existence of evil that is categorically gratuitous. If this sort of evil existed, it would be evil whose gratuitous character is simple, unqualified, and absolute. It would be evil that serves no greater good or prevents no greater evil in any logically possible world in which it exists.

To repeat my argument from the last chapter:

> (1) If a good, all-powerful God exists, absolute gratuitous evil does not exist.
> (2) A good, all-powerful God exists;
> (3) Therefore, absolute gratuitous evil does not exist.

2 In the last chapter I conceded that gratuitous evil exists in a contingent relationship with human freedom. God cannot remove the possibility of such evil without removing the freedom that makes it possible. But this is to say that such evil is not gratuitous after all, since it serves the greater good of a world in which there are free moral agents who can choose good or evil.

3 Literally, a justification of God. The term was coined by the 18th century philosopher and mathematician, Gottfried Wilhelm Leibniz. See his *Theodicy*, ed., Diogenes Allen (Indianapolis, New York: The Bobbs-Merrill Company, Inc., 1966).

4 The Westminster Confession strikes a wise balance on the perspicuity of Scripture:

> All things in Scripture are not alike plain in themselves, nor alike clear unto all: yet those things which are necessary to be known, believed, and observed for salvation are so clearly propounded, and opened in some place of Scripture or other, that not only the learned, but the unlearned, in a due use of the ordinary means, may attain unto a sufficient understanding of them.

The Westminster Confession of Faith, 1.7, found at:
http://www.reformed.org/documents/wcf_with_proofs/

5 A greater good may come only on the other side of (and even through) sorrow and suffering when evil is prolonged and seems gratuitous. Depending on our response, it may grow into

bitterness and resentment, or it may be redemptive. It may lead to a greater evil, or it may contain the seeds of a greater good if, in our lament, we are brought to a place of a humble surrender and openness to God. "He who goes out weeping, bearing the seed for sowing, shall come home with shouts of joy, bringing his sheaves with him." (Psalm 126:6.)

6   C.S. Lewis, *The Problem of Pain* (New York: HarperOne, 2001), p.91.

Eleanor Stump has written:

> Natural evil—the pain of disease, the intermittent and unpredictable destruction of natural disasters, the decay of old age, the imminence of death—takes away a person's satisfaction with himself. It tends to humble him, show him his frailty, make him reflect on the transience of temporal goods, and turn his affections towards other-worldly things, away from the things of this world. No amount of moral or natural evil, of course, can guarantee that a man will [place his faith in God]. . . . But evil of this sort is the best hope, I think, and maybe the only effective means, for bringing men to such a state.

See Eleanore Stump, "The Problem of Evil" in Eleanore Stump and Michael J. Murray, eds., *Philosophy of Religion: The Big Questions* (Malden, MA: Blackwell Publishers, Ltd., 1999), p. 233.

7   There comes a time when we cannot do something because we become entrenched in willing not to do it.   Like an addiction, we can give in to sin until we are trapped by it. As both Jesus and Paul put it, we become slaves to sin. See John 8:34 and Romans 6:16-17)

8   Christians believe that as the joys of heaven surpass all that we know, so the pain and suffering of hell are likely greater than anything we can imagine. If this is true, critics say, then hell is a more serious objection to the existence of a good, all-powerful God than evil in this world. See Marilyn McCord Adams, "The Problem of Hell: A Problem of Evil for Christians," in William L. Rowe, ed., God and the Problem of Evil (Molden, MA: Blackwell Publishers, 2001).

For my part, I don't think we know as much about hell as some people think we do. I am a reverent agnostic about much of it. We are on the surest footing, first, if we stay close to the teaching of Jesus. In an earlier chapter I wrote:

> We are all sons of Adam and daughters of Eve. We have all shared in their sin and know their consequent sorrow.

> This is the condition of fallen humanity. This is what it means to be "by nature children of wrath." The wrath of God is not a bolt of lighting, thrown Zeus-like from the heavens to punish wrongdoers. Wrath is joy rejected. Peter Kreeft is right: "But the opposite of true joy is far worse than anguish . . . . In fact, its opposite is hell." Jesus' description of perdition is no pre-scientific fiction. It is as realistic as anything can be. Hell is a place of weeping and gnashing of teeth. Ultimate sorrow and grief. If joy is found only in the undimmed presence of God, and hell is the darkness of eternal separation from him, there is no other way that it could be. Hell is the place of divine wrath: joy refused and forfeited with finality. It is the unending, unmitigated sorrow of choosing another god. It became one of two destinies the day our first parents took their first steps from the Garden.

We are on sure footing, too, if we follow the trajectory of other beliefs that we have good reasons to affirm. First, we were made for eternity. Second, we are free-willed moral agents, and always will be. Third, God is just. There is a place for those who say "Yes" to him and a place for those who say "No," and no one ends up in the wrong place. Fourth, because God is just, it is not the case, as some object, that hell is an eternal punishment for temporal sin. Hell's inhabitants continue to reject God throughout eternity. Hell is an outpost of rebellion against God, and its inhabitants are "successful rebels to the end." (See C.S. Lewis: "I willingly believe that the damned are, in one sense successful rebels to the end; that the doors of hell are locked from the inside." C.S. Lewis, *The Problem of Pain*, p. 130.)

Fifth, because God is just, the nature and intensity of pain and suffering in hell is no more, no less, and nothing other than, the actual consequences of a sinner's choice to live apart from God. Sixth, we are all moving toward heaven or hell even now. As C.S. Lewis put it:

> Every time you make a choice, you are turning the central part of you, the part that chooses, into something a little different from what was before…you are slowly turning this central thing either into a heavenly creature or a hellish creature…to be one kind of creature is heaven; that is joy and peace and knowledge and power. To be the other means madness, horror, idiocy, rage, impotence, and eternal loneliness. Each of us at each moment is progressing to one state or the other.

C.S. Lewis, *Mere Christianity* (New York: Simon & Schuster. Touchstone Edition, 1996), p. 92.

Finally, God is true to his promise: "You will seek me and find me when you seek me with all your heart." No one who seeks God in this way will fail to find him and their heart's satisfaction in him. Hell is a problem, but one that can be avoided.

9   There are two views, each held by some Christians, which do not include hell as an ongoing, eternal state of affairs. The first is annihilationism, the belief that those who are not bound for heaven will simply cease to exist with their last breath. Hell, according to this view, is a metaphor for the finality of death. The second is view universalism, the belief that in time hell will be vacated as the love of God triumphs in human hearts and heaven is embraced freely and fully. I don't believe that either of these views squares with the biblical witness.

10   See Psalm 16:11.

11   See 2 Peter 3:9.

12   That is, everything that happens serves the interests of the glory of God. It is a means to that greater end.

13   Believers say that *some* pain and suffering is judicially related to God. As the state punishes wrongdoers, with the result that their pain and suffering is just, so God magnifies his justice through the punishment of sin, whether it is served indirectly through moral agents or natural forces, or directly by him. The greater good served in such instances is the glory of a holy and just God.

14   Karl Barth, *Church Dogmatics*, eds., Geoffrey W. Bromiley, T. F. Torrance (New York: Charles Scribner's Sons, 1957), Vol. II, pp. 647, 653, 655.

As C.S. Lewis saw it, "Fully to enjoy is to glorify. In commanding us to glorify Him, God is inviting us to enjoy Him." C.S. Lewis, *Reflections on the Psalms* (New York: Harcourt Brace Jovanovich, 1958), p. 97.

15   In his work, *The Problem of Pain*, C.S. Lewis introduced us to the distinction between a simple good, a simple evil, and a complex good. He wrote:

Suffering is not good in itself. What is good in any painful experience is, for the sufferer, his submission to the will of God, and, for the spectators, the compassion aroused and the acts of mercy to which it leads. In the fallen and partially redeemed universe we may distinguish (1) The simple good descending from God, (2) The simple evil produced by rebellious creatures, and (3) the exploitation of that evil by God for His redemptive purpose, which produces (4) the complex good to which accepted suffering and repented sin contribute.

C.S. Lewis, *The Problem of Pain*, pp. 110-111.

[16] See Jeremiah 9:24, RSV; Micah 7:18.

[17] See my discussion of joy and virtue in the final section of Chapter 4. Jesus perfectly embodied this virtue and this joy, which is why he could say to his followers: "If you keep my commandments, you will abide in my love, just as I have kept my Father's commandments and abide in his love. These things I have spoken to you, that my joy may be in you, and that your joy may be full." (John 15:10-11)

[18] See Colossians 3:8-10.

[19] Although it does not focus explicitly on what God is doing in the midst human suffering, pain, and evil in the world, the comprehensive language used by the apostle Paul in his letter to the church in Rome includes these things:

> And we know that for those who love God all things work together for good, for those who are called according to his purpose. For those whom he foreknew he also predestined to be conformed to the image of his Son, in order that he might be the firstborn among many brothers. (Romans 8:28-29)

There are three important observations to make about this passage. First, the "good" in view is contingently related to loving God and a calling that aligns with the purposes of God. Second, if we ask what this "good" is, the context suggests that it has to do with people becoming like Christ ("conformed to the image of his Son"). Third, the language of predestination invites us to put these issues into an eternal framework in the purposes of God.

[20] See 2 Peter 3:13.

[21] This notion goes back to the Church Fathers, Irenaeus and Origen, who saw humans as incomplete and imperfect, and saw the world as an environment designed by God for their moral and spiritual development, with the challenges of pain and suffering as an essential component in their growth.

See the development of this theme in John Hick, *Evil and the God of Love* rev. ed. (San Francisco: Harper & Row, 1978). See also R. Douglas Geivett, *Evil and the Evidence for God: The Challenge of John Hick's Theodicy* (Philadelphia, PA: Temple University Press, 1995).

People whose souls are being shaped well flourish in joy, whatever life may bring. They embrace the Creator's mandate to fulfill his vision for the world and the human project. They steward the resources of the world as an expression of love for its Maker and love for their neighbors. They are fruitful in the righteousness, peace, and joy of God's Kingdom.

[22] God's gift of moral freedom is a necessary condition for joy. Without moral freedom we are not responsible for our beliefs, our values, our actions, or the development of our character – all of which are essential for joy. Unless we can say a meaningful "Yes" to God, the joy for

which we were created is an empty abstraction. It comes to life in our flesh-and-bones existence when we offer God's gift of freedom back to him, when our hearts affirm, embrace, and treasure his purposes for our lives, and we do this freely. Moral freedom creates the possibility of evil in the world, but it also makes our greatest good possible. We can't have one without the other.

[23] We see this played out, for instance, in Hebrews 11, where faith is defined as "the assurance of things hoped for, the conviction of things not seen" (v. 2), we are told that "without faith it is impossible to please [God], for whoever would draw near to God must believe that he exists and that he rewards those who seek him" (v. 6) and we are then shown a parade of men and women in the Jewish Scriptures who exemplified this faith (verses 7 and following).

[24] Matthew 25:21, 23

[25] 2 Corinthians 4:17

[26] For a development of this theme, see Marilyn McCord Adams, *Horrendous Evils and the Goodness of God* (Ithaca, NY: Cornell University Press, 1999).

[27] See Leibniz, *Theodicy*.

[28] If you are not familiar with the words *eschaton* or *eschatological*, they refer to what Christians call the "last days" or "end times."

[29] See John Piper, *A Godward Life: Savoring the Supremacy of God in All of Life* (Colorado Springs, Colorado: Multnomah, First Edition 1997; New Edition 2001; New Hardcover 2015).

[30] Romans 15:13

[31] Karl Barth wrote, "Most joy is anticipatory. Even in the experience of the fulfillment, and particularly when this experience is genuine, it usually changes immediately into anticipatory joy, i.e., joy in expectation of further fulfillment. In this respect, it normally has something of an eschatological character." Karl Barth, *Church Dogmatics*, Vol. III, Part 4, p. 377.

[32] Featured in the Lord's Prayer:

> Our Father in heaven,
>   hallowed be your name.
> Your Kingdom come,
>   your will be done,
>   on earth as it is in heaven.
> Give us this day our daily bread,
>   and forgive us our debts,
>   as we also have forgiven our debtors.
> And lead us not into temptation,
>   but deliver us from evil.
> For yours is the Kingdom, the power and glory, forever. Amen.
> (Matthew 6:9-13, with traditional ending)

[33] I am indebted to George Eldon Ladd for this insight. See his work, *A Theology of the New Testament* (Grand Rapids: William B. Eerdmans Publishing Co., 1974).

[34] A play on words from Tolkien's description of what he calls *eucatastrophe*:

> The eucatastrophic tale is the true form of fairy-tale, and its highest function . . . . It does not deny the existence of *dyscatastroph*e, of sorrow and failure: the possibility of these is necessary to the joy of deliverance; it denies . . . universal final defeat and in so far is *evangelium,* giving a fleeting glimpse of Joy, Joy beyond the walls of the world, poignant as grief . . . . In such stories . . . we get a piercing glimpse of joy, and heart's desire, that for a moment passes outside the frame, *rends indeed the very web of story, and lets a gleam come through.*

J.R.R. Tolkien, *The Tolkien Reader* (New York: Ballentine Books, 1966), pp. 86-87. (Emphasis in final phrase added.)

[35]   Let me encourage you to re-visit the section "An Epistemology of Joy" at the end Chapter 4 of this book.

[36]   C.S. Lewis, *Mere Christianity*, p. 153.

[37]   Acts 17:27-28

[38]   Augustine, "Confessions" in *The Works of Saint Augustine: A Translation for the 21ˢᵗ Century,* ed. John E. Rotelle, trans. Maria Boulding (New York: New City Press, 1997), I/1, p. 83.

[39]   See Psalm 139:7-12.

[40]   You can start your meditation with Scriptures like the following: Acts 17:28, RSV; Psalm 23:4; 46:1;139:7-10; Isaiah 43:1-5.

[41]   See Psalm 16:8.

[42]   See Psalm 25:15.

[43]   Psalm 73:28

[44]   See, for instance, Psalm 86:11 and 3 John 1:4.

[45]   See Romans 8:29 and 2 Corinthians 3:18.

[46]   See the following: Hebrews 1:2-3; Romans 8:29; Galatians 4:19; Ephesians 4:13.

[47]   John 15:11

CHAPTER 15: JOY AND THE KINGDOM OF GOD

[1]   The content of this chapter is drawn largely from earlier writings of mine on joy, including Chapter 12 in Rick Howe, *Path of Life: Finding the Joy You've Always Longed For* (Boulder, CO: University Ministries Press, 2017) and Chapters 14 and 15 in Rick Howe, *River of Delights: Quenching Your Thirst For Joy*, Volume 2 (Boulder, CO: University Ministries Press, 2017).

[2]   Ours is a narcissistic age. Christopher Lasch described it this way:

> After the political turmoil of the sixties, Americans have retreated to purely personal preoccupations. Having no hope of improving their lives in any of the ways that matter, people have convinced themselves that what matters is psychic

self-improvement: getting in touch with their feelings, eating health food, taking lessons in ballet or belly-dancing, immersing themselves in the wisdom of the East, jogging, learning how to "relate," overcoming the "fear of pleasure."

The contemporary climate is therapeutic, not religious. People today hunger not for personal satisfaction, let alone for the restoration of an earlier age, but for the feeling, the momentary illusion, of personal well-being, health and psychic security.

Christopher Lasch, *The Culture of Narcissism* (New York: Norton, 1978), pp. 4, 7.

Writing two years earlier, Francis Schaeffer warned that the United States, on the heels of its European forebears, had entered a post-Christian era. Values and convictions that once held our culture together no longer did. All that remained of Christianity for many were memories without power, words without meaning, and rituals without reality. He saw frightening portents of what might lie ahead and sounded a prophetic alarm. What he saw, to his dismay, was that many who bore the name of Christ had slowly, quietly, and uncritically come to embrace cultural values that were seriously at odds with Christ and his ways. Chief among them were personal peace and affluence. See Francis A. Schaeffer, *How Should We Then Live? The Rise and Decline of Western Thought and Culture* (Old Tappan, New Jersey: Fleming H. Revell Company, 1976), p. 205ff.

In the same year, Paul Tournier wrote of Christians:

What I am concerned about are the large numbers of people who are victims of a tragic misunderstanding. They take no further interest in worldly matters because their interest has – quite properly – been awakened in regard to the spiritual verities, as if the latter could exist in themselves in the abstract, outside of their incarnation in the world.

Paul Tournier, *The Adventure of Living* (New York: Harper & Row, 1976), p. 202.

[3]   I wrote in *Path of Life*:

Joy engages us as subjects, but it is never merely subjective. It is the enjoyment of someone or something. It always has an outward look. It is always attached. In this sense, there is no such thing as joy in itself. You can't extract joy, as you might cinnamon from a cinnamon tree, and then enjoy the taste in itself. Joy is governed by its objects.

Joy must always be hyphenated in our thinking. It is always joy-in-God or joy-in-his-gifts or joy-in-our-neighbors. Joy in God's creation, for instance, is our pleasure in a rainbow or the song of a nightingale. Joy may linger beyond the encounter, and may even return in memory; it is still, however, attached to an object. . . .

You will never find joy by looking for it in itself. It is always found in an outward look, in an engagement with God, his world, and the people he has created. It can't be found anywhere else.

Rick Howe, *Path of Life: Finding the Joy You've Always Longed For* (Boulder, CO: University Ministries Press, 2017), p. 152.

[4]   Quoted in see William Morrice, *Joy in the New Testament* (Grand Rapids, Michigan: Eerdmans, 1984), p. 107.

5   The highest praise we give a sacrificial act done for another is to say that it was a joy to do it. We see this in the language used to describe Jesus and his redemptive act on the cross: ". . . looking to Jesus, the founder and perfecter of our faith, who for the joy that was set before him endured the cross, despising the shame. . . ." (Hebrews 12:2)

6   Though many have forgotten, this has been central to the Christian story from its opening chapter. See, for instance, Matthew 5:11-12; Acts 5:41; Colossians 1:24; James 1:2; 1 Peter 4:13.

7   Mark 1:15

8   See Isaiah 61:1-2.

9   With traditional ending.

10 See Matthew 4:17, 23.

11 See, for example, the Sermon on the Mount: Matthew 5:3, 10, 20, 6:10, 13, 33, 7:21.

12 See, for example, Jesus' parables of the Kingdom in Matthew 13.

13 See Matthew 12:27-29.

14 Compare: Matthew 12:28 and Luke 11:20.

15 See Luke 9:1-6; 10:1-12.

16 See Matthew 24:14.

17 See Matthew 16:18-19.

18 See Acts 1:3.

19 See Romans 14:17.

20 Many passages speak of the Kingdom as yet future. See, for example, Matthew. 6:10; 25:34, 36-43; Luke 13:28-29.

21 Philippians 2:11

22 I rely heavily on the scholarly work of George Eldon Ladd on the Kingdom of God in the New Testament. See George Eldon Ladd, *A Theology of the New Testament* (Grand Rapids, MI: William B. Eerdmans Publishing Co., revised 1993), chapters 4-9.

23 There are also many passages that speak of the Kingdom as a present reality. See, for example, Matthew 5:3, 10; 6:33; 11:11-13; 12:28; 21:31; 23:13; Mark 1:15; 10:14-15; 17:20.

24 See, for example, Matthew 5:20; 7:21; 18:3; 19:23; 23:13.

25 Mark 1:14-15

26 The Greek word for repentance, *metanoia*, literally means a "change of mind." Gerhard Kittel, ed., *Theological Dictionary of the New Testament*, trans. Geoffrey W. Bromiley (Grand Rapids, MI: Wm. B. Eerdmans Publishing Co., 1964), Vol. IV, p. 978. It is a radical change of mind and change of heart that leads to a change in direction and a changed life.

27   You can read the parable in full in Luke 15:11-32.

28   See 1 Thessalonians 1:8-9.

29   C.S. Lewis, *Reflections on the Psalms* (New York: Harcourt Brace Jovanovich, 1958) p. 32.

It is true that the Scriptures sometimes speak of God's hatred of sinners (e.g., Psalm 5:4-6), but, in light of other clear statements about God's love for sinners, we should interpret those passages to mean that he hates the wicked *with respect to* their wickedness, the evil *with respect to* their evil, and sinners *with respect to* their sin.

C.S. Lewis wrote:

> I remember Christian teachers telling me long ago that I must hate a bad man's actions, but not hate the bad man: or, as they would say, hate the sin but not the sinner.
>
> For a long time I used to think this a silly, straw-splitting distinction: how could you hate what a man did and not hate the man? But years later it occurred to me that there was one man to whom I had been doing this all my life—namely myself. However much I might dislike my own cowardice or conceit or greed, I went on loving myself. There had never been the slightest difficulty about it. In fact the very reason why I hated the things was that I loved the man. Just because I loved myself, I was sorry to find that I was the sort of man who did those things. Consequently, Christianity does not want us to reduce by one atom the hatred we feel for cruelty and treachery. We ought to hate them. Not one word of what we have said about them needs to be unsaid. But it does want us to hate them in the same way in which we hate things in ourselves: being sorry that the man should have done such things, and hoping, if it is anyway possible, that somehow, sometime, somewhere he can be cured and made human again.

C.S. Lewis, *Mere Christianity* (New York: Harper Collins, 2001), p. 117.

30   Luther's Ninety-five Theses began with this assertion: "When our Lord and Master Jesus Christ said 'Repent,' he intended that the entire life of believers should be repentance." See *Luther's Works*, ed., Harold J. Grim, (Philadelphia: Muhlenberg Press, 1957), Vol. 31, p. 25.

31   The apostle Paul contrasts those whose sin keeps them from the Kingdom of God with those in whom the fruit of the Spirit grows. See Galatians 5:19-23.

32   Romans 14:17, RSV

33   This is taught vividly in the story of Joshua before the gates of Jericho. See Joshua 5:13-15.

34   Romans 14:18, literal translation.

35   C.K. Barrett, *A Commentary on the Epistle to the Romans* (New York: Harper & Row Publishers, 1957), p. 265.

Kingdom righteousness in this context is not "the status of righteousness before God which is God's gift." C.E.B. Cranfield, *A Critical and Exegetical Commentary on The Epistle to the Romans* (Edinburgh: T&T Clark Limited, 1979, reprint. 1981), Vol. 2, p. 718. If we let Paul speak for himself, and speak his mind fully, he sees righteousness both as a judicial standing before God, and as action that seeks the well-being of others before God. The first is his doctrine of justification ("righteousness by faith") and is especially in view in chapters

3-5 of his letter to the Romans. The second is a "righteousness leading to sanctification" (e.g., Romans 6:13, 16, 18, 19), and includes the many practical exhortations that seek the good of others in Romans 12-14.

36 See the following: Genesis 18:19; Psalm 106:3; Proverbs 21:3; Isaiah 56:1; Jeremiah 22:3.

37 Contextually, Paul is concerned with those who "put a stumbling block or hindrance in the way of a brother" (14:13, RSV). If righteousness is action taken to help others flourish before God, then acting in ways that cause others to fall is a direct contradiction to this. The positive commitment to righteousness in this sense is found, for instance, in 14:19 – "Let us then pursue what makes for peace and for mutual up building," (RSV) and in 15:2,"Let each of us please his neighbor for his good, to edify him." (RSV)

38 Psalm 97:2

39 From the beginning of the human project, God exercises dominion in developing the world through human agents. This is true of the "cultural mandate" given in creation, and it is true in our era of the Kingdom.

40 See also: Job 29:12-17, RSV; Proverbs 29:7, NIV; Matthew 25:37-40, NIV.

41 Joy is both a centrifugal and a centripetal spiritual force: It reaches out and draws others in. Joy is hospitable: always seeking company and inviting and bringing others home to share its boon. Our own joy is enhanced, enriched, and enlarged as we give ourselves to its largess. James Gilman puts this into the context of our concern for the poor, "The community's joy lies in the privilege of sharing with the poor the same gracious kindness it receives from God, so that in the end both donor and recipient rejoice together." James E. Gilman, Fidelity of the Heart, An Ethic of Christian Virtue (Oxford: Oxford University Press, 2001), p. 61.

42 The biblical concepts of righteousness and justice overlap. Biblical justice is not the same as the classical Greek understanding of this moral quality. In its Aristotelian sense, justice is calculating and disinterested. It is giving a person his due. From a biblical perspective the just person is not merely one who acts justly because it is required of him; he desires justice, loves justice, and delights in justice. It is not disinterested or detached, but passionately involved. It is not giving a person his due on the basis of merit, but acting in ways that will promote human flourishing as an expression of love.

43 See his teaching on this matter recorded in Matthew 25:31-40:

44 Though they are related, and outwardly may appear to be the same, it is important to say here that kingdom righteousness is not an equivalent term for social justice. Donald Bloesch writes:

> Both humanitarian works of mercy and works of social reform are at best approximations of kingdom righteousness. If the church identified itself with the cause of social justice, this might indeed make people more receptive to the kingdom message. Social justice is a partial fulfillment of the law of God; the eschatological kingdom is the perfect fulfillment of the teachings of the law. Social justice is related to the law of God; the righteousness of the kingdom is related to the gospel. Social justice is conducive to human happiness; Christian obedience brings blessedness – contagious, radiant joy.

Donald G. Bloesch, *Freedom for Obedience: Evangelical Ethics in Contemporary Times* (San Francisco: Harper and Row, 1987), p. 84.

45   See Philippians 4:6-7, RSV.

46   See Romans 14:19, RSV.

47   Romans 12:18

48   *Shalom* is a prominent theme in Isaiah. In the following passages, it is translated "peace."
      Isaiah 9:6-7; 26:1, 12; 32:17-18; 48:18; 52:7; 54:10; 55:12; 57:18-19.

49   Cornelius Plantinga, Jr., *Not the Way It's Supposed to Be: A Breviary of Sin*, (Grand Rapids,
      MI: William B. Eerdmans Publishing Company, 1995), p.10.

50   "Healthy joy cannot be full while sisters and brothers are in misery. Joy in a surrounding
      context of misery is insulted and undone." Daniel C. Maguire, *The Moral Core of Judaism
      and Christianity: Reclaiming the Revolution* (Minneapolis: Fortress Press, 1993), p. 279.

51   See Isaiah 32:17-18.

52   "Joy is what humans experience when the way the world is and the way the world ought to
      be converge. For Christians joy is love's delight in God and God's promised kingdom, when
      the way the world is and the way God wills the world converge." Gilman, *Fidelity of Heart*:
      p. 54.

53   In this context, joy as the consummation of *shalom*:

      It is "the fulfillment of our capacity for rejoicing." Maguire, *Moral Core*, p. 236.

      It is to "enjoy living before God, to enjoy living in nature, to enjoy living with
      one's fellows, to enjoy life with oneself." Nicholas Wolterstorff, *Art in Action:
      Toward a Christian Aesthetic* (Grand Rapids: Eerdmans, 1980), p. 79.

      It is "a just peace with joy in God's creation." Donald G. Bloesch, *Freedom for
      Obedience: Evangelical Ethics in Contemporary Times* (San Francisco: Harper and
      Row, 1987), p. 90.

54   Cornelius Plantinga writes:

      The prophets knew how many ways human life can go wrong because they knew
      how many ways human life can go right. (You need the concept of a wall on a
      plumb to tell when one is off.) These prophets kept dreaming of a time when God
      would put things right again.

      They dreamed of a new age in which human crookedness would be straightened
      out, rough places made plain. The foolish would be made wise and the wise,
      humble. They dreamed of a time when the deserts would flower, the mountains
      would run with wine, weeping would cease and people could go to sleep without
      weapons on their laps. People would work in peace and work to fruitful effect.
      Lambs could lie down with lions. All nature would be fruitful, benign, and filled
      with wonder upon wonder; all humans would be knit together in brotherhood and
      sisterhood; and all nature and all humans would look to God, walk with God, lean
      toward God and delight in God. Shouts of joy and recognition would well up from
      valleys and seas, from women in streets and from men on ships.

      Cornelius Plantinga, Jr., Ibid.

55   This is the joy which Madeleine L'Engle sees captured in the Sanskrit word, *ananda*: "that joy in existence, without which the universe will fall apart and collapse." Madeleine L'Engle, *A Swiftly Tilting Planet* (New York, NY: Dell Publishing, 1979), p. 40. It is the joy that binds Being to being, and all created things to each other. It is the aim of creation and redemption alike.

John Calvin wrote:

> [The] Psalmist calls upon irrational things themselves, the trees, the earth, the seas, and the heavens, to join in the general joy. Nor are we to understand that by the heavens he means the angels, and by the earth men; for he calls even upon the dumb fishes of the deep to shout for joy. . . . As all elements in the creation groan and travail together with us, according to Paul's declaration, (Rom. 8:22) they may reasonably rejoice in the restoration of all things according to their earnest desire.

John Calvin, *Commentary on the Book of Psalms*, trans. Rev. James Anderson (Grand Rapids, MI: Baker BookHouse, reprint, 1979), Vol. IV, p. 58.

Martin Luther wrote that in the resurrection people will "play with heaven and earth, the sun and all the creatures." And "All creatures shall have their fun, love and joy and shall laugh with thee and thou with them . . . ." Quoted in Jürgen Moltmann, *Theology and Joy*, trans. Reinhard Ulrich (London: SCM Press, LTD, 1973), p. 57.

56   Emil Brunner, *The Divine Imperative*, trans. Olive Wyon, (The Westminster Press: Philadelphia, 1947), p. 128.

CONCLUSION

1   He wrote: 'Two extremes: to exclude reason, to admit reason only." Blaise Pascal, *Pascal's Pensées*, trans. W.F. Trotter (New York: E.P. Dutton & Co., Inc., 1958), #253.

www.ingramcontent.com/pod-product-compliance
Lightning Source LLC
Chambersburg PA
CBHW071414090426
42737CB00011B/1458